16368

Praise for *The Tr*

"My mother and I had a very ~~ven friends.~~ But now we are, and I praise (

"I loved my grandmother very much and felt inspired to write her a poem to let her know what her life had meant to me. I gave it to her on her birthday shortly before she died. As she read it, tears flowed freely for both of us. She clutched it to her heart and said, 'And to think this poem is about me!' I hugged her and then she said, 'I will take this to heaven with me.' She had every nurse and visitor who came into her room read the poem before he or she left."

"I presented the tribute to my parents on their thirty-third wedding anniversary. We went through a lot of Kleenex that night. Dad said it was the best present he ever got. Mom wrote me a note thanking me for the hard work and love I put into writing it. Those remarks surprised me: both from parents who rarely shared how they felt."

"My sister and I both framed our tributes, and a week later we celebrated my mother's birthday (seventy-ninth) by reading them to her after our dinner. She cried, hugged us, and said she had the two most wonderful daughters in the world. We didn't realize it then, but it would be the last family gathering we would have with her, because just sixteen days later she died of a heart attack. Everyone who had known and cared for Mother (in a nursing home) came into the room while we were packing her things and told us that Mother had asked each one of them to read the tributes to her over the past sixteen days since her birthday. Some even asked for copies! They all had obviously been touched!"

"I presented my tribute to my in-laws, and it was the first time I have ever seen my father-in-law hug a man. I believe that partly because of the bridge my wife and I built just a few months ago, he is now open to the gospel and is reading his Bible every day."

"My dad is sixty-five and I am thirty-four. He is not an emotional man nor am I. As he read my tribute, we saw his face begin to melt. Tears rolled off his cheeks as he began to stutter. Though this (tribute) was personal, he hung it in his office for all to see. It was a wonderful feeling letting my dad know what he meant to me while he is alive to appreciate it."

"When I gave Dad his (tribute) yesterday, he only said, 'That's nice,' and went outside and never mentioned it again. No matter how he feels about it, I sure feel a lot better! Telling him I love him is what I really wanted to do."

"The tribute was given to my family Christmas Day [after their father had committed suicide] and read aloud by me. Needless to say, the reaction was tearful and sweet. My mother hung it in the living room, close to the front door where all could see it, and we have become much closer. It's almost as if she feels a sense of peace that she never had before. A copy was given to each of my siblings, and we have all talked at length about the tragedy for the first time. The tribute alone was more healing than any therapy we could have gotten."

Library
Oakland S.U.M.

The TRIBUTE and the PROMISE

Dennis Rainey
with David Boehi

THOMAS NELSON PUBLISHERS
Nashville • Atlanta • London • Vancouver

Copyright © 1994 by Dennis Rainey

All rights reserved. Written permission must be secured from the publisher to use or reproduce any part of this book, except for brief quotations in critical reviews or articles.

Published in Nashville, Tennessee, by Thomas Nelson, Inc., Publishers, and distributed in Canada by Word Communications, Ltd., Richmond, British Columbia, and in the United Kingdom by Word (UK), Ltd., Milton Keynes, England.

Unless otherwise noted, Scripture quotations are from THE NEW AMERICAN STANDARD BIBLE, Copyright © 1960, 1962, 1963, 1968, 1971, 1972, 1973, 1975, 1977 by The Lockman Foundation and are used by permission.

Scripture quotations noted NIV are taken from the HOLY BIBLE, NEW INTERNATIONAL VERSION ®. Copyright © 1973, 1978, 1984 by International Bible Society. Used by permission of Zondervan Bible Publishing House. All rights reserved.

The "NIV" and "New International Version" trademarks are registered in the United States Patent and Trademark Office by International Bible Society. Use of either trademark requires the permission of International Bible Society.

Library of Congress Cataloging-in-Publication Data

Rainey, Dennis, 1948–
  [Tribute]
  The tribute and the promise : how honoring your parents will bring a blessing to your life / Dennis Rainey : with David Boehi.
     p.   cm.
  Originally published: The tribute. Nashville : T. Nelson. c1994.
  Includes bibliographical references.
  ISBN 0-7852-7175-9 (pbk.)
  1. Ten commandments—Parents. 2. Parent and adult child. 3. Christian life.
4. Aged—Family relationships. I. Boehi, David. II. Title.
[BV4675.R35 1997]
248.8′4—dc21   97-20345
                                                                                   CIP

Printed in the United States of America
6 7 8 9 10 QPV 03 02 01 00 99

To Mom,

In this your 81st year of life, I dedicate this book because you have given me:

life,
moral training and direction,
a granite-solid spiritual legacy,
the ability to laugh when things don't go well,
and a mother's pure love.

Thanks, Mom, for being a woman who is worthy to be honored. You are the reason for this book. I love you.

Contents

Acknowledgments

Writing a book is like planting and maintaining an orchard. It takes time. It requires the attention, energy, and commitment of skilled men and women who want to see an end product that yields a lot of fruit. *The Tribute and the Promise* is no different. This book started a number of years ago as just a single idea, and thanks to the efforts and talents of others, it finally has come together and matured. Whether it is productive in its yield of fruit will be determined by those who read these pages and apply its challenge to their lives.

My friend and partner in ministry, Dave Boehi, deserves a medal of honor for his tireless service and painstaking care in helping shape this manuscript. Dave, once again, your critical eye has proved to be invaluable. I deeply appreciate the work that you did on this book and all that you do at FamilyLife.

I wanted to thank a group of people from different professional disciplines who gave me input on *The Tribute and the Promise* by serving on the reading committee. I appreciated your coaching, encouragement, and time. Thanks to Theresa Beck, Marcie Bostwick, Jon and Peggy Campbell, Barbara Craft, Joan Hemingway, Pam Leathers, Bob Lepine, Myra McCoy, Virginia Robinson, Al Sanders, Jeff Schulte, Jane Ann Smith, Sue Stinson, Dr. Vicki Tanner, and Jerry Wunder.

To the FamilyLife team who added so much to this manuscript, I say a hearty thanks! Thanks to Betty Dillon for the many errands and all of your reading and research. Pam Stauffer, thanks for putting away the stars and butterflies of your upcoming marriage and focusing on this book. Thanks to Julie Denker and Karen Wistrand for your "eagle eye" in proofreading. Thanks to Mark Crull who juggled my automobile problems, did some specialized research, and brought me many sandwiches while I was a writing recluse. Kudos go to Mary Larmoyeux and Sharon Hill for your determined servant-spirit that stood in the gap while I was away from the office. Thanks, too, for all the typing you and Linda Treadway did to make the manuscript come alive with illustrations. A special word of appreciation goes to Lynn Engle for your editorial ability, which was greatly appreciated. You did wonders for this book and are a valued friend.

A special thanks also goes to Gary Davis for providing a private place to write. The 4-H Center team was very helpful!

Thanks to Dan Benson who urged me to write this book. You have been a source of much encouragement over the years. Also, to the editorial and marketing team at Thomas Nelson, thanks for your touch. One final word goes to my editor at Nelson whose keen eye and sword-like typewriter helped put the finishing touches on this book.

I also want to say a special word of thanks to the leadership team of FamilyLife. You guys filled in more than one spot so that I could get away to write this manuscript. An extra portion of gratitude goes to Merle Engle without whom I would be doing no writing, little speaking, and certainly, no radio. Thanks for your Christlikeness and servant's spirit in so many ways. You are a gift from God.

And finally, I want to say a special word of thanks and fully acknowledge the price my family paid in having a dad come home with his eyes glazed over from writing. Thanks for allowing me to get away. You kids are the best. Thanks to Ashley, Benjamin, Samuel, Rebecca, Deborah, and Laura. And to Barbara, my partner, friend, and warrior in life, I want to tell you how much I appreciate you. Thanks for encouraging and coaching me along the way and for being the "wind beneath my wings." Thanks for being a committed woman of God.

Certainly no group of people deserves more acknowledgment than you, the readers. I thank you for your time, and for being obedient in honoring your parents. You are not only investing in your own family, but also in generations to come. Thanks for being faithful. May God grant you favor.

Foreword

My precious and saintly mother, and equally loved and deeply appreciated father, have been with our Lord for many years. They both died at the age of ninety-three.

From my earliest youth, I have loved, obeyed, and honored my parents. They were very special to me. As I recall our relationship through the years, thousands of fond and treasured thoughts flood my mind. Gratefully, I never had any significant negative, unhappy encounters with my parents.

Without question, my love for and happy relationship with my father and mother have greatly influenced and enriched my relationship with God. Indeed, my view of God, my ability to love, trust, and obey Him, and my eagerness to surrender my life completely without reservation to the Lordship of Christ can be attributed at least in part to my godly parents.

Our attitudes toward our parents truly influences our attitudes toward our God, our Lord and Savior Jesus Christ.

The relationship between a parent and a child is one of the most important in our lives, regardless of our age. That is why I have been disturbed by the growing trend of "blaming parents" in our present society. In an effort to understand their own emotional struggles, many adults unfairly condemn their parents rather than take biblical responsibility upon themselves.

I believe that following the command of Scripture to love God with all of our heart, soul, and mind, the mandate to honor our father and mother may be the most important of the Ten Commandments. Throughout my life, I have had opportunity to counsel with many thousands of people and have found in the process that those who have unresolved anger and resentment toward their parents are incapable of loving and obeying God with utter abandonment.

In *The Tribute and the Promise*, Dennis Rainey has found that, for many adults, honoring parents is one of the most important steps of faith they can take. You will read many stories of triumph, about people who have obeyed God in honoring their parents, who in many cases have been harmed or wronged by the very ones whom God has commanded us to honor. God's command is not only for the benefits and blessing of the parents but for the children as well, because unresolved anger and resentment toward parents robs the child of God's blessing.

If you are not satisfied with your relationship with your parents, this could be one of the most important books you will ever read. Honoring your parents and writing a tribute to them could revolutionize your life, your relationship with them, and your relationship with God.

—Bill Bright

1

Into the River

How sharper than a serpent's tooth it is to have a thankless child.
—William Shakespeare

On the outside Bill seemed the very image of a successful attorney. He wore a finely tailored suit and drove a sleek, black Lexus—the type of car men drool over. His finely appointed home was in the most expensive area of town, and on summer weekends his family enjoyed a vacation home on a nearby lake.

Wealth can be deceptive, though. As I sat with Bill one day over lunch, he talked about his failing marriage and the sense of isolation he felt with his two teenagers. I could see that he wasn't nearly as confident in his personal life as he appeared.

Bill felt hurt and confused. Why was he having such a difficult time making his marriage work? Why was intimacy with his wife so elusive? Why was he fearless in the corporate environment and yet so fearful in all his relationships—with his wife, his children, and other men? I listened carefully.

As I sipped my coffee and glanced at his fashionable tie and watch, I couldn't help asking Bill about the family he grew up in. Who had shaped his life? What type of a relationship did he have with his parents when he was a child? How would he describe that relationship today?

As Bill answered these questions, I saw his countenance change. His eyes grew distant. His voice dimmed and faltered at points. His handsome face lost its sparkle.

He talked primarily about his dad, who he felt had emotionally abandoned him. Bill had worked so hard as a child to win his dad's approval and even now as an adult—but it never came. Now a middle-aged man, he had never once felt like an adult in his father's eyes. Their relationship was shallow, he said—cordial and perfunctory, always remaining on the surface. As Bill descended into his description, I heard words that spoke of unresolved longings for a real relationship.

I had felt these deep currents before with men and women as they talked about their parents. It was as if I had plunged Bill into a river—a deep, relentless stream that coursed through his past. The river ran through the bittersweet memories of his childhood—the times of joy and the times of rejection and loneliness. In some spots the water flowed over boulders and around fallen trees, reminders of the pain he'd felt when his father had criticized or ridiculed him.

This forty-something business executive, so successful in the world's eyes, still felt like a boy with his parents. The more he talked, the deeper he immersed himself in the river. His mood changed from sadness to pain, then to anger and bitterness. Even though he lived just two hours away from his boyhood home, he rarely visited his aging parents.

Was he getting even? he wondered. *Or had he just lost hope of ever being truly connected to his parents?*

He was just about to emerge from the river, wet and tired, when I said, "Bill, I think you've got some legitimate concerns about the way you were raised. And yet I see within you something that I've seen in hundreds of other adult children. There is something deep inside of you that longs for a relationship with your mom and your dad before they die."

Bill looked at me thoughtfully but didn't speak.

I went on: "I can't explain it, but somehow our identity is inextricably linked to our parents. Our personal fulfillment and personal peace are tied to the kind of relationship we have with them. To regain a relationship with your father and mother, you're going to have to rediscover what they did right. And you'll need to come to grips with the fact that your parents are human beings with needs."

I paused for a moment as the words penetrated his heart. Then I told Bill, "I'm going to challenge you with one of life's riskiest assignments. You need to determine how you can tangibly honor your dad and mom."

With that, Bill was back in the river. But one thing was different: He was nearing the headwaters, the Source.

The Forgotten Commandment

If you pick up your Bible and turn to Exodus 20, you'll find the Ten Commandments. These ten timeless absolutes were given by God to the Jewish people after He brought them out of slavery in Egypt. Although studies show that most people are unable to recite these commandments from memory, most of the Ten Commandments are at least familiar to us: "You shall not murder," "You shall not steal," etc.

One of those decrees, however, is often overlooked. Even in the Christian community, little is said about the fifth commandment:

> Honor your father and your mother, that your days may be prolonged in the land which the LORD your God gives you.
>
> Exodus 20:12

I call this the "forgotten commandment." Instead of honoring our parents, we've taken the better part of the past three decades to bash, blame, and attack our parents for their faults and failures. Our parents have become a toxic waste site on which to dump the blame of our dysfunction. In the process of analyzing our backgrounds—which I believe is indeed an important part of growing up—we have failed to take responsibil-

ity for our own attitudes and actions. We have failed to obey
that which God clearly commands: to honor our parents.

And yet, surprisingly, this command may be one of the
most profound in all of Scripture because of its accompanying
promise: "that your days may be prolonged in the land which
the LORD your God gives you." As I personally have sought to
apply this concept of honoring my parents, and to encourage
others to do the same, something inexplicable has occurred.
Hundreds of adults have told me that working through this
process has turned out to be one of the most meaningful spiritual and emotional experiences of their lives. These adults
have discovered a "prolonging" to their days—not so much in
length of time, perhaps, but undoubtedly in added meaning
and contentment.

I'm no mystic. But I can only describe these experiences
as I did with Bill: It's like jumping into a deep, swiftly flowing,
powerful river. Many adults never come near this unexplored
and untamed river because they are afraid of where it might
take them; they just don't want to confront their pain and their
responsibility. But I can promise anyone this: By the time
you've run the rapids of this river, you'll climb out soaked and
exhausted—yet your life will never be the same. And you may
find that the experience has changed your relationship with
your parents as well.

I've learned that this command to honor our parents
yields more fruit than most of us realize. Indeed, I believe
there are penetrating and unforeseen benefits that are inextricably linked to one's obedience to this command:

> ▶ Could it be that the quality of life you experience today
> is tied to your obedience to this command?
> ▶ Could it be that a part of your longing and quest to
> become an adult is connected with the commandment
> to honor your parents?
> ▶ Could it be that obeying this commandment is a major
> step toward true spiritual maturity in your life? Or, to
> put it another way, could it be that how you handle this

command will determine whether you keep growing or become stunted in your growth as a Christian?

▶ Could it be you could forge a deeper, more meaningful relationship with your parents by honoring them?

▶ Could it be that your parents, who took the initiative in your life for probably eighteen to twenty years, are now waiting for you to initiate something of substance and meaning back to them?

▶ Could it be that your parents are just as desperate as you are to receive approval and affirmation?

▶ Could it be that a generation of elderly parents is waiting to receive the honor and dignity that belongs to them as our elders? Could their lives become more meaningful as a result?

▶ Could it be that the kind of legacy you leave to the next generation, whether you are married or single, is deeply connected to your relationship with your parents and whether you honor them?

▶ Could it be that God is honored and pleased when we honor our parents?

▶ And, on a broader scale, could it be that the very survival of our nation is tied to its sons and daughters honoring their parents?

I believe the answer to each of these questions is yes.

A Hot August Day . . .

My own journey on this river began in August 1966. The scene is forever etched in my mind.

I stood in the driveway of my home in Ozark, Missouri, leaning against my white, four-door Chevrolet Bel-Air. I was eighteen years old, and I was about to leave home.

Boxes and suitcases filled the trunk and the backseat. My spinning rod could be seen through the back window, bent and pressed to conform to the rear dashboard. Back in the house, my bedroom was abandoned and lonely—littered with reminders of the boy who claimed those four walls as his own for eighteen years. In a few minutes I would drive off to my new home—a dorm room at Crowder Junior College in Neosho, Missouri.

There were Dad and Mom, about to face an empty nest. Mom seemed especially short that day standing next to Dad, his arm around her waist. It was an awkward moment.

Looking back, I was "bushwhacked," as Dad would say, by the emotion of the occasion. No one had warned me that leaving home would be so hard, so crowded with emotion. No one had told me that the metamorphosis of a boy becoming a man would begin in earnest when I left home and headed for college.

I was about to be on my own.

I have only a hint of what Ward and Dalcie Rainey were feeling at that moment. Perhaps they were thinking about the little boy who used to build mountains and roads in the sandbox next to the driveway. Or maybe the fishing pole sparked memories in Dad of us catching a stringer of white bass on Swan Creek.

I don't know what prompted the thing that happened next. Perhaps it just was that an adolescent boy had grown up a little and uncharacteristically thought of someone else's needs other than his own. Perhaps it was God who stirred my soul. But, for the first time in my life, I remember feeling an enormous sense of gratitude and appreciation to these two people who had given me so much of themselves and who had so fashioned my life.

As I looked in their eyes, the emotions rose suddenly in my throat. I remember that I wanted to cry, but as I moved to embrace them I swallowed hard, fought off the tears and said, with a breaking voice, "Mom, Dad, I love you."

It is tough to admit that this was the first time I remember having said those words to my dad and mom.

In typical fashion for parents of their generation, they managed to control most of their tears, too. But their goodbye hug was a little tighter and longer than any in my memory. I remember feeling there was something good and very right about my spontaneous display of love toward my parents.

Looking back, I think I grew up a little bit that day in the driveway. As I backed out the car and waved goodbye, I felt happy that I had done what was right.

Touching a Nerve

During the next ten to fifteen years, as I grew in my relationship with Christ and helped begin a full-time ministry to families, my interest in the subject of the forgotten commandment grew. For several summers I taught a graduate class at the International School of Theology for students who were preparing for vocational ministry. Of my twenty or so lectures, the one addressing "Honoring Your Parents" easily sparked the greatest response. It was intriguing!

After one lecture, three young women came to me and described their dads. The characteristics of each father were generally the same—very successful in providing for material needs, but aloof, detached, distant, and unexpressive. All three of the women had tears in their eyes as each expressed her desire to somehow build a loving relationship with her dad.

As I questioned each woman, I saw that these fathers had made some wrong choices—but I also sensed these young women had erred as well. I counseled them to honor their fathers by taking their share of responsibility for changing the relationship. I suggested they spend some time alone evaluating their responses to their dads. Then, when appropriate, they should call their fathers and confess to having been ungrateful, ask for forgiveness, and say, "I love you."

One girl was immediately convicted of her failure to honor her dad. She said, "I need to call home and tell my dad I'm sorry for being such a spoiled brat."

Later I found out that in each case the father's heart melted. One of the women returned the next morning with tears streaming down her face. "For the first time in my life, my father and I communicated," she told me. "In the past, my father gave me cars, jewelry, piano lessons, nice vacations, everything. I got him on the phone and told him, 'I don't want all this stuff—I just want you. I love you and I want to know you.'

"He began to cry, and I began to cry. For the first time, he told me that he loved me. I don't think our relationship will ever be the same. I can't wait to go home."

Somehow this message was touching a raw nerve in the lives of these three women and the other adults in my class. Many had such difficult relationships with their parents that the command to honor them presented a challenge of immense proportions, a major step of faith. Yet when they took that step, something powerful happened. Even if they didn't see great changes in their parents, they usually reported that their own lives were somehow different.

I remember thinking, "God has put something in this commandment that we're missing today. He wants to do something in our relationship with our parents that I haven't even begun to understand."

A Painful Lesson

My personal odyssey with this idea included one more discovery. It probably was the most significant of all—as well as the most painful.

As I spoke about honoring parents, I shared practical ways to demonstrate that honor. The list included the usual: hugs, kisses, phone calls, cards, letters.

But I began to sense there had to be something more substantive involved than a five-dollar phone call—more significant than a kiss or a hug, more effective than a two-dollar Mother's Day card.

Even today, I can't fully explain it. But something started sprouting back in September 1976—on the day my dad died.

Just a couple of weeks earlier, Dad and Mom had visited my family and me in Little Rock. My father and I worked side by side that weekend, fixing up the house we had recently purchased.

He and I laughed as we went to the hardware store and asked for "quarter-inch putty," which we needed to fill in the space between the molding and ceiling. Neither of us was what you would call a "handyman." After my parents left to go back home, I told my wife, Barbara, it was one of the best times I'd ever had with Dad.

Two weeks later the phone rang. It was my brother calling: Dad had died of a massive heart attack.

He was gone. There had been no warnings, no time for goodbyes. Dad was gone.

In the years that followed, I reflected on my dad's funeral. Sixty-six years of life, forty-four years of marriage, and forty-eight years of business—all summed up in a thirty-minute memorial. It was meaningful for our family; but it still bothered me a bit. It seemed too brief a remembrance for all Dad had meant to us.

Dad was a great man. Impeccable character. Quiet. Hard-working. The most influential man in my life. It didn't seem right that a man's life could be summarized in such a superficial sketch.

I wondered, *Did he really know how I felt about him?* I had worked hard to express my love to him for several years, but my words had seemed so hollow. Had I really honored him as I should have?

I pledged then that I would not wait until Mom died to come to grips with her impact on my life. I resolved to let her know about my feelings for her.

A letter wouldn't do—it couldn't express my emotions adequately. No department store had the gift I was looking for. It could not be manufactured in a factory.

What I had in mind had to be personal. Meaningful. It required some pomp and formality.

So, in the winter of 1984, I began working on a written Tribute to my mom. I jotted down memories. Tears splattered on the legal pad as I recounted lessons she had taught me and fun times we had shared. It truly was an emotional catharsis.

Off and on for about a month I worked on her Tribute. I crafted and honed every word, shaping each phrase with the care a first-time father gives to his new baby, selecting memories that would honor her and bring a smile to her face.

She needed to smile. She was alone now.
Here's the tribute I wrote:

"She's More Than Somebody's Mother"

When she was thirty-five, she carried him in her womb. It wasn't easy being pregnant in 1948. There were no dishwashers or disposable diapers, and there were only crude washing machines. After nine long months, he was finally born. Breech. A difficult, dangerous birth. She still says, "He came out feet first, hit the floor running, and he's been running ever since." Affectionately she calls him "The Roadrunner."

A warm kitchen was her trademark—the most secure place in the home—a shelter in the storm. Her narrow but tidy kitchen always attracted a crowd. It was the place where food and friends were made! She was a good listener. She always seemed to have the time.

Certain smells used to drift out of that kitchen— the aroma of a juicy cheeseburger drew him like a magnet. There were green beans seasoned with hickory-smoked bacon grease. Sugar cookies. Pecan pie. And the best of all, chocolate bonbons.

Oh, she wasn't perfect. Once when, as a mischievous three-year-old, he was banging pans together, she impatiently threw a pencil at him while she was on the phone. The pencil, much to her shock, narrowly missed his eye and left a sliver of lead in his cheek . . . it's still there. Another time she tied him to his bed because, when he was five years old, he tried to murder his teenage brother by throwing a gun at him. It narrowly missed his brother, but hit her prized antique vase instead.

She taught him forgiveness too. When he was a teenager she forgave him when he got angry and took a swing at her (and fortunately missed). The most profound thing she modeled was a love for God and for people. Compassion was always her companion. She taught him about giving to others even when she didn't feel like it.

She also taught him about accountability, truthfulness, honesty, and transparency. She modeled a tough loyalty to his dad. He always knew divorce was never an option. And she took care of her own parents when old age took its toll. She also went to church—faithfully. In fact, she led this six-year-old boy to Jesus Christ in her Sunday evening Bible study class.

Even today, her age doesn't stop her from fishing in a cold rain, running off to get Chinese food, or "wolfing down" a cheeseburger and a dozen bonbons with her son. She's truly a woman to be honored. She's more than somebody's mother . . . she's my Mom. "Mom, I love you."

Making It Special

When I finished Mom's Tribute, I decided something was needed to set these words of honor apart from all the letters I had written in the past. But what?

After several days of thinking through different options, I decided, with Barbara's help, to have the Tribute typeset and framed in a black wooden frame. The effect was simple, but impressive. And on a cold, dreary, overcast day in February, I packaged the finished product and mailed it home to Mom.

Three days later, the phone rang. It was Mom. She was obviously touched by her surprise gift. Immediately I knew that this simple gesture had genuinely communicated things I had clumsily tried to say for years.

I had known she would like it, but I was unprepared for the depth of her appreciation. She hung it right above her table where she eats all her meals. There's only an old clock on another wall in that room—and that clock is no rival for my mom's Tribute.

She has shared it with family members, the television repairman, the plumber (who, she boasted proudly, asked for a copy), and countless others who have passed through her kitchen. Recently she told me, "On days when I'm down emotionally, I'll read that and think, 'How can he write that about his mean, old mom?' " Seeing that tangible representation of my love on the wall above her breakfast table reminds her of the truth. Who knows how often she's read it, just to get a little encouragement?

Now, over a decade later, it's interesting to look back on that gift and reflect on the effects of having formally honored my mom. I think it cemented our relationship as adults: I was still her son, but I no longer felt like her little boy.

Our relationship slowly changed as I began to return a portion of the grace and forgiveness she had given me a thousand times as I grew up. In our conversations, I found myself encouraging her and lifting her spirits more than I had in the past. I related to her as a peer, and started to care for her needs rather than just expect her to recognize mine. I made a greater effort to spend time with her.

Sharing the Idea with Others

The results of honoring my mom with a Tribute were so encouraging that I began to challenge others to write Tributes of their own. "Your parents need a tangible demonstration of your love now. Why wait until after they die to express how you feel?" I asked.

I never presented this idea as a magic potion or a cure-all for healing difficult relationships. Yet, as people began implementing it, I saw that honoring their parents with a Tribute touched a deep nerve in them.

Soon people began sending me copies of the Tributes they had written. They told me remarkable stories about the healing they had experienced in their relationships with their parents. And in choosing to obey the forgotten commandment, many had found that God had begun a work of healing and growth in their own souls.

I began to see there really was more to this command to honor parents than I had realized.

Are You Ready for an Incredible Journey?

As we examine this concept of honoring parents, you may embrace the idea enthusiastically. Perhaps you already have a good relationship with your parents. If so, you'll probably enjoy applying some of the creative ideas you'll find in this book.

But maybe you haven't handled your relationship with your parents very well since you've become an adult. You may feel isolated from them or angry about how they've treated you in the past. Perhaps you have trouble communicating with them, and the idea of writing a Tribute as I did for my mother seems impossible. (See the box, "A Special Word to Children of Abusive Parents," at the end of this chapter.)

Wherever you are in your relationship with your parents—whether it's great, just okay, strained, or estranged—there is hope and encouragement for you in these pages. Whether you have been hurt by angry parents, abused, ignored, or manipulated, you will be given practical ways of dealing with your father and mother honorably.

I'll lead you through a simple, step-by-step process of producing and presenting a Tribute for your parents. I will recount a number of the stories that have gripped me and given me the conviction that this message must be shared. And I'll share several Tributes that accompany these stories from homes just like yours and mine.

I can promise you one thing: If you're willing to step into the river—to take an honest look at your relationship with your parents and seek ways to honor them—**then working through this issue and writing a Tribute may be one of the most profound, mysterious, and incredible experiences of your entire life.**

My own journey down this river—going back nearly twenty-five years to that sun-drenched, emotion-filled driveway—tells me there is something great tucked away in this forgotten commandment. Perhaps your journey begins today.

But before I explain the concept of the Tribute any further, let me tell the story of another man's journey into the river. . . .

A Special Word to Children of Abusive Parents

Perhaps some of you have been wounded so deeply by your parents that you cannot see how God can expect you to honor them. When you were a child, you may have experienced physical, sexual, or emotional abuse. If that's the case, then the idea of writing a formal Tribute is almost repugnant to you. You may feel intense anger just thinking about it. You may feel that I do not understand your personal situation.

I have devoted one chapter—(chapter 15)—specifically to people who have been abused. Yes, God's promise in the fifth commandment holds true even for you. In the meantime, let me gently encourage you to read through this book with an open heart and ask God to show you how He would like you to respond. I have no desire to place on you a burden that you are unable to carry at this time.

Perhaps it will be years before you can work through your pain. Perhaps you need time to work through serious issues from your family background with the help of counseling. Maybe writing a Tribute is not possible at this time.

But I have to believe that, tucked away in a quiet place in your soul, a part of you desperately desires a good relationship with your parents. If so, remember this: God is in the reconciliation business. It could be that honoring your parents through a Tribute will begin to pry open a rusty door in your relationship and let in a fresh wind of healing.

2

The Healing Power of Honor: One Man's Journey

You might say my good friend Robert Lewis* grew up in a 1990s family—forty years ago. He says it was the "modern family before it was modern."

In Ruston, Louisiana, in the early 1950s, Robert's dad and mom got up each morning and both went off to work. Thomas Lewis sold insurance, and Billie worked for a legal firm. (She later became personal assistant to the lieutenant governor and then to a state senator.) While other children were cared for by full-time moms, Robert and his brothers spent a good many of their early years with live-in maids who cleaned the house, washed their clothes, and fixed their meals.

Robert never doubted his parents loved him—but he knew something was missing. His dad never was the type to show affection or approval. Robert never heard the words, "I love you," or, "Great job." In fact, both of his parents were so busy they didn't have much time for three boys who needed daily encouragement and attention. Perhaps that is what fueled Robert's drive to achieve as a student and athlete in high

---

* The personal stories I share in this book are used by permission. If I use a first name only, I have changed some details to enable the person involved to remain anonymous.

school and in college: he was searching for the affirmation he didn't receive much of at home.

Still, Robert never thought of his family as being different. That is, until his dad started drinking heavily. By the time Robert turned ten, he knew something was terribly wrong in his home. Dad and Mom seemed to yell at each other all the time. And as a teenager, Robert frequently was embarrassed when he brought home friends and found his highly intoxicated dad stumbling through the house.

Christmas Eve often was a memorable disaster. Robert's dad usually drank himself through the holiday season. Although the Lewises couldn't be described as being a religious family, Billie always wanted the family to gather for a religious observance such as reading the Christmas story. But it never seemed to work out. Tensions would arise, the drinking started, then the screaming began. And three frightened and confused boys sat watching as Christmas collapsed in chaos.

Caught in the Middle

Robert wrestled within, trying to understand what his parents were feeling. It seemed to him his dad *wanted* to do what was right. Unfortunately, his mom saw more failures than successes, and she had a flair for pointing those failures out to him. So, Dad escaped his troubles through alcohol, and Mom looked for support from her sons. Robert's brothers usually sided with their mother in these disputes. But whenever Robert struggled to explain to his mom what he thought his dad was feeling, she would yell, "You just don't understand!" In attempting to help both of his parents, he often ended up being the "enemy" of both.

There were many good memories, too. He remembers the special fishing trips with his dad, which meant father and son being together all day on a peaceful lake. His father could be such a delight when he was sober.

And then there was that autumn evening which, thirty years later, remains a magical memory. The leaves were changing, the air was crisp, and both parents were in a particularly good mood. Thomas was whistling while burning leaves and listening to a high school football game on the radio, and Billie was inside frying up some of the Gulf Coast oysters Robert loved.

There was something supremely special about that evening—so peaceful and warm. *This is how our family should be,* Robert thought. Yet, even then he knew it was just a moment in time. It was not the way life was going to be.

Turning Points

Each of the Lewis brothers chose a different path in life. But each still had to cope with the common wounds of his childhood. The oldest brother was a corporate lawyer and a talented artist. He eventually chose an openly homosexual life-style, which ended tragically in 1990 when he died of AIDS at age forty-four.

The youngest brother majored in Oriental history but chose not to pursue a career in that field. Instead, he decided to leave home and move to the mountains of Wyoming to hunt, fish, and search for himself. In the years to come, he would find his answer to life in a meaningful relationship with Jesus Christ.

Robert, meanwhile, grew up with a lot of anger and resentment. These became an asset to him in two areas—fights and football. Simply put, Robert was mean.

But he also was fortunate. When he was fifteen, one of his coaches took a unique interest in him. The coach gave Robert much of the affirmation and encouragement he didn't get from his father. He told Robert, "You're a leader—you can do it. You can make decisions. You can be somebody special. I believe in you." Such encouragement worked wonders, and he excelled.

After high school, Robert eventually received a football scholarship to the University of Arkansas. A neck injury prevented him from reaching his athletic potential, but something even more significant happened during those college years: Robert invited Jesus Christ to be his Savior. "I saw in Jesus someone I could entrust my life to—someone who would not leave or forsake me," Robert says. "In Christ, I found stability and direction."

Like most children of alcoholics, Robert learned from an early age not to feel or think about his family's problems. He coped by burying his feelings and denying the harsh reality of his family's dysfunction.

But as he grew into adulthood and began living on his own, Robert started looking more realistically at his relationship with his parents. Soon he began to realize just how much he had missed as a child. Yet he also realized he had to make a choice: He could blame his parents for this and seek revenge by criticizing them or isolating himself from them. Or, he could move toward forgiving them. In other words, he could play the role of victim, or he could take responsibility for his life.

Robert didn't want to deny the pain and hurt he felt. But he knew he couldn't wallow in it either. One side of him wanted to lash out with anger, yet another side knew he would only hurt himself by doing so. He realized he needed to give Christ all the pain, and to rely on Him for the strength and love he hadn't received as a child.

Somehow, Robert began to see his parents through a different filter. For years he had focused on what they'd done wrong. But now, married and a parent himself, he saw how his own children didn't notice many of the good things he did for them. It dawned on him that he had forgotten many of the things his parents had done for him as well.

The Impossible Prayer

Several years later, Robert was pastoring a church in Tucson, Arizona. One evening he was conducting a small-group Bible study in his home. To stimulate discussion, he asked, "What is something you would like to believe God for, but you think is just impossible?"

Each member answered the question. Then came Robert's turn. "You know," he said, "I think it would probably be impossible for my dad to become a Christian."

Thomas Lewis, now seventy years old, had lived his life without any interest in religion. Robert had explained the gospel to him on two occasions, but each time his dad wouldn't even talk about it.

"I'm not saying God couldn't do it," Robert told the group. "But it does feel hopeless. It seems almost impossible to pray for this." The evening concluded with heartfelt prayers, including some for Robert's "impossible" request.

Within twenty-four hours, Robert's world changed. That very night in Louisiana, his parents got into a terrible fight. Thomas had gotten drunk and decided to leave the house. Billie, afraid to let him drive, grabbed his shoulder. But Thomas brushed her arm away, slammed the door behind him, and drove away in his car.

What Thomas didn't see during that brief, angry moment was that when he brushed his wife's arm off his shoulder, Billie stumbled backward and fell. As she fell to the floor, her neck hit a marble coffee table and was fractured.

She lay on the floor, unable to move. Fortunately, a phone had fallen off the coffee table from the impact, and an operator came on the line. Billie somehow forced out enough words to let the operator know she desperately needed help. An ambulance arrived and rushed her to the hospital, where she would remain for three months with steel pins implanted in her skull to support her broken neck.

Thomas stayed out all night and never came home. Some friends located him at his office the next morning, and when they told him what had happened to Billie, he was so shocked he suffered a major heart attack on the spot.

The whole tragic episode had begun on the same night Robert's small prayer-group prayed for the "impossible." Robert didn't learn about any of it until the next morning, when a doctor called. He told Robert, "Your father has had a major heart attack. You need to come, because he's probably not going to live long." Robert quickly called a longtime friend to tell him he was coming home—and his friend told him about Mom.

Reeling from the two devastating blows, Robert boarded a plane in Tucson with a heavy heart. He wondered, *would his dad live? Would his mom? And what was God doing?*

The Blessing

Robert arrived in Louisiana that night and immediately drove to the hospital where his father lay in intensive care. As he sat down next to his dad, an amazing conversation began to unfold.

Thomas, groggy from medication, had a fuzzy look in his eyes. "How are you doing?" Robert asked. His dad replied, "Well, I'm not doing too good. I've done a horrible thing."

As Thomas began describing what he'd done to his wife, Robert realized his father was so medicated he didn't recognize his own son. The older man thought he was talking to a doctor. As Robert listened, his eyes wide, Thomas said, "Let me tell you about my three boys." He began talking about where each of his sons lived and what they did. When he came to Robert, the listening son recalled, "He talked about what a good son I was and that he was really proud of me. That I was pastor of this 'big church' (he exaggerated here) in Tucson."

For the first time in thirty years, Robert was hearing the words of praise a son so needs to hear from his father. It was another magical moment—a father giving his son the gift of acceptance and approval. As they continued talking, Thomas grew aware of who Robert was. Tearfully he confessed what he had done to his wife. "I've done a horrible thing," he cried. "I need to go to hell." Robert had never heard his father speak so directly about eternity. And without hesitating, he replied, "Dad, that's where you're going to go if you don't come to the place of forgiveness in Christ."

"What do you mean?" Thomas asked. For the next hour Robert explained who Christ was, why He died on the cross, and how Thomas's sins could be forgiven. And, that night, the impossible happened. Thomas ended years of rebellion and independence by praying with his son—confessing his sins and asking Christ to forgive him and come into his life.

Robert says, "I walked out thinking, 'This has got to be one of the greatest miracles I've ever witnessed—my dad coming to Jesus Christ and giving me his blessing on the same night.' It was an incredible story. And it all happened within twenty-four hours of a prayer I thought God could never answer."

Reversing Roles

As Robert's mother recovered in her hospital bed, she heard one chorus repeated regularly from her family and friends: "Get a divorce." No one thought she should live with a man who had made her life so miserable and had broken her neck. "You've stayed with this man far longer than you should have," everyone told her. "How could you possibly stay married to him after what he's done to you?"

Only one lone voice said, "Don't do it." It was Robert's. He alone believed something good could come out of this tragedy. For the first time he had seen his father humble himself and repent, and Robert knew this gave the marriage a glimmer of hope.

Robert decided to draft a set of requirements for his dad:

1. He would never drink again.
2. He would seek professional counseling for his drinking.
3. He would live outside the home for an entire year to establish a track record of sobriety and recovery.

Robert took the list to his mother and asked, "If Dad can do all this, would you stay married to him and allow him back into your home after a year?" She didn't think Thomas could do it, but she agreed to wait and see.

Then Robert approached his father. He said, "Dad, you can either be responsible, or you can be divorced. I can't stop the divorce because Mother can choose that. And she's got everybody on her side telling her to do it. But I've gotten Mom to agree that if you'll live responsibly, in time she'll receive you back."

By standing up to his father and setting up conditions for the marriage to continue, Robert was in a way reversing the earlier roles of father and son. He was helping his dad to take responsibility. And it worked: A year later his reborn father, clean and sober, moved back home.

"Some people would say my parents had a miserable life," Robert says. "They were inept in a lot of ways, and they certainly experienced a lot of pain. But when they finally had some help and direction, they responded. It wasn't a perfect end, just a faithful one.

"My mom often said, 'I don't want a divorce, but I don't have any choice.' I showed her how she could have a choice, and she responded to that. Dad also was given a choice, and he chose not to drink and to work his way back home. And I loved him for that."

A Tribute

Robert eventually moved his family to Little Rock, where he became my pastor. One Sunday morning Robert allowed me the privilege of giving the sermon. I took the opportunity to speak on God's commandment to "Honor your father and your mother."

I challenged the congregation to consider writing a special Tribute to their parents. By this I meant a formal, typeset, framed document thanking and honoring them for what they did right as parents. I had no idea how seriously this simple suggestion would affect Robert. Even though he and I had developed a good friendship, I wasn't aware of the drama surrounding his family and how he would apply this message to his parents.

A couple of years later, Robert was on a retreat in Colorado and had a free afternoon. The idea of writing a Tribute had been germinating in his mind for some time, and now the time seemed right to act on it.

Years before, he had confronted his feelings of bitterness and had forgiven his parents. But now his mother and father were growing old, and he sensed he ought to put together something special for them—a document to formally honor them for what they had done right.

He took a pen and paper, sat in the lodge in front of a fire, and began to write some recollections from his childhood. To his surprise, a flood of memories coursed through his mind: the terrible moments of his childhood as well as the happy ones . . . all the anger and joy and sadness and longing. The explosion of emotion overwhelmed him. He had thought he would simply sit down and write a letter—but now he was crying and weeping as he never had before. People began staring at him. Soon he had to leave and return to his room.

For the next four hours, through tears and sobs and writing in between, Robert released much of the pain he had built up through the years. "It's hard to describe what happened, because I've always been more of a cerebral type," he says. "This flood of emotion showed I was getting in touch with a part of myself that I didn't even know was there. The closet door came open and all this 'stuff' flooded out. It was powerful and potent. And bittersweet. But it was also thrilling, because I felt the healing winds of freedom rushing within me."

When he was finished, he had written a document he titled, "Here's to My Imperfect Family." The title is startling. But Robert knew he couldn't paint a rosy picture of the past— his family was too honest for that. They all were painfully aware of the trials they had gone through. Yet, at the same time, Robert wanted to remind them of the good things he had discovered in a fresh way.

A Christmas Ceremony

Robert had the document typeset and framed. On Christmas Day, he and his family drove to Louisiana. After all the other gifts were opened, Robert stood up and turned to his mother and father. He said, "You know, there are a lot of things I've always wanted to say to you that I've never known how to say. So I've tried my best to put them all into writing. I'd like to read it to you." With his wife and four children standing by his side, Robert read the following Tribute:

"Here's to My Imperfect Family"

When I think of family, I think first of you, Mama, and you, Daddy. I will never understand the forces that drew or held you two together all these years. Clearly, it has not been easy. But, then again, I have now learned that few marriages are. Each carries its own crucible. Reflecting back as one of your three sons, it's not hard to say that our family was less than perfect. The "imperfect family" would be a much more descriptive term for our home. To be sure, we never had enough or did enough together. We fell short of many ideals.

Those things have little if any hold on me now. Instead, I frequently recall "particular" things that are now forever imbedded within me . . . things that need to be stated in writing, for they are the secret successes of my imperfect family.

I am glad you never divorced. Today I do not think of a way out because you never got out. My children know about divorce from their friends but not from their family. They will grow up carrying permanency in marriage in their heritage; and though that in itself will not ensure success for them, it will help as it helped me.

I am more appreciative than ever for your sacrificial involvement and investments in me. I will never know them all, as my children will never know all of mine. But I do know some. Your presence at my school programs and Little League games is one. Responding to late-night fever and upset stomachs and crises like the "chicken bone affair," caught in the throat of a frightened third-grader. I needed you, Mom, and you were there. I also remember the genuine compassion I received after being heart-broken that I stood and watched rather than starred in my first organized football game. And the hours you expended talking with me, exploring and sur-facing my thoughts, feelings, and ambitions. How that helped!

I think of fishing at Kepler's Lake with Daddy. Boy, was that fun! I still enjoy it every time I relive it in my mind. And through your help for a young black man named James, I have a deeper social con-sciousness toward those "not like me." And thanks, Daddy, for saying "I'm sorry" when you wrongfully hit me in anger one day. You don't remember the incident, I know, but I do. It's deep inside me now—and it comes back to me every time I need to say those words to my children and my wife. Seeing that day in my mind makes the humbling process easier.

I owe both of you a thousand "thank you's"—for Florida vacations at the Driftwood Lodge . . . for all the oysters I could eat on my birthday . . . for the constant encouragement during my teenage years . . . for teaching me about inner toughness. I can still hear you saying, "If you can't take it, you can always quit" . . . for struggling in December to give Christmas its real meaning. Mom, I got the picture now . . . for teaching Sunday school at Trinity . . . for traveling to all those ball games . . . for standing behind me when I turned down LSU . . . for saying "I love you" because I needed to hear it . . . for the new car in college (I now know somewhat how that must have hurt finan-cially) . . . for not panicking when it seemed your son had become a religious fanatic . . . for letting me know the financial "ride" was over after college and I was on my own . . . for not getting too in-volved in shaping my direction. . . .

There is much more, of course. Much more. I

guess if I were offered one wish, it would be for one day of childhood in time past . . . when I could again be your little boy. It would be a crisp, fall evening with the smell of burning leaves and a Bearcat football game in the air. I would be outside enjoying the bliss of youthful innocence. Mom, you would be frying those oysters, and Daddy, you would be calling out to our faithful dog, Toddy, "What a dog!"

So here's to my imperfect family. One that fell short in many respects, but one whose love makes the shortcomings easy to forget. Here's to the family that never had it all together, but one just perfect enough . . . for me!

I love you,
Robert

Robert had to stop several times because his eyes flooded with tears. He saw his dad's eyes welling up, too. Thomas couldn't bring himself to cry, but obviously he was touched deeply. Robert's mom was simply stunned. She just sat, weeping silently with tears of happiness.

When it was over, everyone was still in a moment of sweet silence. No one in the Lewis family was used to hearing such transparent words. And now nobody knew what to say.

However, the next day, the first thing Robert saw when he walked into his parents' home was the Tribute, hung in the room's most prominent spot. It stayed there until Thomas and Billie died, showing the world that even though they had made mistakes in their lives, they also had done other things well. And in the life of at least one of their sons, everything now was being reconciled in love. "We all knew the imperfections and warts," Robert says, "but here, in this Tribute, my mother and dad finally had been honored for what they'd done right. And it was wonderful."

That was December 1985. Just nine months later, Thomas died of a heart attack. Yet for Robert, the pain of that moment was eclipsed by a deeper chorus of positive feelings. Robert recalls thinking as he stood before his father's open casket, "There is nothing I wish I would have said to you, Dad, because I said it. I have no regrets. I am healed, and now so are you. We can both rest in peace."

He Chose a Different Path

I never fail to be amazed when I hear Robert tell his story. As he says, "God's Word holds unique, special, and powerful experiences for those who will radically grab hold of it and see it through to the end."

Many people would say that Robert had every right to criticize and even reject his parents. Yet he chose a different path, the path of honor. As a result, Robert saw God's power at work in an unusual way.

By the way, Robert's mother made a recommitment to Christ during her later years and died in 1990. Today the Tribute he wrote for his parents hangs in his study at home.

3

Whatever Happened to Honor?

What is honored in a land will be cultivated there.
—Plato

Anna Jarvis, born eighth of eleven children and reared in Grafton, West Virginia, made history by honoring her mother.

Sonora Smart Dodd, who grew up in Spokane, Washington, as the only daughter among six children, secured her spot in the history books by honoring her father.

You've probably never heard of those two names. But each year your calendar reflects their influence—they were the founders of Mother's Day and Father's Day.

Anna Jarvis was at her mother's bedside on the night she died in May 1905. Two years later, Anna convinced her church—Andrews Methodist Church in Grafton, where both she and her mother had taught Sunday school for years—to hold a special Mother's Day service in honor of mothers on the anniversary of her own mother's death. That Sunday morning, Anna gave a white carnation—her mother's favorite flower—to every mother who attended. The response: four-hundred and seven children and their mothers came.

An idea was born. From that point on, Anna began seeking to honor all mothers. In Philadelphia she organized a Mother's Day Committee, with such notables as food manufacturer Henry J. Heinz, department store founder John Wanamaker, and the editor of the *Philadelphia Inquirer*.

In 1910, West Virginia became the first state to recognize a formal Mother's Day. State after state, from east to west, followed that lead. And on May 10, 1913, the U.S. House of Representatives passed a resolution officially recognizing Mother's Day. All of this was at Anna Jarvis's bidding and prodding.[1]

Meanwhile, in Spokane, Sonora Smart Dodd sat in church on one of the first Mother's Day celebrations and listened as mothers were extolled for their personal sacrifices in rearing their children. Sonora's own mother, however, had died during childbirth. She knew that it was her father—Civil War veteran William Jackson Smart—who deserved to be honored.

She persuaded the Ministerial Society of Spokane to salute fathers by holding special church services. Church leaders agreed, and the observance was scheduled three weeks later (on June 19) to allow pastors time to prepare sermons on the subjects of fathers. National newspapers reported the events, and interest in creating a "Father's Day" began to grow.

Panati's Extraordinary Origins of Everyday Things records that Father's Day was not accepted as quickly as Mother's Day. In 1924 "President Calvin Coolidge recommended that states, if they wished, should hold their own Father's Day observances." He wrote to the nation's governors that "the widespread observance of this occasion is calculated to establish more intimate relations between fathers and their children, and also to impress upon fathers the full measure of their obligations." It wasn't until 1972, though, that Father's Day was permanently established nationally by President Richard Nixon.[2]

A Schizophrenic Culture

Because of Anna Jarvis and Sonora Smart Dodd, each May ten million of us call a florist to send flowers to our mothers. Card companies sell 150 million Mother's Day cards and 85 million Father's Day cards to us each year.[3] And we rack our brains, thinking, "Let's see, last year it was slippers for Mom, and the fishing rod for Dad. So, what are we going to do this year?" To some people, these observances seem more an obligation and a nuisance than a special occasion.

Each year on Mother's Day and Father's Day, we witness a temporary burst of stories in the media on motherhood and fatherhood. A television reporter features his mother and tells his audience about her love and sacrifice. A national magazine asks celebrities, "What lessons did you learn from your father?"

Yet, during the rest of the year, we see the other side of our relationships with our parents. We read of celebrities revealing how their parents abused them when they were kids. We hear adults blaming their parents for their problems—everything ranging from alcoholism to repressed sexuality to overeating. We see television sitcoms in which parents are portrayed as incompetent buffoons.

We read that "barely half of the American public believe it is the children's responsibility to look after their parents."[4] We hear about the new trend called "Granny dumping": Unwilling to care for their parents and grandparents, adult children are abandoning them on the doorsteps of hospital emergency rooms.

Are these the same children who send millions of cards to their mothers and fathers? What is going on? It's as if we are schizophrenic when it comes to honoring our parents.

Plato wrote, "What is honored in a land will be cultivated there." Who receives honor in our culture today?

Sports heroes receive honor. If you can slam-dunk a basketball, knock the breath out of a running back, or throw a baseball ninety-five miles per hour, you can make millions of dollars in contracts and endorsements.

Entertainers receive honor. Hardly a week goes by without some television show presenting awards to music, television, and movie performers.

Soldiers and policemen earn medals for acts of courage and heroism. Employees often are honored for top performances or for years of service to a company.

And what usually accompanies all these honors? Pomp and pageantry. A pedestal. An ovation. Applause. Photographs. A handshake. Hugs. Public recognition and words of appreciation. Tears. Prestige. Feelings of significance.

Have you ever watched someone receive an honor who was not expecting it? You see shock, gratitude, and appreciation streak across his or her face. And chances are, he or she will never forget the moment.

Yet, think about who does *not* receive much honor in our culture: those in authority. We have declared an "open season" on authority figures. Our leaders have become easy prey for the investigative reporters on the evening news. One wonders if Lincoln or Washington could have escaped the carnage today's media creates.

In addition, leaders in businesses, churches, and other organizations face a steady stream of dishonor in the crushing demands and expectations put upon them by their staff or employees. At present we are experiencing a crisis in a shortage of competent leadership. This could easily be traced to the fact that bright men and women are simply unwilling to risk the possibility of public dishonor that can come simply from stepping up to the front of the pack.

Most disturbing, though, is the general lack of honor given to perhaps the most important segment of our society—parents. I can't help wondering if the decline in the birth rate over the last three decades is in some way related to our failure to honor our parents. Perhaps fewer people are willing to take upon themselves the job of parenting when so little honor is ascribed to it.

Unfortunately, we are modeling for the succeeding generation how to dismantle and disgrace one another. We encourage the ravenous human appetite for ripping others apart.

We have become a nation of dishonor. And no nation—or person—ever moves forward in an atmosphere of dishonor.

Honor: A Weighty Matter

Honor, according to Webster's College Dictionary, is "high public esteem; fame; glory; to earn a position of honor." When God commands us to honor our fathers and our mothers, however, He provides some additional meaning. In the original Hebrew language, the word for *honor* meant "heavy" or "weight."

Its literal meaning was "to lay it on them." Today, when we use this phrase—"lay it on them"—we typically mean flattery. Not so here. To honor someone meant, "I weigh you down with respect and prestige. I place upon you great worth and value." That, in fact, is what a Tribute accomplishes—it's the most personal, practical, and powerful way I have ever come across to "weigh down" a parent with honor, respect, and dignity.

It is fascinating to observe how God used the concept of honoring parents as one of the foundational elements in forming Israel into a nation. Think of the setting: God had brought His people, held captive for so long in Egypt, into the wilderness of Sinai. He had promised them the land of Israel, but up to this point He never had given them any written directions. They needed a constitution that would teach them how to relate to God and how to live with one another. They needed instructions that would govern their behavior and preserve their identity as a nation.

God gave them the Ten Commandments. And to best appreciate the significance of the command to honor parents—the fifth commandment—note where it fell:

"You shall have no other gods before Me.
"You shall not make for yourself an idol, or any likeness of what is in heaven above or on the earth beneath.
. . . You shall not worship them or serve them; for I, the LORD your God, am a jealous God. . . .

"You shall not take the name of the LORD your God in vain. . . .

"Remember the sabbath day, to keep it holy. . . .

"Honor your father and your mother, that your days may be prolonged in the land which the LORD your God gives you [emphasis mine].

"You shall not murder.

"You shall not commit adultery.

"You shall not steal.

"You shall not bear false witness against your neighbor.

"You shall not covet your neighbor's house; you shall not covet your neighbor's wife or . . . anything that belongs to your neighbor."

Exodus 20:3–17

I believe God had a purpose in placing the fifth commandment where He did. By doing so He highlighted two important truths about honoring parents. The first is:

1. Honoring your parents should grow out of a strong relationship with God.

Note that the first four commandments deal with how man relates to God. With these mandates, God established that He is the One who should be exalted above anyone and anything else. A nation's life—and an individual's life—is defined by its relationship with God.

Then comes the fifth commandment: honoring our parents. Its placement indicates it should be a direct result of our faith in God.

Look carefully at the commandment again. Whom did God command us to honor? Only perfect parents? Only Christian parents? Parents who are spiritually mature and insightful? Only those who never made major mistakes in rearing us?

No, God commands us to honor our parents regardless of their performance, behavior, or dysfunction. Why? Because honoring parents demands that we live by faith—we have to trust that God in His sovereign wisdom will use our parents to help shape us into the people He wants us to be.

For some of us, honoring our parents may be a "spiritual barometer" of our relationship with God. And if we want to walk in His ways, and experience His love and power, then we need to obey His commands. Jesus said, "If you keep My commandments, you will abide in My love; just as I have kept My Father's commandments, and abide in His love" (John 15:10).

God knew we need to live by faith—to be obedient to Him without always seeing the reason or understanding the "why" for everything we do. Yes, honoring your parents may stretch your faith. You may do it only because God commanded it, not because you feel your parents deserve it. But because you exercise faith, you will grow spiritually in the process.

God ordained the "office" or position of parents, and He wants us, in obedience to Him, to honor the officeholder. It matters not whether the person holding the office is worthy of honor; our responsibility is simply to honor.

Our Helper

Another important truth to remember is that God did not leave us powerless to obey this commandment. Deuteronomy 30:11 states, "For this commandment which I command you today is not too difficult for you, nor is it out of reach."

This may seem preposterous, because no human being in history—except Christ—has ever been able to obey the Ten Commandments perfectly. But that is why God gave us the Holy Spirit—to give us the power to obey Him. Read these encouraging words from Jesus:

> If you love Me, you will keep My commandments.
> And I will ask the Father, and He will give you
> another Helper, that He may be with you forever;
> that is the Spirit of truth, whom the world cannot
> receive, because it does not behold Him or know

Him, but you know Him because He abides with
you, and will be in you.

John 14:15-17

If you have received Christ as your Savior, God has given
you a power source that you may hardly have tapped.

The second reason God placed the commandment to
honor parents where He did is because:

2. Honoring your parents should be the cornerstone of a nation.

By divine decree, the commandment to honor one's parents was listed *before* the remaining directives about murder,
adultery, stealing, lying, and coveting. In establishing Israel,
God assigned priority status to the institution of the family and
its relationships. And in doing so, the Lord makes a clear statement: Do you want your nation to live a long time? Do you not
only want to survive, but also have peace in your homes and
nation? Then begin by esteeming and respecting your parents.

A nation's greatest defense is not its military, but the family. Our nation's greatest asset is not the national treasury—it's
the family. The moral spine of our country is not in lawmakers
—it's in the family, which spawns and nourishes character.
That is why the health and life expectancy of a nation can be
measured by the way its people honor or dishonor their parents. A nation's very survival is at stake over how its children
treat their parents.

Indeed, all of the basic components necessary for a
healthy society find their origins in the family: respect and love
for others, submission to authority, commitment, and character, to name a few. John MacArthur says it well:

A person who grows up with a sense of respect
for obedience to his parents will have the foundation
for respecting the authority of other leaders and the
rights of other people in general. . . . Children who
respect and obey their parents will build a society

that is ordered, harmonious, and productive. A generation of undisciplined, disobedient children will produce a society that is chaotic and destructive.[5]

The Warning

God thought this honor so important to the health of the nation of Israel that He commanded their leaders to put to death any child that struck or cursed his father or mother (Exod. 21:15, 17). The Lord amplified this command later in Deuteronomy 21:18-21, with a chilling and sobering decree:

> If any man has a stubborn and rebellious son who will not obey his father or his mother, and when they chastise him, he will not even listen to them, then his father and mother shall seize him, and bring him out to the elders of his city at the gateway of his home town. And they shall say to the elders of his city, 'This son of ours is stubborn and rebellious, he will not obey us, he is a glutton and a drunkard.' Then all the men of his city shall stone him to death; so you shall remove the evil from your midst, and all Israel shall hear of it and fear.

The severity of a death penalty for cursing parents certainly grabs our attention. It's as if God underlined the fifth commandment and put an exclamation point at the end to say, "This is absolutely critical for your nation and its families." And we can be certain that after this warning was given, thousands of Jewish boys and girls heard some stern and grave warnings from their parents and spiritual leaders!

In prescribing such severe consequences for sin, God was shaping Israel's conscience. He was making a statement that teaching and training children to honor their parents was a divine priority for the nation.

Honor or Consequences

The Bible is filled with stories of real sons and daughters who honored or dishonored their parents as adults. As you read through the following list of biblical characters, ponder the weight of each person's choices and their consequences:

▶ Ham dishonored his father, Noah, by taking delight in catching him in a naked and drunken condition and mocking him to his brothers. But Shem and Japheth honored their father by covering his nakedness (and thus "covering him" in his sin). The result: Ham's descendants became Canaanites and were cursed to become servants to his brothers. The descendants of Shem and Japheth became entire nations that prospered and were blessed by God.

▶ Esther, who honored her surrogate father, Mordecai, ended up becoming a queen, which resulted in the saving of the Jews.

▶ Lot's daughters deceived their father by getting him drunk, seducing him, and becoming pregnant by him. The children of these two daughters became two nations which were deadly enemies of Israel.

▶ Jacob, with the help of his mother, deceived his father Isaac, to receive the blessing meant for his older brother. As a result he spent the rest of his life paranoid, running from Esau. Later, eleven of Jacob's sons dishonored him by selling their brother, Joseph, into slavery and deceiving their father.

▶ Moses honored his father-in-law, Jethro, by taking his advice to delegate decisions. The result was that the people got answers to their disputes and problems.

▶ Samson dishonored his parents by lusting after a Philistine woman and going against their counsel by marrying her. His choice was his demise: He ultimately lost favor with God, and the Philistines took over and desecrated Israel.

▶ David honored Jesse by being faithful to shepherd his

father's flock, a lowly job for a boy from a wealthy family. But David ultimately became king, and Israel grew as a nation under God's favor.

▶ Amnon raped his half-sister Tamar and brought disgrace to his father, King David, and his rule. This resulted in hatred and intense sibling rivalry in the king's household.

▶ Absalom led a rebellion against his father, King David, competing with him for the throne. Absalom later died while still a young man, without the blessing he could have received. And his rebellion divided the nation of Israel.

▶ Ruth honored her mother-in-law, Naomi, and God blessed her with a wealthy husband, Boaz. The long-range result, though, was that she became a part of the lineage of David and an ancestor of the Savior of the world, Jesus Christ.

Note the far-reaching effect these choices had. Usually they affected the entire nation of Israel. When these children honored their parents, God honored the nation with blessing —but dishonor in Israel was followed by calamity.

As I look at the priority God places on the fifth commandment and its accompanying warnings, I'm astounded that the Christian community today is so silent when it comes to honoring parents. Honoring our mothers and fathers is a command of God that He wants us to take seriously.

What Honor Is, and What It Isn't

Honoring parents is a command for all children, regardless of age. There is no exception clause in this commandment that exempts the adult child from responsibility. As we shall see, the command to honor parents is just as important for an adult child as it is for a younger child still at home.

Chances are that at this point you're starting to squirm in your seat. Yes, honoring your parents seems risky. Perhaps you fear that honoring them by writing a Tribute would convey that you approve of their wrong choices or actions, of how they live, or of the mistakes they've made. Or, possibly, you fear such a Tribute would place you back under their emotional control—and you've had enough of that.

Honoring your parents does not mean endorsing irresponsibility or sin. It is not a denial of what your parents have done wrong. It does not mean you flatter them by ignoring or denying the emotional or physical pain they may have caused you.

First of all, honoring your parents as an adult child cannot place you under their authority. It does not give them authority to manipulate you. That's because a Tribute isn't written to seek approval. It doesn't mean crawling back into the cradle and becoming a helpless child again. Rather, honoring your parents means:

- ▶ choosing to place great value on your relationship with them.
- ▶ taking the initiative to improve your relationship.
- ▶ obeying them until you establish yourself as an adult.
- ▶ recognizing what they've done right in your life.
- ▶ recognizing the sacrifices they have made for you.
- ▶ praising them for the legacy they are passing on to you.
- ▶ seeing them through the eyes of Christ, with understanding and compassion.
- ▶ forgiving them as Christ has forgiven you.

Honoring your parents is an attitude accompanied by actions that says to your parents: "You are worthy. You have value. You are the person God sovereignly placed in my life. You may have failed me, hurt me, and disappointed me at times, but I am taking off my judicial robe and releasing you from the courtroom of my mind. I choose to look at you with compassion—as people with needs, concerns, and scars of your own."

Honoring Parents Brings Rewards

Many years ago, renowned soprano Marian Anderson was asked by a reporter to name the greatest moment in her life. She had many big moments to choose from. There was the night the famous conductor Toscanini told her that her voice was the finest of the century. There was the private concert she'd given at the White House for the Roosevelts and the King and Queen of England.

In addition, she had received the $10,000 Bok Award as the person who had done the most for her hometown, Philadelphia. And, to top it all, there was the Easter Sunday in Washington, D.C., when she'd stood beneath the Lincoln Memorial and sung for a crowd of 75,000 that included Cabinet members, Supreme Court justices, and members of Congress.

Which of these big moments did she choose?

None.

The greatest moment in Marian Anderson's life was the day she had gone home and honored her mother by telling her she wouldn't have to take in washing anymore.[6]

As the famous soprano obviously knew, honoring one's parents may be one of the most rewarding and memorable deeds of one's life. In the next three chapters you'll discover why.

4

The Promise

*When I was a boy of fourteen, my father was so ignorant I
could hardly stand to have the old man around. But when I
got to be twenty-one, I was astonished at how much the old
man had learned.*
—Mark Twain

Lien Mersha was only five years old when her parents were killed in an automobile accident. When she lost her family, something inside her died as well.

"I started stuttering, didn't speak until spoken to, never talked to kids, never played outside," Lien says. "I'd come home after school and go to my room."

Lien had many rooms over the years. She, her sister, and two brothers were made wards of the state of Minnesota and sent to live in separate foster homes. Lien was quickly labeled a "problem child" and lived in fourteen homes during the next six years. She shoplifted, broke windows, pulled pranks on neighbors, and began taking drugs. "I was always in trouble. They told me I was going to end up in jail. I believed it for a long time."

Then she met Nhon and My Le.

In April 1975, Nhon was a pilot in the South Vietnamese Air Force. On one of the last, hectic days before Communist North Vietnam took control of South Vietnam, Nhon and My fled the country with their two young children, Dat and

Tuyen. After several months in a refugee camp, the family was allowed to emigrate to the United States.

Nhon and My both were committed Christians, and they wanted to give something back to the country that had given them a new life. They wanted to do something to make a statement of appreciation to their new homeland. So they approached the state social services agency and asked to be foster parents for the "worst case you have."

The social worker came up with several possible children. But in each case Nhon and My shook their heads—they told the astounded social worker the child was not bad enough! They wanted a truly needy, problem child.

They ended up with Lien.

When Lien learned that her new foster family was Vietnamese, she thought it was a joke. But this time, with this family, things really were different.

No matter what Lien did, Nhon and My stuck with her. "They went through hell and back with me," Lien says. "Dad said it was almost like getting shot at by the enemy. He took shot after shot after shot. I would keep shooting bullets at him, but they never really harmed him because he knew in the end there would be so much good that would come out in me."

The turning point came one evening after a conflict that had started when Lien lied to Nhon and My. "We were in the den, watching TV, and he said, 'Lien, why do you take the love I have for you away?' "

For the first time, Lien realized someone actually loved her. "I started crying and said, 'I didn't know you loved me.' I began to realize that the Les were important to me, and that if I continued doing drugs, I would lose them. I realized I had something special here, and I needed to make it work."

After that, Lien began to change. She decided she would honor her parents by obeying them and trying to please them. "When they told me to do something, I did it. If they told me to be home at midnight, I was home at midnight, not at 12:30 or 1 a.m."

Nhon and My convinced Lien to go through treatment for her drug problem. They told her about their faith in Christ, and at age seventeen she received Him into her life at a church retreat.

A couple of years later, a newspaper reporter sat down for a meal at a Vietnamese restaurant. She was surprised to see that her waitress was an American teenager—Lien. The reporter was further intrigued when she learned Lien's parents were the Vietnamese owners of the restaurant. She arranged for an interview, and that gave Lien the opportunity to write a Tribute for her parents.

The newspaper printed the entire Tribute, verbatim. Here are some excerpts:

When my father came here five years ago, he started as a kitchen cleaner, a housekeeper, a butcher. He worked for $2.05 an hour. He worked as a keypunch operator, then advanced to a programmer. Now he's a systems programmer, owns his own restaurant, and is the owner of a five-bedroom, colonial home in southeast Minneapolis. Last year both he and my mother became American citizens. They have helped eleven people come over here from Vietnam.

I treasure them so. They can never do any wrong in my eyes.

My mom worked for Control Data before they started the restaurant. I can talk to her about anything. I admire the way she always stands behind my father in his decisions and supports him. They knew I was on drugs, but they wanted to help me. They took a chance that nobody else would. They saw that I wanted to be good—that in order for me to be good, I had to be around good surroundings.

I don't mind authority now. I think it's everything in the way they show me they care. If I have a problem, it's theirs. No matter what time of the day, I can go to them and say if I have a

problem, and they take time for me. It doesn't matter
what they're doing. They always stop and talk to me.

Nobody has ever taken the risks that my parents
have with me. They trust me to run the restaurant.
They trust me with their cars. They trust me with
their children, Dat and Tuyen.

The kids are very precious to me. I have so
much insight now for when I raise my own family
. . . things I'd do differently. I'd want them to know
that when they're in trouble with me, I don't hate
them and don't like disciplining them. I'm doing it
because they made a decision and even though it isn't
right, they're responsible for the outcome.

The main thing is that [they] have shown me
that there is a chance. I've seen a life now that I want
—that I didn't want before. I've learned the past will
never leave you, but you don't have to worry about it,
because it's gone. It's the present and the future that
you have to look forward to.

Today Lien is married and has adopted children of her
own. "We hope one of our children will adopt when they're
older, and carry on their grandparents' legacy," she says.

Lien Mersha is a walking miracle. But her remarkable
story demonstrates more than the power of loving and committed parents. It also illustrates a remarkable truth of Scripture—that when you honor your parents, God gives you a tremendous blessing. Her life began to change when she finally
began to honor the parents who demonstrated so much love to
her.

The First Commandment with a Promise

If honoring your parents is the "forgotten commandment," then the second part of the fifth commandment must
be the "forgotten blessing." In the last chapter I addressed the
first half of the fifth commandment. Now I'd like to discuss the
second:

Honor your father and your mother, *that your days may be prolonged in the land which the* LORD *your God gives you.*

Exodus 20:12 (emphasis mine)

Deuteronomy 5:16 adds another phrase to the promise: "and that it may go well with you. . . ."

Paul mentions in Ephesians 6:2 that this is "the first commandment with a promise." But what does it mean? How can your "days be prolonged" by honoring your parents? And in what ways will things "go well with you"? Does God actually promise we will live longer if we obey this commandment? Yes! You can't get around what God clearly promises in these verses of Scripture. Yet there is one condition: *You must be obedient to God in all areas of your life.*

Deuteronomy 30 contains some very specific promises, and they boil down to this: If you obey God's commandments, He will bless you and "prosper you abundantly" (v. 9). But if you disobey God, He will withdraw those benefits:

See, I have set before you today life and prosperity, and death and adversity; in that I command you today to love the LORD your God, to walk in His ways and to keep His commandments and His statutes and His judgments, that you may live and multiply. . . .

But if your heart turns away and you will not obey . . . I declare to you today that you shall surely perish. You shall not prolong your days in the land where you are crossing the Jordan to enter and possess it.

Deuteronomy 30:15-18

From a human perspective, I do not always understand how this happens. But it does seem that God is fully capable of blessing our lives with more years than we would have enjoyed had we not been obedient to Him. When a person walks in obedience to God, he or she generally is more peaceful and joyful, and better able to handle tragedy, failure, and anger.

Theologian and author Martin Lloyd-Jones comments on this part of God's promise:

> What it is meant to convey is that God is very well pleased with people who observe this commandment, and that if we set ourselves to observe these commandments, and this one in particular, for the right reason, then God will look down with pleasure upon us, and will smile upon us and bless us. Thank God for such a promise![1]

Do you want to live your life with the favor of God upon you? Would you like to feel the blessing and the good hand of God upon your life? Your life can be transformed by fulfilling this command to honor your parents. Obeying this verse could do more to increase your life expectancy than jogging!

It's obvious that if we honor our parents, we'll benefit from better communication with them, the possibility of peace with them, and greater freedom in our relationship with them. But I believe there are some hidden benefits as well. In the next three chapters, I want to explore this promise more fully, because it is one of the most mysterious and powerful in all of Scripture.

Chapter 5 will focus on how *you and your legacy will benefit from being "connected by honor" to your parents.* And chapter 6 will explain how *your parents will profit from a better relationship with you from your act of honoring them.*

But first let's consider another profound way that "it may go well with you": *Honoring your parents will help you finish the process of growing into adulthood.*

Putting Away Childishness

In 1 Corinthians 13:11, the apostle Paul writes of our need to grow up: "When I was a child, I used to speak as a child, think as a child, reason as a child; when I became a man, I did away with childish things." Paul knew that kids will be kids—that as children we behave childishly. But he also pointed out that as we grow up, we must set aside childish behavior and become mature.

Children are by nature petty, hurtful, and fault-finding in their relationships. They speak rashly, rudely, and selfishly, with little concern for how their words will affect their parents and others.

Children think life revolves around them. They're self-righteous. They think they're always right and that others are at fault, even when the evidence has declared them guilty.

Paul's challenge to us is that we lay aside our childishness and finish the process of becoming an adult. And part of maturing as an adult is the growing realization and conviction that we are just as responsible for our relationship with our parents as they are. And, if your parents are elderly or in poor health, you may be even more responsible than they are.

One-Way Streets

For most of your first eighteen to twenty years of life, your relationship with your parents probably could be compared to a one-way street. Your mother nursed you and changed your diapers—and your dad walked the floor with you at 2 a.m. She taught you how to walk—he taught you how to ride a bike. She read to you—he told you stories.

The "traffic" of love generally flowed in one direction—from them to you.

Of course, you brought your parents some joy and fun along the way. But as an infant you probably never looked up into your mother's eyes after she'd changed one of your especially fragrant diapers and told her, "Wow! Thanks, Mom. I really needed that!" No—instead, you probably fought her, resisting her clean-up efforts!

It was a one-way street. And it probably remained that way through high school and most of college. The problem with some parent-child relationships, however, is that they continue as one-way streets even when a child is in his or her thirties and forties. The adult child fails to assume responsibility for making the relationship a *two-lane* highway. A Tribute can help you begin the construction of a second lane in the two-lane highway you want to build back toward your parents.

A Rite of Passage

"I never felt my mother treated me like an adult."

Sound familiar? How often have you felt this same way about your parents? And how often have your friends echoed these words?

This statement came from Diane, who otherwise seemed happy with her life. She lived in the same town as her mother, but their relationship seemed strained and shallow. "She and I had a fairly cold, awkward relationship," Diane says. "We very rarely laughed together. I had a hard time letting down my guard with her, and she had a hard time letting down her guard with me."

When they talked, the conversation always centered on superficial things—how work was going, what the kids were doing. "We wouldn't talk about feelings at all," Diane recalls. "She still treated me and my other siblings a lot like kids. I felt a lack of respect."

To Diane's mother, there was only one way to do things— her way. "She couldn't see that other people saw things in a different way. She had no respect for our ideas, even on things like what we ate for dinner, or what clothes we picked out."

Over the years, Diane began to withdraw from her mother. She saw her mom every couple of weeks, but she removed herself emotionally. For a while, she didn't feel she was missing anything.

Her feelings began to change, however, when she heard about the idea of writing a Tribute for her parents. "I had dwelt on the negative for so long, there was a wall between us," she says. "It was just one of those things I knew I needed to do."

As Diane worked on the Tribute and remembered good things her mom had done for her, God slowly gave her a different perspective on her mom. "As I was going through [the Tribute], I learned to appreciate her more than I had. I always wondered what it meant to honor her in the midst of all these negative things that had happened. Even though she did things wrong, I felt I needed to forgive my mom. Honoring her was a concrete way of forgiving her."

While Diane was working on her document, she and her mother had a big argument. "I was very, very angry with her. It was a really big decision on my part to still do the Tribute. But with my husband's encouragement, and with God giving me the courage, I did finish it, and I gave it to Mom at Christmas."

As her mother read the Tribute, she immediately broke down in tears. "I think part of the problem was that all those years, while I was feeling she didn't respect me, she didn't feel any respect and appreciation from her kids," Diane says.

The Tribute allowed Diane and her mother to set aside their differences and begin building their relationship. "I feel she's more relaxed with me," she says. "I feel like some walls have been broken down. The other day she called and we were laughing about something over the phone. My husband heard us and said, 'I just can't believe how much your relationship with your mom has changed.' "

Even though Diane's mother appreciated the Tribute, it may have meant more to the daughter. "In a way, it was for me as much as anyone else. I knew it was something God wanted me to do, but I didn't know all the positive benefits that were going to come out of it. I really saw how fruitful obedience to God and His commands can be.

"It's been hard for my siblings to deal with how I handled this. They're not Christians, and they have absolutely no understanding of why I would ever look at these good things that my parents did.

"I'm not sure how to deal with that. But I do know that whereas I felt like a kid with my mom, after I did the Tribute I felt I was more on her level. I was able to relate to her more. It was sort of a rite of passage."

Maybe you find yourself facing problems very similar to Diane's. Perhaps you're waiting for your parents to respect you, recognize you as an adult, and "let you go." But, at the same time, your parents are waiting for you to honor them.

It's a standoff. You each may be like the wife who described the impact on her marriage of always waiting on her husband to act: "There's nothing I wouldn't do for him, and there's nothing he wouldn't do for me. And that's exactly what we do for each other—*nothing!*"

It is only as we choose to take responsibility for *our* part of the relationship that we begin to establish ourselves as mature adults—both in our parents' eyes and in our own. I can see at least three reasons why this maturing process begins to occur when you honor your parents:

1. Honoring your parents requires you to take initiative in the relationship.

When I wrote my mom's Tribute, something occurred within me that I could not describe for years. Later, I realized the Tribute was also a formal statement that her little boy had grown up. On my own initiative, I recognized her worth and value to me as her son who was now a man.

I do not pretend that honoring parents by presenting them with a Tribute is the total answer to a lack of self-confidence or identity crisis in a man or a woman. Nor can I guarantee it will mark a decisive turning point in a person's relationship with his or her parents.

On the other hand, I have heard and read enough stories to recognize that something mysterious happens in men and women who reach out through a Tribute to honor their parents. Perhaps this is because the act of honoring demands that we *initiate and give*. It is indeed significant whenever a forty-five-year-old business executive reveals that honoring his parents helped him to develop an identity as a man and to feel like an adult for the first time in his life.

As adults assume the responsibility to honor their parents, they begin to change the dynamics of a relationship that has always been a one-way street. And the result usually is that a *friendship* finally takes root.

2. Honoring your parents helps you to set aside the "victim" mentality.

It's an old idea, but it seems to be more in vogue than ever these days: "It's not my fault!"

The idea is that your problems and flaws are the result of your environment rather than of your personal choices. Popular psychology de-emphasizes the concept of personal responsibility—after all, we don't want to feel guilty for the wrong choices we make. Instead we are encouraged to blame others —often our parents—for our difficulties.

I'm reminded of the story of a little boy who came home from school with yet another bad report card. When he handed the report to his dad, the boy looked up and asked, "What do you think it is this time—heredity or environment?"

In his recent book, *A Nation of Victims*, Charles J. Sykes discusses this victim mentality:

> But perhaps the most extraordinary phenomenon of our time has been the eagerness with which more and more groups and individuals—members of the white middle class, auto company executives and pampered academics included—have defined themselves as victims of one sort or another. This rush to declare oneself a victim cannot be accounted for solely in political terms. Rather it suggests a more fundamental transformation of American cultural values and notions of character and personal responsibility.[2]

I need to state clearly here that many people deserve to be called victims. I've already discussed the extraordinary impact a parent has upon a child, and I do not want to appear to deny that many emotional or relational difficulties adults face can be traced to deficiencies in their parents' skill in rearing them.

What is happening in our culture now, however, is that too many people are blaming and bashing their parents for their problems and using "victim status" to avoid a prickly question: *When am I going to be responsible for my own life?*

Maturity and adulthood begin to occur when you honor your parents because it *moves you away from being the victim and toward a new perspective—that of taking responsibility for your life and for your relationship with them.*

A certain family cycle is worth noting at this point. You and I were born from a womb in which we were 100 percent dependent upon our mothers. During our early years we continued to depend on them to meet most of our needs. The older we grew, the more independent we became.

On the other hand, our parents were 100 percent independent of us when we were born. And now, as the aging process takes its toll, they become increasingly dependent upon us. Some parents find themselves completely dependent on their children at the very end of their lives. This is the way it should be—the cycle of a family—and yet it will work only if we, as adult children, assume more and more responsibility for our parents.

This leads us to the third reason honoring our parents helps us to grow up and mature:

3. *Honoring your parents helps you to mature by taking a hard, honest look at your parents.*

As I've watched many individuals go through the process of honoring their parents by writing a Tribute, several common threads begin to emerge. One is that when a person sits down over a period of time to collect positive memories and recount what his or her parents did right, a number of emotions surface: Gratitude. Appreciation. Joy. Love. A flood of happy memories that were lost are recaptured.

Other emotions may surface as well—anger, bitterness, disappointment over unmet expectations, broken promises, failed relationships. In fact, these negative emotions often hold positive memories captive. Many adult children have spent their lifetimes denying the truth and reality about their parents.

But when memories and emotions—both negative and positive—are buried, we are unable to honestly deal with them. Maturity demands that we confront our pasts, our circumstances, and our emotions genuinely and truthfully. No one will ever experience the benefits of growing up if he or she denies or refuses to face the reality of having been raised by fallen human beings known as parents.

Writing a Tribute is simply not possible if you have not faced your past in an honest way—grieving over mistakes and pain while also acknowledging what your parents did right. For that reason, the process of writing a Tribute also can bring a further benefit to your life: *healing*.

Leave the Results to God

God is challenging us to grow up by honoring our parents. He is calling us to responsible, thoughtful acts of love toward those whom he says we must honor. You are not accountable for your parents' response. They may refuse your love and honor. They may not forgive you for your mistakes. They may never ask you to forgive them for how they have hurt you. *But your responsibility is simply to obey God, to trust Him, and to let Him work in their hearts.*

One woman wrote me:

> Please tell people that not everyone will have a happy miracle to tell after calling their mother or father (or both) and asking forgiveness. Two months ago I decided that was the step I needed to take with my father—so I called him and very humbly apologized and asked him to forgive me. He would not. I was attacked verbally and made to feel very guilty.
>
> The conversation ended in tears. My comfort is not in a happy ending—yet—but in knowing that I have obeyed my God.

Her story didn't end there: Before she sent me the letter, she happened to talk with her father again. She added this postscript:

> I just got off the phone with my father—I didn't think my happy ending would come so soon. My father's world is crashing in around him—he declared bankruptcy yesterday.
>
> As a result I lost my place to live at school next year and will have to postpone my senior year so I can work full time. A number of other comforts also have been denied.
>
> But as I talked to my father I found that I had no bitter feelings, no hatred, and no anger. Instead, I heard myself asking him if there was anything I could do for him—I felt compassion and concern. And when I started to say good-bye, I heard myself tell my father, "I love you."

Our Lord's words in James 4:6 ring true in this example: "God is opposed to the proud, but gives grace to the humble." This woman realized that, in order to honor her father and create a two-way street, she needed to humble herself and ask for forgiveness.

Even though she didn't receive the forgiveness she desired, her step of faith may have changed their relationship. She became a giver instead of a taker. She became an adult.

"The Little Boy Hates Saying Goodbye"

A Tribute from Mark Bontrager to his parents, DeWayne and Judy Bontrager of Plantation, Fla.

At the FamilyLife Parenting Conference, I speak about the need for parents to prepare to "release" their children into adulthood. Listening to Mark Bontrager, it's obvious to me that his parents had that in mind. Mark grew up in a Christian home, the son of a pastor and a schoolteacher, and his parents knew they were preparing Mark to live on his own.

One story illustrates the atmosphere of trust that the Bontragers built in their home. "In high school I was dating a girl named Nancy, and she lived just down the street," Mark says. "A lady dropped off Mom after work one day, and the woman noticed another car in our driveway. 'Whose car is that?' she asked. Upon learning it was Nancy's, the woman expressed surprise: 'You mean you let them stay home alone?'

" 'My son is seventeen,' Mom replied. 'If I can't trust him by now, when can I trust him?' "

Mark had the opportunity to give his parents a Tribute at an opportune time—at age twenty-three, as he was beginning his new life in the Air Force. To him the Tribute was a chance "to open up my heart and express what I was feeling in a way that would encourage my parents and show honor to them."

Following is a slightly condensed version of the Tribute Mark gave his parents.

What the Little Boy Wanted to Say

He started off small,
    so small that they wondered
    if the little boy would ever grow up
    to fulfill all of the wonderful dreams
    that they had for him.
They prayed, and they hoped, and they prayed some more . . .
Then one day, they took him home from the hospital,

he was going to be okay.
The little baby grew,
   much too quickly for them but they loved
   to watch him grow.
(He was Dad's favorite play-toy.)
He learned to crawl,
   then talk,
   soon he was walking, laughing, and playing.
He loved stories,
   just like the one you are hearing,
   he would always say, "more book!"
He wanted to learn how to read.
He kept growing.
   He went to school,
   came home the first day of first grade and said,
   "I didn't learn how to read today."
   He learned to read. . . .
Then it seemed like no time, he was away . . . in
   College.
Five years later,
   he is home again,
   twenty-three years old
Soon to make the jump into the real world.
And the same hands
   that brought him home from the hospital
   will be hugging him good-bye
As he heads off on his own.
Well, this little boy
   hates saying goodbye
   He loved to remember
   all the little things that they did for him—
   because
They loved him.
   So he thought, and he remembered . . .
   when Dad used to come home from work, and
   he was just home from school, and Dad would
   open the door to the house and he and his little
   brother would run down the stairs and jump

into Dad's arms—Dad would laugh and hug
them—and he always loved the way Dad's co-
logne smelled. He'll never forget that. . . .
Then he remembered . . .
how Mom used to tie his shoes as he sat on the bed
before school. She always tied them the best—boy
was she quick! Everyone else always did it too tight.
He'll never forget that. . . .
Then he remembered . . .
how Dad would always give him a dime so he could
get a Coke at church. He'll never forget that . . .
He remembered . . .
Mom, undoing his boots after his playing in the
snow. It was so cold, but *she* would warm him right
up. . . . He'll never forget that. . . .
He thought some more and he remembered . . .
Dad, taking the training wheels off of his bike and
helping him learn to ride his bike. . . . He'll never
forget that. . . .
He remembered . . .
how Mom faithfully fixed his lunch every day for
school. Whether it was cream cheese and jelly, tuna
fish, or peanut butter and jelly—everything was always good, and she always had a little surprise. . . .
He'll never forget that. . . .
He remembered . . .
trying to keep up with Dad as he walked so quickly
to the nursing home, to help the people. . . . He'll
never forget that. . . .
He remembered . . .
Dad writing him in college about girls, going shopping for clothes with Mom, looking for tent spikes on
the railroad tracks with Dad, Mom typing his pa-
pers for him in high school—at the last minute. Dad
taking sound movies at all of the football games,
Mom putting up with his banging on the piano, Dad
helping him with his roller coaster . . . It goes on.
. . . But he'll never forget those things. . . .

There were two more things that he remembered:
> the family devotions; in the living room of the
> house, Dad would ask the family to kneel at their
> seats, it was right to show reverence to God in that
> way. . . . Then Mom would tuck him into bed, and
> say his prayers with him. They knew it was those
> prayers that allowed the very small baby to stay with
> them a few years longer. . . . He'll never forget
> that. . . .

There is one more thing that he will always remember . . .
> how Dad loved his wife—the little boy's mom, it
> made him feel so good knowing that Dad loved
> Mom. It set an example for him to follow. He also
> remembers how Mom served and loved Dad—it set
> a standard for him when he looks for a wife. . . .
> He'll never forget that!

Neither of them were perfect, but neither was the little
boy.

They were just right for each other—God planned it that
way . . . just as Mom and Dad want the best for the
little boy, so the little boy's heavenly Father wants the
best for him too—that's why He gave him such a great
Mom and Dad!

I guess the little boy just wanted Mom and Dad to know
that he loves them!

5

A Lifeline to Your Legacy

What a father says to his children is not heard by the world,
but it will be heard by posterity.
—Jean Paul Richter

Gilbert Beers was editor of *Christianity Today* for a number of years. In 1987 he wrote an article containing one of the most remarkable stories I've ever heard. It's about his great, great, great, great, great, great, great, great-grand-mother and the legacy she left her descendants:

> Catharine duBois, my great-great grandmother to the eighth great, never heard of crisis management. But if she had not honored the Lord in the greatest crisis of her life, I would not be here today.
>
> One day in 1663, Minnisink Indians swept down from the Catskill Mountains, killed several inhabitants of the little settlement now known as New Paltz, New York, and took a number of women and children captive. Among them were Catharine duBois and her infant daughter, Sara. For ten weeks they were held captive in the mountains, while search parties looked for them in vain.
>
> Certain they had avoided reprisal, the Indians decided to celebrate their success by burning

Catharine and Sara. A cubical pile of logs was arranged, upon which the bound mother and daughter were placed. When the Indians lit the torch to ignite the logs, all of Catharine's descendants were about to be annihilated with her.

How we die is a profound reflection of how we live. A life-threatening crisis somehow distills all our theology into a single, pungent drop.

A most human response at that moment would have been for Catharine to scream at her tormentors, curse them for her suffering, or even curse God (as Job's wife advised him in his life-threatening crisis; Job 2:9).

Instead, she burst into song, turning the foreboding Catskill forest into a cathedral of praise with a Huguenot hymn she had learned in France. The words were from Psalm 137, "There our captors asked us for songs, our tormentors demanded songs of joy; they said, 'Sing us one of the songs of Zion!' " (v. 3 NIV).

The Minnisink Indians, of course, had not asked her for a song, but they were now so captivated with Catharine's singing that they demanded another song, then another, and then still another. (Psalm 137 proved prophetic!) And while she sang "the songs of Zion," her husband, Louis, and his search party burst upon the scene and rescued her (and me!).

I have pondered the meaning of this event many times. Like each of us, Catharine was the narrow neck of the funnel where heritage and legacy meet. We draw upon her heritage, much of it bought with a heavy price by those we have never seen. And the way we bring that heritage to bear upon our present circumstance determines the legacy we bestow on unborn generations. Catharine could not have known that her decision about how to die would tell her succeeding generations much about how they should live. Nor can we know how some decision today will affect generations to come.

Who cares how one woman chooses to die in a lonely Catskill forest? Who cares, indeed? Eight generations have cared, and I suspect at least another eight will care as well.

At the burning bush, where Moses was managing his own crisis, the Lord said, "This is my name forever, the name by which I am to be remembered from generation to generation" (Exod. 3:15 NIV). Like individuals, generations do not stand alone but draw faithfulness or unfaithfulness to God from earlier generations, and bequeath their legacy to generations to come.

The God I prayed to this morning is the same God Catharine sang to eight generations ago, the same God who will listen to one of my faithful descendants eight generations from now. The God who heard Catharine's Huguenot hymn 324 years ago hears my prayer of thanksgiving today for her faithfulness. The God of Abraham, Isaac, and Jacob —and Catharine duBois—is my God and the God of my descendants. He transcends all generations.

My concern today is that I will faithfully fulfill my role as that narrow neck of the funnel, for the faith of some young man or woman 324 years from now may come to focus on how Christianly I handle a momentary crisis this afternoon.[1]

Honor Connects Generations

Gilbert Beers's story illustrates a profound truth: *Who you are and what you do with your life can have an impact on others for generations to come.* As Beers wrote, "Catharine could not have known that her decision about how to die would tell her succeeding generations much about how they should live."

But there is another lesson hidden in Beers's article: Children are influenced by family stories passed down from one generation to another. It's remarkable that Beers even knew that story—obviously it was told over and over through the years by parents and grandparents who wanted their children to know about the God who rescued their ancestors.

I believe it is just such linkage between generations that God wants to cement firmly in place by calling us to honor our parents. How you relate to your parents and speak about them today can demonstrate for your children a powerful statement of love. And it can allow the wisdom of one generation to pass to another. The result is the promise of Deuteronomy 5:16: "that it may go well with you. . . ."

In the previous chapter we saw that by honoring our parents we take responsibility for the relationship—that we can make a two-lane highway out of a one-way street. And, in the process, we can take a major step toward maturity.

In this chapter I want to look at a second way "it may go well with you" when you honor your parents: *It allows the legacy of one generation to continue unbroken to the next.*

The Power of Legacy

I'd like you to ponder this question: If you died right now, how would your children, friends, and family describe the legacy of your life? If you could have them say anything about you, what do you wish they would say of you?

Now, stop and consider your parents. What positive statements could you make about their lives? What kind of legacy have they left you? And what of it is worth passing on to the next generation? In other words—what could you honor them for?

By honoring your parents for their positive contributions in your life, you highlight the *legacy* of their lives. And in doing so, you pass on to succeeding generations stories of lessons learned and wisdom gathered.

To explain this principle more fully, I'd like to highlight three ways in which honoring parents keeps a legacy alive:

1. Honoring your parents allows you to learn from your parents.

As I look into Scripture, it becomes clear to me that God's most important structure for passing along spiritual truths is the *family*—parents teaching their children, grandparents teaching their grandchildren, and so on. Consider these words from Psalm 78:5-7:

> For He established a testimony in Jacob, and appointed a law in Israel, which He commanded our fathers, that they should teach them to their children; that the generation to come might know, even the children yet to be born, that they may arise and tell them to their children, that they should put their confidence in God, and not forget the works of God, but keep His commandments.

God calls each generation to pass down spiritual truth to the next. And for any family to carry on this type of spiritual relay, they must maintain an honorable multi-generational connection.

As you read through Proverbs, you recognize the priority God places on this connection of children to their parents. And through such a connection, children learn the discipline and wisdom needed for life:

> My son, do not forget my teaching, but let your heart keep my commandments; for length of days and years of life, and peace they will add to you. Proverbs 3:1

> A wise son accepts his father's discipline, but a scoffer does not listen to rebuke. Proverbs 13:1

> My son, observe the commandment of your father, and do not forsake the teaching of your mother; bind them continually on your heart; tie them around your neck. When you walk about, they will guide you;

when you sleep, they will watch over you; and when
you awake, they will talk to you. For the
commandment is a lamp, and the teaching is light;
and reproofs for discipline are the way of life.

Proverbs 6:20-23

From these verses, we see God wants parents and children
to be vitally connected. He knows children are born with sinful
natures, and they need to learn *wisdom, discipline,* and *obedience*
from their parents.

Some of the Tributes I've seen clearly illustrate the way a
parent can influence a child. In his Tribute to his mother,
Nancy, Joe Blanchette of Charlotte, Vermont, wrote, "You in-
stilled in me the importance of doing well no matter what job I
was doing. 'Set yourself apart from the other boys,' you'd tell
me. 'Shovel a path *two* shovels wide instead of just one.' Or,
'Don't just be on time, be a little early.' "

Do you think Joe's children will learn the same things
from him?

What Can You Learn from Your Parents?

Your parents are part of you. Their blood runs through
your veins. I've counseled enough people to realize that, even
when they deny it, they feel a terrible pain by isolating themselves from their parents.

I know of a man who lives in the same town as his parents,
and he has not spoken with them for years. He says he's better
off this way, and I'm sure that in some ways life is easier for
him. But my guess is, deep inside he feels incomplete without
a relationship with them. *Because he* is *incomplete without this
relationship.*

When adults do not honor their parents, they *isolate themselves from two of the most important people God has placed in their
lives.* If you have godly parents, this is not difficult for you to
understand. But if your parents are not believers, or if they
have failed you in their roles as parents in the past, you may

have a hard time believing your parents have something to offer you.

It could be that in many areas you *have* gained greater wisdom than your parents. But you probably could not honestly say there is absolutely nothing you can learn from them. It could be you need to look for ways to draw upon their advice.

Perhaps there isn't a spiritual legacy in your family. But is there something about God you learned from your father? Your mother? I have found that even those who came from nonreligious backgrounds still learned something of God's character from each of their parents.

2. *Honoring your parents allows them to remain connected to your children.*

Recently I heard about a woman who visited her mother along with her husband and teenage son. The son began discussing male and female roles with his grandmother, arguing that her ideas were old-fashioned.

What really hurt the grandmother most, however, was that her own daughter and son-in-law were sitting there, encouraging their son. "It felt to me like they were cheering him on," she said. "They were on his side, and I was the one who was completely outdated." Her concluding comment helps us to understand what happens when we fail to honor parents: "I feel no link to my grandson." In other words, *another way a legacy is poisoned through a lack of honor is that grandparents become cut off from their grandchildren.*

Children should be taught to respect their elders, even if they disagree with them. One aspect of honoring them is to respect their views, try to understand them, and refrain from challenging them in a condescending way. It could be their ideas *are* outdated—but many times their "old" ideas work much better than our "new" ones. We need to respect their insight and experience.

I am part of the "Baby Boom" generation and grew up in an era when authority was challenged. We invented the term "generation gap" and once warned ourselves never to trust anyone over thirty. We began to believe old values and old morals were outdated.

With this type of mindset, it's easy for children to pick up the attitude that "old ideas" are not even worth considering, simply because they're old. Yet when elders are ignored rather than honored, and when parents begin believing there is nothing worthwhile their children can learn from their grandparents, *we cut ourselves and our descendants off from the wisdom of the past.*

I ask you: Why are so many old people so bored and under-challenged? What keeps them going as they approach the end of their lives? Why do so many waste so much time chasing little white balls around a golf course? Here they are at the end of their lives, and many don't have any compelling vision to focus on, let alone to pass on to the next generation.

Something tells me that, in many cases, the problem may lie in their relationships with their adult children. If you said to me, "I wish my parents would start setting aside time to be grandparents to my children," I would ask, "How much time do you spend with your parents? Are you pursuing a relationship with them?" Perhaps if we value the older generation by honoring our parents, they will value the younger generation by getting involved in their grandchildren's lives.

Do your parents feel close to you? Do they feel loved, appreciated, and needed? And if they are needed by you, is it for something other than just babysitting? If they are loved and honored, perhaps they would make an effort to be involved.

Jack Turpin of Dallas, Texas, is a busy man, but not too busy for his eleven grandchildren. Several times a year he picks up a number of his seven grandchildren who live in the Dallas area for what he calls "Grandpa Day." Starting at 7 a.m., they go to a traditional spot for breakfast and then to his office. There he has a closet filled with games and books that the grandkids enjoy during the morning. Then they have lunch and return home.

God gives grandparents a special role in a child's life. A child may learn some character qualities more from his grandparents than from his parents. That's the type of vision I'd like to see grandparents embrace—one that shows they're helping build another generation.

I realize not all grandparents are able to do this. I also realize your grandparents make their own choices. Even if you as an adult child fulfill your responsibility to honor them, they may not take on the role you'd like them to. But by honoring them, you at least make an attempt to connect your children to the family legacy.

3. Honoring your parents may result in your children honoring you.

Do you want your children to regard you as wise when you are older? Would you like for them to listen to you when you're as old as your parents are now?

Your children are watching you, and they will follow your model. If you don't honor your parents, you run the risk of having your children do the same to you.

There's a story in *Our Daily Bread* about a wealthy widower who left his property to his only son and daughter-in-law on one condition—that he would be allowed to live in the country with them for the rest of his life:

> After a few years, when the inheritance had been spent, the daughter-in-law got tired of having the elderly gentleman around and told her husband he would have to leave. The son agreed and broke the news to his father.
>
> A short time later he and the feeble old man walked down the dusty road to a state-supported home for senior citizens. Being very unsteady on his feet, the father finally asked if he could rest for a few moments on a sawed-off stump to regain his strength for the last mile of the journey.
>
> As he sat there, he suddenly put his head in his hands and began to sob. The son, pricked in his conscience, tried to make excuses. Finally, the father

controlled himself enough to say, "I'm not crying so much because I'm going to this lonely home for the poor and unfortunate. I'm weeping because of my own sins. Forty years ago I walked down this road with my father and brought him to the very same place. I am now seeing the results of the evil deeds I have sown!"[2]

One of my favorite quotes, which I often use when I'm speaking at a FamilyLife Parenting Conference, concerns the downward spiral the Christian faith can take from one generation to another: "To our forefathers, the Christian faith was life. To our parents, it was a ritual. To us, it was a necessary evil. To our children, it will be abandoned." In the same way, if you casually dishonor your parents, your children may dishonor you more aggressively.

The Legacy of a Slave

Peter Loritts was a man whom most people never would have considered successful—but he certainly is having an impact on our culture today.

Peter began his life as a slave in North Carolina more than a century ago. Released after the Emancipation Proclamation, he eventually acquired some land to farm. He never learned to read or write.

Two things were important to Peter. First, he loved the Lord. His niece, Vera, now in her eighties, remembers him as a "singing and praying man." He often had his children and grandchildren read him passages from the Bible, which he committed to memory. And when his church needed land for a building, he donated part of his farm.

Second, he was committed to his family. He provided for them and raised them to love the Lord. He passed on to them a heritage of honesty and integrity and strong male leadership.

Peter's son, Milton, grew up with these values, and he passed them on to his own son, Crawford. A man who believed in commitment and responsibility, Crawford could be counted on to keep his word. If he promised something, he'd do it. He used to tell his children to "never walk away from responsibility. You look it in its eye and you deal with it, but you don't just walk away."

Once when his own son, Crawford Jr., was sixteen, he wanted to quit a job he had just begun. His dad asked why. "I just don't like it there anymore, Dad," he replied.

"Son, you gave the man your word that you'd show up. Not liking something is no reason to quit. Your word is everything. You said you'd be there, so you are not going to quit."

The elder Crawford grew up in the rural South in the heyday of the Ku Klux Klan. He faced the terrible discrimination most other blacks faced. But he never allowed his children to use race as an excuse for anything. "Throughout life he would remind us to rise above that, to look beyond that," Crawford Jr. remembers. "And he would refuse to typify white people as being all the same. He had a number of white friends he worked with and shared with. And he would bring us in contact with people who loved us for who we were. He would always point out the differences, and he would just give us tongue-lashings if we ever generalized all white people."

Crawford Jr. grew up to attend a Bible college and become a minister. Today he is director of Legacy, a ministry of Campus Crusade for Christ, and one of the most popular speakers for FamilyLife Marriage Conferences. He also helped found the Urban Family Conferences, an adaptation of the FamilyLife Marriage Conference messages intended to reach families for Christ in the urban community.

Most important, Crawford Jr. is a husband and a father to four children. And he is passing on to his children the same lessons he learned from his ancestors.

"It's funny how you catch yourself saying the same things your dad said to you," he says. "I have two boys in sports, and I tell them, 'If you play, you stay. I don't want to hear any nonsense about you quitting because you don't like it, or because the coach yelled at you.'"

Crawford Jr. and his wife, Karen, have made a special effort to pray for their children. "We've prayed they would come to know Christ at an early age, and that they would trust Him and love Him. Karen and I have made a commitment to try to live our lives in such a way before them—in honesty about our shortcomings, seeking their forgiveness when we sin or make a mistake in front of them—so we can pass on that heritage."

Whenever Crawford travels, he writes his children letters. He's involved in their lives. He leads them in family devotions, and he has an individual Bible study with each of his kids.

When he arrives home late at night from a trip, he slips into the children's rooms and prays for them. He asks God to protect them from the perversions of society, to keep them pure and holy. He prays they will develop their own supernatural relationships with Christ and that they won't merely imitate their parents. He prays they will gain wisdom in making biblical choices. He prays for the men and women they'll marry in the future.

He and Karen take the children up to visit his father. "They love to sit on the porch with their grandfather and listen to his stories," Crawford Jr. says. "The sense of connectedness and destiny this gives them is absolutely incredible."

Crawford Jr.'s oldest son, Bryan, now attends the same college his father did. Recently Crawford told me how his son introduced him before he spoke at a conference: "There are three men in my life who mean a lot to me," Bryan says. "The Lord Jesus, my grandfather for what he stands for, and my dad. I want to be like those three."

And to think it all began with an illiterate slave. Peter Loritts probably had no grand scheme for passing on godly character from one generation to another, but that's exactly what happened. Every person Crawford and Karen Loritts influence for Christ today is a part of Peter's legacy.

This legacy is especially meaningful when you consider the terrible crisis black families experience today. In the past thirty years, the family structure among many African-Americans has virtually collapsed, and millions of children today are growing up without the influence of a father. Sadly, how many of these kids will miss hearing the type of stories the Loritts family has told for decades?

Recently, Crawford and I were taping a segment for FamilyLife's nationwide radio program, "FamilyLife Today," and he told me his father was in poor health. At the end of the program I asked Crawford if he'd like to give a verbal Tribute to his dad for what he'd meant to him. By the time he finished, I was crying with him. Here's what he said:

> Dad, I love you, and thanks for the sacrifices of working over thirty years at the A&P warehouse. Thank you for choosing not to get paid triple-time on those Christmases and other days when we needed the money living in that small apartment in Newark, because you wanted to spend time with your kids.
>
> Thank you for not buying new cars until after we were grown because you wanted to have money for vacations and you wanted to show us things. Thank you for teaching me and telling me that I'm a man and standing with me during hard times.
>
> Everything I am today is because of you, and nobody may ever know who you are. You never made a big splash of it and you never blew your own trumpet, but you quietly did the deed. Thank you.[3]

Crawford is determined his children will remain linked to the past and will continue the connection into the future. His life demonstrates the power of a godly legacy.

Yet, I wonder how many families have squandered a spiritual heritage by failing to honor their parents and breaking the connection from one generation to the next.

It's sobering to consider how quickly a legacy can be lost. The choice to honor parents is one each generation must make.

6

Your Parents Are Waiting

*Children never figure that their parents have expectations and
are disappointed, or that they need something in return for
their love. They don't see their parents as vulnerable human
beings who can be hurt.*
—Erma Bombeck

The headline grabbed my attention:

Toddler's Reign of Terror
Costs $2,300 in Repairs

I proceeded to read one of the most humorous, true-life stories
I've ever seen:

GRAND RAPIDS, MICH. (AP)—At age 2,
Robin Hawkins already is a homewrecker.
When she is old enough to ask for an allowance,
her father intends to show her a bill for almost
$2,300 worth of family belongings she has destroyed
in a two-month rampage.
It all started when Alice the Cat went down the
drain.
"I heard her saying 'Bye-bye, fluff-fluff, bye-
bye,'" her father, Rowlf Hawkins said Tuesday. "I
ran into the bathroom just in time to watch Alice the
Cat go down the toilet."

Cost: $2.50 for the stuffed animal and $62.75 for the plumber.

One week later, Teddy Bear was placed in the dishwasher—on top of the heating element.

Cost: $8 for Teddy Bear, $25 for smoke damage done to the kitchen and $375 for the dishwasher.

When the Hawkinses returned from a weekend trip, they opened the refrigerator and everything inside it was warm.

The repairman found little magnetic letters in the vents.

Cost: $3.50 for the magnetic letters, $120 for the ruined food and $310 for the refrigerator.

"That evening, we sat down to watch TV. When I turned it on, everything was green," Hawkins said. "Robin had twisted the fine tune so far that it broke inside."

Cost: $115 to repair the television.

The next day, Robin's mother, Bernie, went to pick up her husband at work. Robin was sleeping in her safety seat, so Mrs. Hawkins decided to leave her while she ran in to get him. She put the keys in her purse and left the purse in the car.

Robin drove the car about 400 feet before running into a tree.

Cost: $1,029.52 to repair the car.

Robin has also lifted $620 out of the cash register at a supermarket, drilled 50 holes in the walls of a rental property owned by her parents and painted walls with nail polish.

When the Hawkinses returned from grocery shopping one afternoon, they parked the car halfway in the garage and decided to keep Robin strapped in her safety seat while they unloaded the groceries.

Then they heard a loud, grinding noise.

Robin had locked herself in the car and was pushing the control button to the electric garage door and bouncing it off the hood of the car.[1]

Right now I envision Robin as a teenager, driving that car with the wrinkled hood. If I knew her parents' address I would send them a sympathy card—because if Robin is finishing anything the way she started, they'll need it!

Perhaps you never gave your parents the same type of headaches, but you may have tried. Yet, regardless of how pleasant a child's disposition may be, parenting is always a drain physically, financially, mentally, and emotionally. You can never repay your parents totally for what they gave to you.

But you can try.

Your Parents Need It

In previous chapters, we examined God's promise that "it may go well with you" when you honor your parents. Now I'd like to look at this promise from the parents' perspective. I'm convinced parents need to be honored as much as children need to honor them.

Quite a few middle-aged parents call themselves the "caretaker generation." They care not only for their own aging parents but for their adult children who remain dependent on them as well.

In *Newsweek* I read a column by one of these "caretakers," who was tired of still having to mother a troubled twenty-nine-year-old son on drugs. She grew up in a time when more women took nurturing seriously. Her words provide an X-ray picture of a broken heart caused by her son's lack of appreciation:

> This society neither respects nor rewards nurturing skills. Is it any wonder then that many of our young people do not seem interested in acquiring them, only taking advantage of them? I believe that we have earned quite enough stars for our heavenly crowns. We do not want to drown in a morass of unappreciated and unrewarded nurturing.[2]

Here is a woman who's tired of her one-way street. She constructed it and maintained it, and now she has a growing resentment at what that street is costing her. It's easy to see in such an example that a failure to honor parents can contribute to a deadly bitterness in elderly people.

Why Parents Need Honor

There are hidden benefits for the person who orders his or her life according to God's Word. And the benefits in the fifth commandment are both to us *and* to our parents.

There are two primary reasons why parents need honor:

First, *the Bible declares parents worthy of honor.* From Genesis to Revelation the Bible places a premium upon those with "gray hair." Old age should be a time of honor in a person's life; it was when a person had the most wisdom to share.

> A gray head is a crown of glory; it is found in the way of righteousness. Proverbs 16:31

> You shall rise up before the grayheaded, and honor the aged, and you shall revere your God; I am the LORD. Leviticus 19:32

In our youth-oriented society, however, the elderly are increasingly seen as a drain on our resources.

The second reason parents are worthy of honor is because *honor gives parents hope and encouragement when they need it most.*

Throughout all of the interviews we did in preparation for this book, it became clear to us that parents today can suffer from intense loneliness. Instead of reliving wonderful memories and enjoying the fruits of their years of child-rearing, many parents experience an intense ache in their hearts because they no longer are vitally connected with their children.

Perhaps they made some wrong choices and have lived their lives according to wrong values. Perhaps they have never expressed their loneliness and may even deny it still. Regardless, most parents need their children to give them love and appreciation.

The Golden Years?

In her dreams, her family is young again, and the sun is always shining. Her daughters are playing house on the back porch and arguing about who gets to play the mommy today. Her son is playing baseball at the park. Everyone is at the table for dinner each night.

She remembers those tender moments in the morning, when the kids would climb into her bed. She recalls the piano lessons, the football games, the camping trips, the school plays, the birthday parties.

She forgets most of the arguing, the petty bickering between the kids—and, later, the independence and defiance. Instead, she thinks of those years when her children loved to spend time with Mommy, when they turned to her to comfort them whenever they scraped a knee.

Were those days really so long ago? She always knew her kids would grow up someday, that they would need to live their own lives. But did it have to happen so fast?

And why does it seem to be so difficult to spend time with her kids now? With one child living across the country and her other two a few hours away, she doesn't see them—or her grandchildren— as often as she'd like. And when they do come together, she always feels an undercurrent of stress.

She feels they take her for granted now. Don't they remember all the sacrifices she made for them? Don't they remember those days when they loved being with her?

Though many would hate to admit it, those words describe the feeling of many middle-aged and elderly parents today. Introspective and lonely, they wait. They may not know what they are waiting for—so they busy themselves in the twilight years of their lives with hobbies, church work, travel, or their homes.

Many hold a special place in their hearts for the years

when their children were young. Those years may have occurred decades ago—twenty, thirty, or forty years in the past—but with the right spark, the good memories come flooding back.

You may be in the middle of those "golden years" right now. If so, then let me ask you: How often do you think, "Someday my kids will thank me for this"? Do you believe that on some wonderful day, when they are adults, they will thank you for the vacations, birthday parties, places you took them, the braces, the doctor visits, the car insurance, and the Little League games, the laundry, the nutritious meals, the books you read at bedtime?

Don't you secretly look forward to that kind of prophecy coming true? I do—occasionally. In fact, whenever I have to discipline one of our children, I frequently tell him or her, "Someday you'll probably thank me for taking the time and energy to discipline you. Someday you'll come back home and say, 'Dad, thanks for caring enough about me to discipline me!'"

Yet here is the irony: *Many adult children have never returned to their parents to give them this honor.*

That's why a lot of parents are still waiting.

If a person has to wait too long, he or she can lose hope.

Looking for Some New Construction

About two years ago, the state began construction of a 4.2-mile section of road that I travel daily to and from work. Yet, for the past eight months there's been no action—nothing.

I've grown angry from enduring all the detours and dodging monster chuckholes. I'm beginning to feel that the road is going to be left that way forever, partially completed. At times, it looks hopeless—all that machinery just sitting there day after day, motionless. I'd like to see just a little dirt moved. Even a *little* movement by a living construction crew would be encouraging!

When you wait long enough for something and yet never see any sign of fresh, new construction taking place, you lose hope. Can you imagine how parents might feel? They wonder if any of their children care—especially when they see their kids removing what little construction equipment there has been in the relationship. They watch their children withdraw from them as the years go by. They replay all the things they did for them. And they get angry.

Finally, they lash out. They say some things they know they shouldn't. And they end up repelling those they love most.

Honoring your parents with a Tribute can show them some significant soil is finally being moved—soil used to construct the second lane of a two-lane highway back to your parents. For many adults, a Tribute has done just that. It has opened up the traffic to finally flow both ways. And it has been the first step toward having a truly mature relationship with parents.

A Parent's Love for a Child Is Incomprehensible

Many of us do not comprehend the remarkable power we have to bring life and happiness into our parents' lives.

The Book of Genesis tells the poignant story of what happened to Jacob when he learned his son, Joseph, was alive. As you recall, Jacob's other sons, jealous because he favored Joseph, sold their brother into slavery and then told their father that Joseph had been devoured by a wild beast. Years later they traveled to Egypt and learned that their brother was now an important government official. Genesis 45:25-28 records:

> Then they went up from Egypt, and came to the land of Canaan to their father Jacob. And they told him, saying, "Joseph is still alive, and indeed he is ruler over all the land of Egypt." But he was stunned, for he did not believe them. When they told him all the words of Joseph that he had spoken to them, and when he saw the wagons that Joseph had sent to carry him, the spirit of their father Jacob revived.

Then Israel said, "It is enough; my son Joseph is still
alive. I will go and see him before I die."

Jacob's love for his son actually restored life to his old, tired
body.

I am reminded of another, more recent story I heard from
a friend whose mother was dying of cancer. As my friend sat
with his mother during the final hours of her life, she told him
she didn't want to die until she could see her other son one last
time. The problem was this son lived 1,200 miles away.

Yet, as she uttered those words, the other son was indeed
in his car, pushing the speed limit to make it to his mother's
side. Throughout the night, my friend stayed up with her, listening to her labored breathing. "She was breathing very shallow and very slowly. I listened all night," he recalled. "I honestly thought each breath was going to be her last."

In the morning, somehow, she was still alive. Finally my
friend heard a car screech to a stop outside the house. In
rushed his brother, asking, "Is Mom still alive?"

They went to the bedroom, and my friend's brother
leaned over his mother's face. "Mom, I'm here," he said, hugging her gently and kissing her. Weakly, she opened her eyes,
smiled, and nodded. The brother turned to my friend and
exclaimed, "I can't believe she's still alive!"

But when they looked at her a few seconds later, she was
gone.

Her love for her son had kept her alive.

Your love for your parents can give them life. Even if they
are not dying, you have the ability to revive their spirits by
loving and honoring them.

The Prodigal

I think most parents can relate deeply to the parable
Christ told about the prodigal son. Many know what it's like to
see a child leave home, establish independence, squander the
resources given to him, and cut off communication. They feel

the pain of a child who dishonors them by rejecting their values.

Whenever I read this story in Luke 15, I'm struck by verse 20, in which the humiliated son finally returns home. "But while he was still a long way off, his father saw him, and felt compassion for him, and ran and embraced him, and kissed him."

I can almost see the father looking toward the horizon several times a day, hoping and praying continually that his son would return. And I can feel the father's joy when this wayward child honors him by begging his forgiveness: "Father, I have sinned against heaven and in your sight; I am no longer worthy to be called your son" (v. 21).

One woman who wrote me knew what it meant to have a prodigal child. Her oldest daughter, Anne, was a problem child at an early age. "From age two she had a very 'anti' personality," the mother wrote. "She disliked what everyone else liked. She enjoyed what others disliked."

When Anne was a third-grader, her parents took her to see a professional counselor. He described her behavior as that of a typically rebellious teenager—and she was just eight years old! "There were many prayers and many tears for many years," the letter stated. "At various low points in her life we took her for counseling, but it usually ended with her feeling resentful, angry, and worthless."

When Anne was in her twenties, she agreed to see a Christian counselor with her parents. After several years of visits, "finally the wall was broken down." Anne is now a wife and mother herself. Several years ago she presented her mother with this Tribute on Mother's Day:

A tribute to my mother
whom I hated for many years
her graying head hung down
hurt and sadness in her eyes
knees bent beside her bed, hands
and fingers clenched in prayer,
rejection and bitterness causing her despair.

I had, through walls of anger and resentment,
withheld my love from her
because I thought she didn't care.
And yet she did care and took that
all-important step,
she asked me to go with her.
Together she and I surged ahead
in sorrow and joy
through years of sharing and counseling.
Forgiving each other and forgetting the past
we learned to accept each other
for who we are,
mother and daughter,
and friends.

Your story may read like that of the prodigal son. Maybe you actively rebelled against your parents as a teenager and never grew out of it. Perhaps you adopted a lifestyle that flagrantly communicated your rejection of their values. And yet now you've become a Christian—you've seen God change your life. *But you've never asked your parents to forgive you for the way you hurt them.*

It's time to start building a road back home. It's time to go home and give your parents what they need: honor—and a relationship with you. If you do, you'll benefit from it beyond measure. You have God's Word on it.

With all these benefits available, you'd think it would be easy for us to honor our parents. But many of us—*most* of us—still don't honor them, do we?

"We Will Be a Family"

A Tribute to Marjorie Schulte of Dayton, Ohio, from her six children.

Most of us have no idea where we were or what we did on September 23, 1966. But for six children in Dayton, Ohio, that date will always be one of the most significant of their lives. It was the day their mom decided they would be a family.

Just before Christmas in 1965, thirty-four-year-old Marjorie sat stunned in the living room as her husband announced that he was leaving her for another woman. Three daughters and three sons, ranging in age from three months to fourteen years, sat with her in the living room and cried.

Marjorie walked shell-shocked through the next nine months, watching helplessly as her family slowly unraveled. But something happened in her heart on that September day— her anniversary—when she returned from a meeting with her now ex-husband. She realized that the family would fall apart unless she did something to pull them out of their downward spiral. So she gathered all six kids around her and said, "With or without your dad, we will be a family."

I truly believe some of the biggest heroes in our culture are single parents like Marjorie—parents who struggle to meet their families' needs and to somehow raise godly and responsible children.

Marjorie made one amazing commitment. She would do whatever it took to provide for her family, but not at the expense of being a mother. She decided that, no matter what, she would be at home when her kids returned from school, and she would be involved in their lives.

She sewed draperies, mowed lawns, nannied other children, and shoveled sidewalks. She delivered newspapers with her kids. She watched every penny and not only put food on the table but also helped put most of her kids through college.

She would lie in bed at night and cry out to a God she hardly knew at the time, "Please help me raise these children. I can't do it on my own."

And God answered her prayers. Against all odds, her children are solid, responsible adults today, with families of their own.

One of Marjorie's sons, Jeff, served as my personal assistant for several years and, as I write these words, he is studying at Western Seminary in Portland, Ore. I wish you could see his face swell with pride as he talks about his mother.

It was Jeff's idea in 1989 to put together a special book as a Tribute to his mother. It didn't take much coaxing to get his five siblings to join in—that's how proud they were of her.

Each wrote his or her own Tribute, and Jeff had the manuscript bound. It's a bestselling book—eight copies were made. The cover reads, "We Will Be a Family . . . September 23, 1966 . . . A Tribute to Our Mom." It's published by "J. Schulte Publishing"—Jean, Jack, Jim, Joanne, Jeff, and Judy (they also had a dog—Joker). I also like the line on the second page: "For more information: Contact any of the authors personally and they will gladly tell you more about their mom."

On Christmas Day, 1989, all six kids and their families gathered for a family celebration. After other gifts were opened, they sat Marjorie on a couch, showed her the book, and all the kids took turns sitting next to her and reading their passages aloud. I've seen the video of these events, and it is so emotional it ought to be rated "K"—for Kleenex!

Following are excerpts from the book—all written to a woman who truly is worthy of honor.

"When I smile at you today it's because I feel our hearts are one."
—Jean

Every morning I can remember hustling downstairs dressed for school always to find you at the kitchen counter packing lunches or completing the task of sorting out the butter and the peanut butter toast while we headed straight for the large pan of cocoa simmering on the stove. Off we would go without a care or worry. We

knew where you were and we needed that feeling of home and the love that was always there.

You went to each of our school activities and sporting events, trying to at least get to see each person. You became involved in our school and let us know how important we were as well as the people we were with and the activities we participated in. You not only coached for twenty-five years, but you found time to even be the St. Helen athletic director.

Mom, thank you, not so much for being in the role of my mother, because this was God's gift to us and I am grateful to Him for that. But thank you for choosing to be my companion and friend on the journey walking through life and death with me and freely and unconditionally loving me. Those have been your gifts to me.

I want you to know that when I smile at you today it's because I feel our hearts are one. And when I cry it's because I feel your closeness.

"You have managed to fulfill yet another dream . . . something special . . . done out of love."

—Jack

You are the most complete package of love God could have ever provided to me as an example on this earth of Him. The selflessness of your actions in all areas of your life has been a constant reminder of the attitude Jesus came to show us. Thanks, Mom.

So many wonderful thoughts and memories come to mind when I focus in on what you have been to me. You have always been with me; to comfort, to hug, to hold and be held, to laugh, to cry, to talk to, to care, to share in the joys, to weather the frustrations, to share the wins, to share the losses and to show me that all I had to do was my best and it was enough. You never expected a star, just a son, and I could grow up with that peace of mind.

I'm sitting with you in the living room on the couch

staring out of the front window. I'm twelve years old and it's pretty late at night. I heard commotion downstairs and the front door open and close. We watch Dad's car pull away from the front of the house. We cry and we hug and I'm praying to God for strength. I love you and I hate so very much for you to hurt. "We'll make it," you tell me. "We have to stick together and we'll make it." And I believe you and trust in what you say because you're my mom.

You have made this "our family." We can share our innermost thoughts, dreams, and desires within this household. We don't have any concerns or worries that information passed inside these walls will leak to the outside world. There is peace within our home and a confidence and togetherness few families experience.

I can always come home to open arms and a wonderful hug with a warm and loving smile. The values, morals, and example you exhibit are above reproach. The consistency of your word is undeniable.

Yours is an unconditional, undying love proven in the way you have raised your children. Here, again, you have assisted by providing me with the greatest example of how to raise the children God has blessed me with in this lifetime. I pray to be empowered with the same spirit in my role as their Dad.

"I wanted to scream to the world, 'This is my mom!'"

—Jim

Not a day goes by that I don't thank God for the privilege of being your son. I thank Him for allowing me to grow up and live in a home which, under normal circumstances, would have weakened and collapsed but instead strengthened and grew. But, most of all, I thank Him for blessing me with a mom who has given her love and life to her family and, in particular, to me.

Thank you for always being there when I needed

you. The security, warmth, and understanding always helped the difficult times pass.

Thank you for enduring both my questions and my silence. I realize now the total frustration they can generate.

Thank you for planting in me the seeds of Christianity. They are the seeds of true life.

Maybe one of my favorite memories describes my feelings best. It was senior night at Wilbur Wright. The announcer called, "Number 42, Jim Schulte, son of Mrs. Marjorie Schulte." We walked out to mid-court with our arms around each other. As we stood there, the words rang in my ears, *son of Mrs. Marjorie Schulte.* There I was, standing before the crowd with the World's Greatest Mom, and I was her son. I could not believe how fortunate I was. I wanted to scream to the world, "This is my mom!"

I thought I would burst from emotion that night just as I feel now as I write this letter. I want you to know that I cherish you, honor you, and thank God for you every day.

"I beam with love and pride when I tell others of you."

—Joanne

I always felt I had a tough childhood—wearing mostly hand-me-downs, getting teased and called names by my brothers, not being liked by my sister because I liked to play with dolls, never seeming to fit in anywhere, and not having a daddy around to hold me and love me. I always felt I had to prove myself in some way or another, to measure up; anything I could think of so as not to be overlooked.

But I understand now, as a parent and as a mom, that you can't do everything, be everywhere, and protect everyone at all times. You just do the best you can. And I see now, you did do the best!

I want to go back in time a bit and share with you some of the times I remember.

▶ The time you saved every penny you could so you could take all of us kids to Stop-N-Go for a ten-cent Icee. That was the best Icee I ever had.

▶ The time you tried teaching me to throw a softball in the fourth grade (when I decided I wanted to, of course) and I looked really uncoordinated until I asked you if I could try throwing with my left arm. We both knew then that there was hope for me yet.

▶ The slumber parties I'd have down in the basement were always so much fun. Since we didn't seem to go to sleep, I'm sure you didn't either with your bedroom right above us.

▶ I have to admit, I really felt special being the first one to give you a granddaughter, Christina Nicole, March 22, 1986, and then Kelly Jo, July 19, 1988. I can't begin to tell you how much I needed you, too. It meant so much to me when you took a week's vacation to come help me after Kelly was born. I really missed having that time with you after Christy.

When I think of you and all you've done, I picture God smiling and looking at you, saying, "Well done, good and faithful servant."

I know life has dealt you some difficult blows, but you have come out like a beautiful rose in a world filled with thorns.

I think of the countless times I tell people about you and how incredible you are—how you managed to raise six children on hardly any money—yet you were willing to stay home and not go out to work so you could always be there for us. You sure sacrificed a lot for us. And I beam with love and pride when I tell others of you, your love, faith, and dedication to keeping us a family.

"You are more than just a great mom—you are a woman to be honored."

—Jeff

The Bible speaks of the importance of parents training their children to live wisely. Wisdom is defined as "skill in everyday living." You have taught me how to live skillfully. I have especially noticed since I've been out on my own how so much of what I do, I don't even think about, I just do it—because I saw it done by you: managing money, making the most of little, taking care of my belongings, fixing things, learning by doing, working hard.

In addition to teaching me practical things, you gave me a heart. You modeled and entrusted to me a set of values that I look forward to passing on to the next generation. There is no way you could have done much for yourself all those years since most all of your energy was saved for us. I want you to know I benefited from each unselfish decision you made on my behalf. It couldn't have been easy much of the time. But you were, and still are, always there for me.

My memory takes me back to those tough, lonely years in grade school. How many nights would I come home crying? You always held me and loved me. You knew me, and I could really be honest with you about how I felt. You even stood behind me when, after two years of being teased, I broke my fist on a classmate's head.

Thanks for all the times you spanked me, made me sit in a chair, or washed my mouth out with soap. Because your word was good, I never doubted that you were going to follow through with what you said you were going to do. As a result, I learned that there were real consequences for wrong behavior and I needed to take responsibility for my actions.

When Dad left home some twenty-three years ago, there were so many things you could have done. You could have turned inward—feeling sorry for yourself.

You could have become angry—inevitably taking that anger out on us. You could have given up—blaming Dad for all our problems and leaving the "world" to raise us in its mold. But you didn't.

I believe God has His hand upon your life. Just look at what He has done in and through you. To God be the glory—our family is a miracle. The Lord told the apostle Paul in 2 Corinthians 12:9, *"My grace is sufficient for you, for power is perfected in weakness."* Paul's response was, *"Most gladly, therefore, I will rather boast about my weaknesses, that the power of Christ may dwell in me."* In verse 10 he continues, *"When I am weak, then I am strong."* Mom, because you were weak, God's grace made you strong.

The result: You are one of God's heroes. I have more respect for you than for anyone I know. I admire you. I esteem you. I love you. And I am deeply grateful to you. I am who I am because of what God has done through you. I live everyday with that thought.

I, like my five brothers and sisters, am forever indebted to you for the decision you made on September 23, 1966, to "be a Family." You made us one, and by God's grace we will spend eternity as one.

"As the many tears fell from my face, I knew that you loved me and that I had at least one true friend."

—Judy

I wish at times that you could know my heart because it's difficult for me to put into words the depth of love I feel or the emotion that wells up inside me when I think of what you mean to me. I get frustrated sometimes trying to express how I feel because I'm not very good with words and the best I can usually do is cry to get it out. But at least I'm able to get it out.

I have fond memories as a little girl coming downstairs in the middle of the night when I was sick or had a bad dream. You would pull back the covers and tell me to crawl in with you. No matter what the problem was, I usually fell fast asleep. And to this day, you have the most comfortable bed in the house.

Our love and friendship continued to blossom as you helped me make it through high school. When I didn't think I had a friend in the world, you were there to hold me or give me an encouraging word. And as the many tears fell from my face, I knew that you loved me and that I had at least one true friend. Even though I tried some things to fit in, resulting in disobedience and dishonesty on my part, I believe you knew deep down I was vulnerable and just wanted to be liked and accepted. I'm so thankful I never really became friends with those people because I might not be where I am today. Mom, thanks for being my friend anyway.

Now, I sit here as a mother myself, watching Jennifer grow up and feeling the tremendous love I have for her. Oh, what excitement I feel inside as she learns something new or just puts a smile on her pretty little face—or what pain I feel when she is hurt and cries. I feel helpless, and the only thing I can do is hold her tight in my arms just as you did with me.

I just went in to look at Jennifer tonight as she called out my name in her sleep. I stood there realizing the love I have for her and hoping I could be the kind of mother she needs, one that will love her through thick and thin and be there for her always, as you were for me.

I would consider it a blessing to have as good a relationship with my children as I have with you. I look forward to staying up late with them talking, going to their ball games, being their biggest fan, as you were mine, and holding them close through good times and bad, letting them know I'm there for them and I love them. And, I know I can do those things only because I have experienced a wonderful example of what a mother should be. I am proud and thankful that you are my mom. You've been a mother and a friend, and I love you, Mom, very much.

7

Making Room for Honor

She wonders when it first began, this gap between her and her parents. Perhaps it started as a teenager, during those early lurches toward independence. She found her dad and mom unyielding and incomprehensible at times—but what child doesn't feel that way about parents?

Did it develop when she left home for college? She felt so homesick at first and wrote them several times a week. But after a few months she discovered she was actually enjoying her new life. She wrote them less frequently after that. Only later did it occur to her it must have been heartbreaking for her parents to release her; they knew it had to take place, yet they mourned the loss of a special daughter who once needed them so much.

They didn't always understand the choices she made—such as the time she decided not to become a doctor after all. They wanted her to have so many things they never had when they were young, and now she seemed to be throwing it all away. But they supported her and kept on paying her tuition. Did she take them for granted?

Soon after college she moved back to her home state and began a career in pharmaceutical sales in a city a couple of hours from home. She enjoyed the times she spent with her parents, but she felt awkward around them. She made a good salary and was considered a successful salesperson by everyone who knew her. But when she saw her parents, she seemed to slide back into the same old roles from the past.

Now she realizes she had never felt close to her father. He'd always spent such long hours trying to build his business that he didn't have much time for his children—at least not that she could remember. She recalled the year he cut short their vacation to California because he had an important meeting at the office he said he couldn't miss.

Whenever she visits, she hardly knows how to talk to him. "What are his interests?" she wonders. "What does he think of the new President?" He's always glad to see her and is happy for her success, but they never talk about anything important. "How's the weather been here? . . . Oh, the new job's going fine, just fine. . . ."

And her mother—well, it's easier to talk to her, but all Mom seems to care about is her latest project at work. And she never seems to run out of advice to give her grown daughter. She still remembers those days when she thought her mother was the most wonderful woman in the world. But that seems a lifetime ago.

She knows something is missing. She's formed her own life, and her parents' lives have taken a different course. "I feel like we're all strangers," she thinks.

When they see each other, it seems as if they walk gingerly around each other, wondering what to say. They speak of such trivial and safe things—what they've been doing, what friends or family members are doing, what the kids are doing, when they would see each other again. The conversation never dives below the surface.

She used to think she didn't really care, but lately she cares a lot. Perhaps it's because she has her own children now. She remembers the miracle of seeing them emerge into the world, the joy of holding them in her arms for the first time and thinking, "I helped make this possible." Is it really possible her parents once felt the same way about her? And how do they feel now?

She watches with curiosity as her father and mother seem to spend little time with the grandchildren. She thinks cynically,

"They really don't have anything more important to do. They could spend a little time spoiling my kids. They're just being selfish with their time."

But in spite of these feelings, she can't shake the sense that her parents are part of her in a deep, profound way she can hardly comprehend. She looks in the mirror and sees a flash of Mom in the color of her hair and a glimpse of Dad in her eyes. She chuckles to herself when she says things to her husband and children that are the same phrases she heard from her mom's lips.

She begins to feel an ache in her soul when she thinks of her own kids leaving home. She wonders how her parents felt when she left—and now, what it must be like to have a child approaching forty—wondering what she's doing each day and what she's thinking about. How does it feel to receive so few letters from her? Mom and Dad always mention those letters, don't they? What other things are so important that she can't write or call them more often?

She recalls those times she has spoken ill of her parents, carelessly picking them to pieces in the company of others. Her own teenagers are now becoming aware of Grandma and Grandpa's weaknesses. Why did she dwell on their faults instead of what they had done right? Looking back, she could see how their unique strengths and weaknesses had worked together to make her the person she is today. And now, as they grow older, she wonders if she has ever told them that.

She wonders which one will die first.

When the phone call will come.

And what she will wish she had said while they were still alive.

You may find yourself in the same position as the woman I've described here. You can sense a gap between yourself and your parents. And perhaps you're intrigued with the idea that honoring them will help bridge that gap.

If there is a gap in your relationship, it doesn't have to continue. There is hope—if you can understand what is preventing you from honoring your parents.

Excuses, Excuses

You may feel the desire to honor your parents. But you also come up with a host of justifications for not doing it:

▶ "Yes, this would be good for me to do—sometime."
▶ "When my parents earn my honor, then they can have it."
▶ "I'm not good with words."
▶ "My parents will be critical of me."
▶ "We just aren't an emotional family."
▶ "My parents will use this to manipulate me."
▶ "They'll just use this to say, 'See, we were right—we were good parents!' "
▶ "They've never given me their approval. Why should I give them mine?"
▶ "Honor them—after all they've done to me? You've got to be joking!"

Perhaps you need to take a close look at your heart—in the same way I did many years ago as a college student. For several years I had compartmentalized God in my life, allowing Him to rule only small portions of it. But after several spiritually apathetic teenage years, I finally began to grow spiritually.

That year I read a booklet by Robert Boyd Munger, *My Heart, Christ's Home*, which had a profound impact on my life. It challenged me to give Jesus Christ full access and authority over every "room" in my heart—every area of my life. I recall opening some dirty rooms and dark "closets" that I had sealed and declared "off limits" to God all my life. My dating life was an example, and the cleaning job He did on that room was a floor-to-ceiling scrubbing and redecoration. I'm glad, too, because later I met, dated, and married Barbara.

This simple booklet helped me confront several areas of my life that I'd hardly been willing even to think about. As you examine your life to determine what would prevent you from honoring your parents, you may need to do the same.

I'd like to lead you to several rooms of the heart—rooms

that many people have declared "off limits." Perhaps it's time to unlock those doors and allow Christ to do some "spring cleaning."

Room Number One: Lost Convictions

We cannot neglect God's commandment to honor our parents. But putting it to work in our hearts and actions is another matter entirely. I believe many people have rooms or closets where they store such lost convictions.

So often we live as though God doesn't exist, or as if He has no real claim on our lives. As a result, we have no convictions or commitments. And without commitment, a relationship will wither and die.

As a nation we no longer believe in absolutes. We have abandoned the spiritual values that shaped our country. In fact, we have jettisoned our system of beliefs because they got in the way of our having a good time.

In their book, *The Day America Told the Truth*, authors James Patterson and Peter Kim surveyed some 2,000 Americans. Among the authors' many astonishing findings was that only 13 percent of all Americans now believe in all of the Ten Commandments. A dismal 40 percent believe in only five![1] Our most cherished standards have now become multiple choice—take your pick!

The book of Judges contains a telling phrase that describes a nation with no absolutes: "Everyone did what was right in his own eyes" (Judg. 21:25). Beliefs—or the absence of them—do shape our behavior. Convictions create a conscience, a core that repels temptation and compels us to do what is right.

As Ted Koppel said in his address to the graduating class of Duke in 1987, "God did not give us the ten suggestions, but the Ten Commandments."[2] The command to honor parents is not some obscure, optional opinion in the middle of the Old Testament Law, but a clear charge and mandate if a healthy nation is to be full of vibrant families and peace-filled people.

If you've lost your convictions, perhaps you need to open

up the closet door and find the ones that matter. The Ten Commandments were given to us as a tutor, to remind us and convict us of what's important—that we need God—and we're not good enough to get into heaven on our own (Rom. 3:21-31). Our first conviction should be to acknowledge our need for God and to trust the One who can cleanse us, redeem us, and bring us back to Him—Jesus Christ.

Room Number Two: Improper Attachment to Parents

Bill Cosby provided a glimpse into the mind of a parent when he addressed the graduating class of almost 3,000 students at the University of South Carolina. He said, "All across this great nation, people are graduating and hearing they are 'going forth.' My concern is whether they know where 'forth' is. The road home is already paved. 'Forth' is not back home. We love you and we are proud of you, and we are not tired of you . . . but we could get tired of you. 'Forth' could be next door to us, but you pay the rent."[3]

God designed the family as a place where children are nurtured and then, at the appropriate time, are released by their parents. If we as adult children are to finish the process of growing up, then we must leave.

If you marry, leaving is accomplished more easily. The Scriptures command those who wish to be married to leave, cleave, and become one flesh (Gen. 2:24-25). A failure to leave can actually bring dishonor to your parents.

For those who marry, leaving means forsaking our dependence upon our parents and transferring our trust, loyalty, and dependence to our spouse. To continue being dependent upon Mom and Dad for emotional nurturing, approval, or financial support not only undermines the marriage relationship, but dishonors parents as well. Whether parents like it or not, they are not to have the weight of a dependent adult child in their old age—unless, of course, there are unusual circumstances, such as mental retardation or an extreme physical handicap.

For single adults, the process of leaving isn't usually as clearly defined as it is for those who marry. There is, however, a distinct point in which a single adult must assume responsibility for his own life, independent of his parents. It may occur upon graduation from high school or college, in taking a job, or at some other point, but the time comes when he or she must honor Mom and Dad by becoming independent of them.

In either case—whether you're married or single—your parents are honored when you grow to adulthood and become responsible for your own relationships and commitments. Indeed, your parents may want you to leave. But as Bill Cosby said, often it's the children who do not take this responsibility seriously.

I'm reminded of a story I once heard about an encounter between a father and his son.

The father found a baby bird under a tree and assumed it had fallen from its nest. Then, when he got a ladder to put the baby back, he found another baby bird on the ground.

Looking up, the father noticed that the babies' mother was ejecting her offspring from the nest. He turned, walked into the house where his son was watching television and said, "Get a job!"

Both single and married adults need to determine if they are dishonoring their parents by taking advantage of their generosity. I believe young men and women should avoid living permanently at home, unless absolutely necessary. They should be careful not to remain financially dependent upon parents. This doesn't mean parents should avoid helping their children get started in business, marriage, or family, or to help in emergencies. No, the issue is whether we are failing to honor our parents by having an unhealthy dependence on them to rescue us whenever we get into trouble.

Interestingly, when you properly honor your parents, the reverse often occurs—they begin to recognize you as adults.

Dan and Rebecca had been married for more than ten years before they wrote a Tribute to honor Dan's parents. Dan's parents were "controllers." They expected Dan and Rebecca to attend all family functions, even if that meant missing Rebecca's family gatherings at Christmas. Dan could not say "no" to his parents. If he did, his mom would manipulate him by making him feel guilty.

After years of struggling, Dan and Rebecca concluded they must do something to honor them and establish that Dan's "leaving" had occurred. They had a plaque made at a local trophy store. Engraved on the plaque were words of affirmation for all Dan's parents had done for him—a recognition that they had given to his life so he could leave and cleave to Rebecca.

Dan used the opportunity of a Tribute to discuss and carefully establish with his parents some boundaries that would prevent their control in the future. And it worked.

Whether it's parents like these, who refuse to allow their children to leave, or children who refuse to leave—this "room" needs to be swept out totally so that true and proper honor can be given.

Room Number Three: The Desire for Revenge

For some children, the only revenge available against their parents is to withhold love and honor from them. Their attitude is, "I won't honor my parents until they earn it." Like a torture chamber in the basement, this room is a place of punishment, filled with bitterness.

Do you harbor any anger toward your parents? If so, what are you angry about?

- ▶ Their harsh, critical words?
- ▶ Their divorce?
- ▶ Their abandonment of you during your teen years?
- ▶ Their lack of physical affection to you?
- ▶ Their spiritual apathy?
- ▶ Their failure to protect you?
- ▶ Their emotional dysfunction?
- ▶ Their addictions?
- ▶ Their character flaws?
- ▶ Their _____?

Barbara and I are just past the halfway point in raising our brood of six. You would not have to quiz us for long to get a substantial list of failures, regrets, and mistakes we know we have made. If our children want to find something to be angry about and to punish us for, they do not have to look far. I believe our parents are aware of their errors and faults in rearing us, probably more than you or I could imagine.

If you are punishing your parents, at some point you'll need to come to a decision: Are you going to allow your bitterness and anger to control your future, or are you going to release it by forgiving them?

He Didn't Recognize His Own Son

I know a man named A.J. Laubhan, a lawyer in western Oklahoma. His parents divorced when A.J. was five, and he rarely saw his father as he grew up. His father left the family, moved to another state, married and divorced three more times, and had another son. A.J.'s dad mostly ignored him. So naturally, A.J. grew up without hearing any approval from his father.

After a rare visit with A.J. in 1984, his father moved and never told him where he lived. For several years A.J. didn't even know if his dad was alive. "I prayed for several years that we would have a chance to reconcile," he says. "But I didn't have any idea how to get in touch with him."

Then, in March 1990, A.J. heard from his father's fourth wife, who said his dad was in a Long Beach, California, hospital with leukemia, pneumonia, and emphysema. So A.J. caught a plane, rented a car, and drove to the hospital. When he walked into his father's room, the old man was awake. They had talked for a few minutes when A.J.'s father suddenly asked, "Who are you, anyway?"

Imagine the thoughts that must have flown through A.J.'s mind: *I dropped everything, paid hundreds of dollars to fly out here to see my father—and he doesn't even recognize me!*

But A.J. was there to love and honor his father, not to make a last-ditch plea for approval. By honoring his father he was honoring God. Whether or not he received approval from his father, he knew his actions were pleasing to God.

This story did have a positive outcome. At the end of that visit in the hospital, A.J.'s father pointed out to a nurse, "This is my *son!*" A.J. says now, "That really helped me, because it was obvious he was excited and proud of me."

A.J. visited his father for two more days before flying back home. His father said he'd call and write after he left the hospital, but he never did. Two months later, he died. "I don't think the relationship really changed much from his standpoint," A.J. says. "But it did for me. I had the chance to tell him I loved him and kiss his forehead. If I hadn't had that chance before he died, his death would have been difficult for me."

My guess is that most people would not have blamed A.J. if he had decided to ignore this man who had ignored him. But even though his father did not deserve honor from a human perspective, A.J. decided he needed to obey God. And his life is richer for it.

Room Number Four: Fear

I have seen the fear of honoring parents in the eyes of those I have counseled. It's real. It's powerful. It's controlling.

Fear is an emotional pain that can create paralysis in relationships. The door to this room is big, heavy, and foreboding. And it isn't easily opened.

You may fear that honoring your parents will cost you. Honor exacts a price in money or time, yes—but mostly in our emotions. Perhaps to you that price means facing a pain so deep it just doesn't seem worth it.

Barbara and I were enjoying lunch with some out-of-town friends, Charlie and Linda. They had just returned as alumni from our FamilyLife Marriage Conference and had attended the session on "Honoring Your Parents."

The casual mood of the lunch changed abruptly when I asked Linda if she had ever written her parents a Tribute. I'll never forget Linda's expression. She began tearing up, and her face flushed. She began to sob quietly, and her husband's hand gently touched hers knowingly.

I immediately apologized to Linda, but she assured me through her tears it was okay that I had asked the question. After a few minutes, she said, "I just can't honor them yet. The pain is just too great."

People like Linda may be afraid of their parents because of past abuse and pain that's never been dealt with. Perhaps, too, they are afraid of their own emotions—of the possibility of losing control in rage and anger. Or it could be the fear of having to take responsibility for their own feelings. Whatever the case, such fear is real—and it is powerful.

Another common fear is that our parents will dismiss or even demean our efforts to honor them. Their approval is so important to us (and often so infrequently given) that the very thought of doing something so risky feels threatening.

Jesus Christ needs to be given complete access to this room in you, in order to free you from all fears. Indeed, we are commanded to give Him our fears: "casting all your anxiety upon Him, because He cares for you" (1 Peter 5:7). You can do this by making a list of all your fears concerning your parents and "casting" them on Christ through prayer.

Room Number Five: *Pride*

This room has a small door, but a big ego lurks inside. It's the reason many don't honor their parents: pride. They are not willing to humble themselves and take responsibility for how they've offended them in the past—through neglect, passivity, rebellion, or cruel statements. It's far easier to blame someone else than it is to prayerfully look inward and ask, "How have *I* offended my parents? How has *my* attitude been wrong?"

At the extremes are those parents and children who are estranged from each other and unwilling to take the first step to mend the relationship. Too often these grievances last for years; both sides desperately wish they could reconcile, but both are unwilling to be the first one to admit their failures.

When did you last hear someone confess a sin to another

person and ask his forgiveness? Or, more to the point—when was the last time *you* confessed an offense to one or both of your parents? Sometimes we don't confess sin because we don't want to give it up. By admitting a fault, we acknowledge we cannot keep on practicing it.

But the truth remains that your relationship with your parents will never deepen unless you are willing to humble yourself. Genuine humility can bring healing to an estranged relationship with your parents. It is absolutely necessary.

Let Jesus Christ replace your ego and be Lord of this room and your life. You will find as I did that when Christ becomes Lord of your entire life, your heart begins to function the way God created it to.

Room Number Six: Unfair Expectations

In most hearts, there is a room that is filled with longings, desires, and unmet expectations. We know people aren't perfect, and nobody can be. But something within us desperately wishes our parents could have been perfect and met all of our needs.

The result is we are disappointed with our parents and don't believe we can honor them. Larry Crabb puts it well in his book, *Inside Out*:

> Many of us have wonderful parents, and I do, for whom we are deeply grateful. But all of us long for what the very best parent can never provide: perfect love. Love that's always there with understanding, deeply and sacrificially concerned at every moment for our welfare, never too burdened with its own cares to be sensitive to ours, strong enough to handle a full awareness of our faults without retreating, and wise enough to direct us properly at every crossroads. No parent measures up to those standards, yet our heart will settle for nothing less. And because every child naturally turns to this primary caregiver for

what he desperately wants, every child is disappointed.[4]

Some of us need to acknowledge our unrealistic expectations and disappointment. We need to admit that we may be unfairly judging our parents. Most important, we need to turn to God for that perfect love that we need so much. He is the only perfect Father we'll ever have.

Room Number Seven: *Selfishness*

Studies have revealed that 75 percent of us live within minutes of a parent. Some 23 percent are within hours. Only 2 percent of us need to drive for days to see a parent.[5]

So why do so many of us see them so seldom?

We are selfish.

This room is always filled with "more important" things we have to do. There's not much room for anything or anyone else.

Barbara and I each struggle over how often we call or visit our parents. Sometimes it seems the energy just isn't there to crowd one more family need onto the calendar. We don't claim to have achieved balance—but we are determined that our parents will become more of a priority in our lives as they grow older. That decision has already extracted sacrifices. Undoubtedly there will be more.

Here are some of the questions we've asked ourselves:

▶ Do we give our parents the same attention and priorities that we give to our hobbies, sports, and recreation?

▶ Are all of our vacation days spent in other places, or are some reserved to just be with them?

▶ Are we as creative in finding a way to squeeze in a visit to them as we are in going shopping, playing a round of golf, or visiting a friend?

These are difficult questions, but they help to bring the command to honor parents to a clear application.

Yet, simply visiting doesn't solve everything. In fact, if you aren't careful, it will create even more problems. I experienced that firsthand.

As a twenty-five-year-old, I enjoyed a further extension of my childhood by being selfish. I often went home and expected my mom to treat me just as she had all her life—cooking my favorite meals, letting me sleep in, etc. It wasn't until a family member gave me a swift verbal kick to the posterior that I realized how selfish I had become whenever I visited Mom.

Today I am much better about helping with meals, cleaning up, and washing clothes. But many of us may need a verbal, high-voltage jolt to jar us from our selfishness and into acts of love.

As children, we are by nature takers instead of givers. And as adults, we can become too selfish to take responsibility for our relationship with our parents. It just takes too much effort. But our parents need us to become givers.

Selfishness and Neglecting the Commandment

Predictably, Jesus' words slice through the fog like the noonday sun and bring focus to the issue of self-centeredness and honoring parents in Mark 7:6, 8–13:

> "Rightly did Isaiah prophesy of you hypocrites, as it
> is written, 'This people honors Me with their lips,
> but their heart is far away from Me. . . .' Neglecting
> the commandment of God, you hold to the tradition
> of men. . . . You nicely set aside the commandment
> of God in order to keep your tradition. For Moses
> said, 'Honor your father and your mother'; and, 'He
> who speaks evil of father or mother, let him be put to
> death'; but you say, 'If a man says to his father or his
> mother, anything of mine you might have been
> helped by is Corban (that is to say, given to God),
> you no longer permit him to do anything for his
> father or his mother; thus invalidating the word of

God by your tradition which you have handed
down. . . .' "

In those days, when a Pharisee went to visit his parents, he
would pause between the gate and the front door, put his hand
on his billfold, and declare, "Corban!" This term meant all his
money was dedicated to God and was unavailable to meet any
physical needs of his parents.

The issue, according to Jesus, was that they had nicely set
aside the commandment of God in order to keep their tradition. Basically, they were selfish—they did not want to have to
care for their parents.

Perhaps our excuses for failing to honor our parents are
not religious—but I wonder if Jesus isn't putting His finger on
the core issue today: our selfishness.

No, we don't say "Corban" in our church today—but we
do have our traditions that can invalidate the command of
God. A nice card on Mother's Day can become an empty
counterfeit for our failure to call Mom or visit her regularly. A
costly tie for Dad may be a stingy substitute for pursuing a
relationship with him. We can give our expensive, pious gifts
while staking our hearts with a "No Trespassing" sign.

In our hearts, many of us long to have a relationship with
our parents like the meaningful, deep relationships we have
with our closest friends. But many of us are unwilling to deny
ourselves by giving the time, energy, and thought to the relationship. This is one relationship that will extract a sacrifice.

Right now you might be saying, "Wait a second, Rainey!
You're making me a dumping ground for all kinds of guilt! I've
tried to honor my parents. And as best I can tell, there really is
not much to show for my efforts. In fact, I've just spent the
past three years in therapy trying to recover from parents who
really did damage me. Aren't you playing God a bit by laying
all this stuff on me?"

I'm glad you got that off your chest! Some *have* really
worked at honoring their parents, written Tributes, and have
generally gone the extra mile with their parents. If that's you,

then relax. If you have been faithful to really try to honor your parents, then don't let these words create false guilt.

But my feeling is that the majority who read these pages need to admit whatever attitude prevents them from honoring their parents. We've had enough time to think about what is wrong with Mom and Dad; it's now time to think about what they did right. And to honor them for it.

It may be time to allow God to do some radical house-cleaning in our lives.

I can guarantee that if you don't confront these attitudes, you are going to face many regrets. I am reminded of a country ballad that captures the urgency to honor our parents *now*:

Roses for Mama

I had two weeks of vacation coming.
I thought I'd spend it in Florida
    with some old friends—party and date a few
    girls.

I called Mom in Chapel Hill, Tennessee.
She asked, "Are you coming by?"
"No, too busy a schedule—wouldn't have time.
I'll be by in a week or two."

Going through Georgia, I remembered it was Mom's
    birthday. I stopped in a flower shop to wire my
    mom some flowers.

A little boy was leaving, he was very sad.
"What's wrong, son?"
"I wanted to buy my mother some flowers—haven't
    seen her in a year. I live with my grandma now.
Today is my mother's birthday and I promised her
    some roses.
All I have is a dime. I wanted to buy five roses
    because

that's how old I am and roses are her favorite
    flower."
My heart was touched. "Charge them to me," I told
    the lady.

I wired a dozen roses to my mother in Chapel Hill,
Tennessee. I turned around and the boy was gone.
The boy rushed back in and said, "Thank you,
    Mister."

I got in my car and was driving on to Florida.
I saw the little boy again.
He was by a grave in a cemetery.

I stopped. The little boy said, "This is where my
    mom stays.
She's been here a year. I talk to her all the time.
She thanks you for the flowers."

I had to leave.
I went back to the flower shop and asked,
"Have you sent that dozen roses yet?"
"Not yet," was the reply.
"Never mind. I'll take them back with me."[6]

CHAPTER 8

The Gift of Understanding

Christians are like schoolchildren who like to look at the back
of the book for the answers rather than go through the
process.
—Soren Kierkegaard

The phone rang at the Army warehouse. The private on duty answered the phone, and immediately the gruff voice at the other end demanded to know the present inventory of vehicles.

"Well, sir," the private replied in a sarcastic tone, "we have eleven armored jeeps, sixty-five troop carriers, forty tanks, five medical vehicles, and one long, black limousine for some big fat general."

Instantly infuriated, the voice at the other end said, "Son, do you know who you're speaking to?"

"No, sir," answered the private.

"This is General John D. Smith, commander of the Third Army," replied the rigid voice.

"Well, General," replied the private, "do you know who I am?"

"No, but I intend to find out. And when I do, you are going to be in big trouble for insubordination," the general threatened.

The private interrupted, "See you later, Fatty!" And he hung up.

Do You *Know* Who Raised You?

Whether you realize it or not, you may be like that general when you call home and talk to your parents. Do you really know who you're talking to? Do you understand them—their background, their way of thinking, their needs? When many adult children analyze their parents, they do it from their own selfish perspective. They know a lot about their parents, but they've never sought to *understand* them.

In order to honor your parents, it's important that you give them three gifts: the gift of *understanding*, the gift of *compassion*, and the gift of *forgiveness*. I'm beginning in this chapter with *the gift of understanding* because many people have found it to be the major key to unlocking their ability to honor their parents.

Proverbs 24:3-4 explains the importance of understanding: "By wisdom a house is built, and by understanding it is established; and by knowledge the rooms are filled with all precious and pleasant riches." If you have difficulty relating to your parents, or if your parents have hurt you in some way, you may need to step back and look at them in a fresh way—*as people.* By looking at your parents more objectively, by seeing them through the eyes of Christ, you may be able to understand more clearly why your problems with them are occurring.

At the same time, you may gain some insight into your own shortcomings as a child—and how your failures have affected your parents. Many of us have not begun to know our parents, let alone understand the grief we have caused them. A second conviction should be that we obey God by honoring our parents.

An Angry and Rebellious Teenager

Dan Jarrell's father died when he was fifteen, leaving Dan's mother with three teenagers to raise alone. The kids did not handle their dad's death very well. In fact, at times, this single-parent mom saw her family teeter on the edge of disaster.

Spiritually, Dan was dead. If God would take his dad, Dan reasoned, then he wanted no part of God. This strong-willed, angry teenager rebelled.

Dan turned to drugs and alcohol to fill the father-shaped void in his life. At eighteen, Dan was arrested for criminal activity in narcotics. While serving the resulting probation, Dan continued to ignore his mom's pleas to change his ways. At six-foot-three and two hundred-forty pounds, he was big enough to intimidate her and refused to submit to her authority.

A few years later, at age twenty-two, Dan became a Christian. As God became increasingly real to him, Dan began to shed the baggage of anger he had carried for years. His attitude toward his mom began to change—but, unfortunately, the relationship grew more distant. Later he began to understand part of the reason why. When he had told his mother about his spiritual rebirth, she'd seen it as a rejection of all he had learned growing up in their church.

The strain grew for more than a decade. Finally, Dan decided to write and present a Tribute to his mother.

"It was a watershed in our relationship," Dan told me.

As Dan worked on his Tribute, he sought to understand his mom. As he reflected on the memories, both good and bad, he began to realize the price she had paid in raising three children after the sudden death of her husband. Now a father himself, Dan weighed the struggles he was experiencing in raising children. The more he reflected, the more she seemed a heroine rather than an adversary.

Writing his mother's Tribute took time and care. He crafted it. Formed it. And he sweated. *Will it communicate what I want to say to her?* he wondered. The final product was, he says, "a Tribute full of praise and respect for the hard choices she had to make to raise three teenagers. It focused on her strengths."

Here is Dan's Tribute to his mother, Dorothy Jarrell of Ashland, Oregon:

"To Mom"

I *Respect You, Mother*, for the courage it takes to get up and keep living when everything in your world falls apart. Few women left alone with three teenagers to raise could face that reality with the steadfast determination you have shown. With wisdom beyond your experience, you refused to control me. You had the courage to let me fail and then to help me face the wages of my own choices. From you I learned that courage and confidence are not the same thing. Courage is a commitment to do what is right even when you have no confidence at all. I saw such courage in my father, but I learned it from you.

I Honor You, Mother, for the strength it takes to deny your own needs for the sake of those who need you. Strength to be both mom and dad to a hard-headed boy who thinks he's a man. Strength to work full-time in the marketplace and yet never let home be a second priority. Every morning of my life I woke up to breakfast before school. Every time I needed you, you were there. You said "no" to me, knowing I would fight you. You challenged me when I was certain to argue, and confronted me when you knew I would defend myself and accuse you of being unfair. From you I learned that strength is usually a silent virtue. Strength quietly sacrifices for the sake of higher good. It never expects honor and seldom receives it. You have shown me what it really means to be strong, and it has marked my life.

I Praise You, Mother! You were faithful when many would have given up. You were flexible when many would have refused to grow and change. You were fun even in the midst of some painful times for our family. The quality of my life and the substance of

my character are largely of your making. The sacrifices you made to invest in me will impact my children and my children's children. For all that you are and all you have done . . .

. . . I Love You, Mom!

Dan did it right. He typeset the Tribute on parchment, matted and framed it, and called his mom to tell her he was coming home. He didn't tell her why.

He left his wife and kids at home to take a week of vacation on the coast of Oregon with his mom. They spent six days playing, laughing, and fishing together—the things she liked to do. "It was just Mom and me," he said. "A mother and her son."

On the last evening of the trip, Dan took his mom out to eat at a nice restaurant. He told her he had something he wanted to give her in private. So, after dinner, they went back to her hotel room and Dan brought out the Tribute. Sitting side by side on the bed, Dan read it to her. "It was only a few paragraphs long," he said, "but the tears came rolling down her cheeks almost as soon as I began to read."

Recounting the emotions of the moment caused Dan to cry as he told me the story. He went on, "She just sat there on the edge of the bed, weeping and hugging the Tribute like it was a baby."

Dan gave his mom the Tribute she deserved, but it was his gift of understanding that reconnected his heart to hers. It wasn't until he had become a parent himself that he truly comprehended the hardships she'd faced—and the heartaches he'd given her as a son.

"She wondered if I really believed some of the wonderful comments I made about her," Dan said. "It wasn't flattery. It was the truth."

It just took him a few years to understand his mom and to recognize the truth about her.

Focusing on the Flaws

As we move through our teenage years and into adulthood, most of us begin to see our parents as human beings, with their own unique weaknesses and blemishes. And because of our natural bent toward the negative, it's easy to focus our 20/20 vision on the mistakes they made. It is often at this critical crossroads that many adult children make the wrong choices. Rather than seek to understand and honor their parents, they judge and condemn them.

By the time Barbara and I brought home the last one of our six children from the hospital, we understood fairly well what to expect from a newborn. A baby is fun—he grins, giggles, and "coos." At the same time, a baby is self-centered and demanding. Yet, experience had taught us that when a baby cries or throws a fit, we don't reject him. We love him and try to discern his need.

Unfortunately, we do not have the luxury of learning from five sets of parents before we start with our real ones. Most of us have to live with the mistakes we make on one set of parents. The question is, do we learn from our mistakes and try to understand our parents—or do we take the easy route and distance ourselves from them?

Understanding our parents will move us from rejecting them for their mistakes and toward honoring them for what they did right. When I first read the Tributes adult children had given to their moms and dads, I began to see the power of this understanding at work. When we see our parents as people with needs just like ours, we are compelled as their children to reach out and give back to them a portion of the love they have attempted to give us.

"The Pedestal of Our Imaginations"

In an article in *Christian Century* magazine, J. Wesley Brown urged adult children to take a realistic view of their parents:

"Honor your father and mother." Negatively, it means not to confuse parents with God in your life. Positively, it means to accept them as they are— human beings, frail creatures whom God loves no less than God loves little children. And when parents get to be sixty or seventy years old, they have not ceased to be God's children. That they did not have total wisdom when they raised us, that they did not always know exactly what to tell us, what to let us do, and what to prevent us from doing, does not mean they did not love us and intend to do well by us. . . .

Perhaps the greatest honor we can do our parents is to let them down off the pedestal of our imaginations, where we are inclined either to idolize them or to flog them as gods who failed (as indeed they must fail), and to accept them as people—people who need forgiveness as well as respect, who need honest relationships with their children perhaps more than with anyone else.[1]

Something happened inside me when I realized two things: First, much of what I had longed for and expected from my parents were needs that could only be met by God. And second, my parents were human beings with needs, just like me. That's when I took my parents off the pedestal and decided to let them be human. Soon I began to understand them as people with hurts and struggles of their own and a deep need for love.

How to Better Understand Your Parents

To begin the process of understanding your parents, consider these steps:

Step One: *Look at your parents' needs.*

When you look at your mother, what do you see?
A sixty-year-old woman who still seems to treat you like a

child? Or do you picture her as a twenty-five-year-old, striving to earn the approval of her own mother? Do you see her as a woman trying to keep her own marriage together? Or do you see her as a cranky, elderly woman whose body is starting to fall apart and who doesn't know how to cope emotionally?

When you look at your father, what do you see?

A successful businessman who spent too little time with you and your siblings? Or a lonely, insecure man who had so many holes in his life created by his parents that the only way he knew to cope was by working harder and longer hours? Do you see him as a man who never said, "I love you"—or as an eight-year-old boy, continually being criticized by his father? Do you think that now, at the end of his life, he feels successful in what really matters—or like a failure, haunted by his poor choices and wrong values?

Take a fresh look at your parents. A long, careful gaze. Sometimes it's easy to forget that within an elderly parent beats the heart of a small child, a teenager, a parent, and a frightened and helpless human being who desperately needs love and care.

I don't know who wrote the following poem, but it makes a powerful statement about the human needs of the elderly:

Crabbed Old Woman

What do you see, nurses, what do you see,
What do you think of when you look at me?
A crabbed old woman, not very wise,
Uncertain of habit, with faraway eyes,
Who dribbles her food and takes no reply
When you say in a loud voice, "I do wish you'd try."

Who seems not to notice the things that you do
And forever is losing a stocking or shoe.
Who, unresisting or not, lets you do as you will
With bathing and feeding, the long day to fill.
Is that what you're thinking, is that what you see?
Then open your eyes, you're looking at me.

I'll tell you who I am as I sit here so still,
As I eat at your bidding, as I eat at your will.
I'm a small child of ten with a father and mother,
Brothers and sisters who love one another.

A young girl at sixteen with wings on her feet
Dreaming that soon now a lover she'll meet.
A bride soon at twenty . . . my heart gives a leap
Remembering the vows that I promised to keep.

At twenty-five now I have young of my own
Who need me to build a secure, happy home.
A woman of thirty, my young now grow fast,
Bound to each other with ties that should last.

At forty my young now will soon be gone
But my man stays beside me to see I don't mourn.
At fifty once more babies play round my knee;
Again we know children, my loved one and me.

Dark days are upon me, my husband is dead.
I look at the future and shudder with dread.
For my young are all busy rearing young of their
　　own.
And I think of the years and the love I have known.

I'm an old lady now and nature is cruel.
'Tis her jest to make old age look like a fool.
The body it crumbles, grace and vigor depart,
And now there's a stone where I once had a heart.

But inside this old carcass a young girl still dwells
And now and again my battered heart swells.
I remember the joys, I remember the pain
And I'm loving and living life over again.

I think of the years all too few—gone so fast
And accept the stark fact that nothing can last.
So open your eyes, nurses, open and see
Not a crabbed old woman—please look—see me.

Every time I read this poem, my mind swiftly carries me back to the nursing homes I have visited. And I see them all again—aging people filling room after room on both sides of a long hall. I can feel the loneliness that resides in each of those rooms. And I see real people, alone with real needs—longing for someone, anyone, to understand them.

Step Two: *Learn more about their backgrounds.*

I suggest you take a step back, take off your title of daughter or son, and take a brief but realistic inventory of your mom and dad:

▶ How did they get to this point in their lives?
▶ What events, circumstances, and choices made them who they have become?
▶ What did they have to overcome to achieve what they accomplished in life?
▶ What have been their major disappointments?
▶ What kind of families did they grow up in?

Take off the glasses that got smudged from the mistakes they made in your childhood; ask God to give you clear vision, a new perspective of your mom and dad.

Take time to talk to your parents to get to know them as people. Over a period of time, ask them questions about their family backgrounds. Begin working on a family history; interview them about their experiences. Ask them why they made the choices they made. Probe them with questions that will force them to reveal more of who they are. If my dad were alive today, I'd fire a hundred questions at him that I'd love to hear him answer. (For a further discussion of this idea, see chapter

17, "Beyond the Tribute: Twenty Building Blocks that Bring Honor and Build Relationships.")

Talk to your parents' friends and relatives. Look for clues that tell you about the values and expectations passed on to your parents from their culture. How did their homes compare to those of other families in their area?

If your grandparents are alive, look closely at your parents' relationships with them. You might see that your parents experience many of the same frustrations that you do as an adult child.

A young woman recently described her shallow relationship with her domineering mother. Then she mentioned her grandmother: "Every time I see my grandmother, it reminds me of why my mom is the way she is. Mom feels her mom is critical. They relate to each other, but they don't ever relate about feelings."

A careful inventory of your parents' backgrounds will enlarge your heart to better understand them.

Step Three: Put yourself in their shoes.

If you are disappointed in how your father and mother raised you, try to imagine the struggles and pressures they must have felt during your growing-up years. Economic pressures. Social pressures. Health struggles. Extended family problems. Emotional struggles. Maybe they experienced a business failure or an unexpected financial setback they never told you about.

If you have children of your own, think of how your parents must have experienced some of the same pressures you are working through now: two-year-olds and teenagers who constantly press the limits; helping a child cope with peer pressure; the onslaught of hormones and the roller-coaster emotions of adolescence.

Many adults complain that their parents continue to treat them like young children. If you have children, think about how you relate to your kids now—and then visualize how difficult it will be to let them go and relate to them differently.

Imagine a professional tennis player who spends twenty years honing his craft. You approach him and say, "It's time for you to give up that skill. You're now going to play golf—and by the way, I've entered you in a tournament next week."

That's how difficult it is for parents. They spend years developing skills and habits in parenting—then all the rules change overnight once their birds have left the nest. They may never have been told, "You need to be working toward the day when the nature of this relationship is going to change."

Step Four: *Think of what they did right.*

Many adults have a difficult time gaining a proper balance in how they view their parents. They don't want to let go of a negative, critical view of their dad or mom. Sometimes it's easier to maintain a victim's mind-set: "They blew it and I'm paying the price. I'm the one who's messed up. I'm the one who's having a problem in my marriage. I'm the one who gets angry with my kids."

In reality most parents did the best they could with what little wisdom they had, but they make the mistakes that have plagued the human race since the beginning of time.

I could judge my father harshly for some of his weaknesses and mistakes. I never saw my dad pray, apart from those special thanksgivings offered before supper and occasionally at church. He was a very private man.

Dad never led our family in devotions. He did teach Sunday school to a handful of rambunctious fourth-grade boys. But he rarely was open with his emotions. He was reserved in his words and with his hugs. As an adult, I began to probe him with questions that demanded he share more of himself. He responded, but I could tell it was difficult for him.

My dad made his fair share of mistakes. He and Mom had a quarrel when he brought home a car he'd bought without consulting her. He never did admit he was wrong. Having been a husband myself more than twenty years, I've now got my own list of errors much like that one to compare to his.

Maybe he worked too much at building his own business. He probably watched too much television on the weekends. He was too strict with my brother and too lenient with me; he should have asked me a lot more questions about where I was going and where I had been.

But all things considered, Dad was very effective as a father. He was a winner. As a boy, I measured him and my family against my friends' family experiences. I always liked my dad and my home best.

I always knew he loved me. The scrapbook he secretly kept of my athletic career throughout high school and college told me that.

Dad taught me character, integrity. He showed me how to be successful and how to compete fairly as he coached my Little League team to the semifinals of the city tournament.

And he lived responsibly. He had difficulty getting a credit card in the late sixties because he had no credit references; he had always paid cash and never borrowed any money!

He left me with a thousand vivid memories of playing catch; of three Canadian fishing trips; of hunting for rabbit, deer, and quail; of skipping rocks; of teaching me how to drive (I sat on his lap while driving down a deserted gravel road); and of visiting and caring for his mom—all the things that feed a relationship and make it thrive.

Now, as an adult, I look back on what my dad did right and wrong. If I wanted to, I could focus on his deficits and errors. I imagine I have some character flaws because Dad did not raise me as well as he might have. Yet, because I've sought to honor my dad, I haven't spent much time focusing on his shortcomings.

You see, I now understand his roots. In fact, the older I become, the more amazed I am that Dad turned out to be the man of character he was.

Dad grew up in a log cabin with seven brothers and sisters. His own father deserted the family when Dad was a teenager. Dad literally helped raise his brothers and sisters and trapped wild animals to help put food on the table. All of this gives me an even greater appreciation for what he did right.

He raised his family in an age when fathers were expected to be providers more than communicators. And yet he did his best to communicate with me as much as he was able. He was involved in my life.

I believe there comes a point when every son and daughter needs to consciously lay aside the mistakes of their parents and focus on what they did right. Just as I did with my dad.

Understanding Your Parents Results in Honor

When you move toward understanding your parents, you're well on your way to honoring them. And you can tell when you're beginning to understand your parents: Their behavior toward you may not change, but you discover that you don't react the same to them. You find it is easier to extend grace to them because you view them differently. You have some understanding of them and their needs.

I had to continue growing out of my childish self-centeredness and my desire for them to meet my needs. As I began to understand what their needs were, I was prompted to move toward them and to want to meet *their* needs.

For many adults, this new understanding leads naturally to the next step of honoring—the gift of compassion.

"Do you remember July 19, 1960?"

A Tribute from Dawn Crane to her mother, Malina Lyons of Crete, Ill.

This Tribute requires a long preface. In her letter to me, Dawn Crane of Chatsworth, California, described a woman of remarkable commitment—her mother:

"My father was an alcoholic and a wife-beater. He had put my mother in the hospital a few times, but back in the fifties she was at a loss as to what to do. She also loved him, and, as she says, when he wasn't drinking he was a wonderful, loving man. When I was four years old, however, he threatened Mom by telling her that he was taking me and moving to California. When she heard this, she began praying that God would somehow stop him from following through on this threat.

"Dad had several massive strokes when I was five years old. Mom had to go back to work, as Dad was "committed" to the V.A. Hospital in North Chicago, Illinois. Occasionally, he escaped from the hospital and hitchhiked the seventy miles to our home to "surprise" us. It was quite traumatic for my mother and me, because he wasn't a "normal" person anymore. He was severely brain-damaged and fairly dangerous.

"When I was six and in the first grade, he showed up before I left for school and chased me around the house with a pair of scissors because he thought my waist-length hair was much too long. So he cut it all off.

"Another time, he came home and impregnated my mother. At the time, she was a basket case, but her faith in the Lord carried her through. Eventually my father's physical condition began to deteriorate and he couldn't run away anymore.

"Dad was in the V.A. for eighteen years. Every Sunday after church, Mom and I would load the car with my sister, the adorable "accident" for whom we are very grateful, and lots of goodies for Dad. We would then trek to the hospital to visit Dad for about an hour.

"He had his stroke when Mom was thirty-four, and she stayed loyal and devoted to him until his death in 1983. She"

*has not even dated a man since Dad, even though she would
like some companionship. Before his death, physicians counseled her to divorce him due to the situation, and although he
was quite a burden and had abused her in the early days, she
refused and remained dedicated to his care.''*

"To Mom, With Love"

Another Mother's Day is upon us this year and I
wanted to do something different for a very extraordinary mom.

Do you remember July 19, 1960? I sure don't, thank
the Lord! I'm sure it was traumatic enough for one of us,
let alone both of us having to go through it! Although I
don't remember the day, I know it was extremely special, because that is the day the Lord delivered me into
your arms. Your loving, caring, gentle arms. He knew
what a unique woman you were going to be, and that's
why He gave you to me.

One of my most vivid memories as a small child is
of you washing the dishes and listening to me ramble on
and on about how Joy Lynn, my "male" doll, and I were
going to accomplish great things when we grew up. You
were so patient with me, and I really believed that Joy
Lynn would turn human one day. You knew better, of
course, but never burst my bubble!

Babies meant so much to me. Remember when we
went to see the movie *Hawaii*, just you and I? Well, you
just wrapped your arm around my shoulders when I began to cry after the native drowned the baby in the
ocean. Such a compassionate, loving gesture.

You were always patient with me. Even when I
wanted to watch the *Wizard of Oz* for the umpteenth
time on television. Even though you knew I would jump
on your lap and bury my face in your shoulder when
Dorothy and the gang had to go into the haunted forest
and be abducted by those ugly, wicked, little flying mon-

keys! You would let me cry and get your pretty sweater all wet with my tears. And of course, you knew I would react that way, and I still do. The only difference today is that I don't have your shoulder to get wet when the monkeys attack!

All the things you did for me, and for others, will stay in my memory forever: when I used to sit on your lap and you would teach me to read, and to tie my own shoes, and to tell time; when you really cared about what I thought we should name the new baby; how patient and kind you were when teaching me how to bake and cook; being supportive when the music teacher told me I should choose to play the viola instead of the drums! You were as bound and determined to let me play the drums as I was. You even put up with a decade of having to listen to me practice! Not to mention having to lug those silly drums back and forth all over creation!

Remember when I broke my leg skiing? I'm sure you do! And we had to get those drums into the school for our last concert—we both tripped over my cast going into the front doors of Hubbard Trail. Yikes! What a sight we must have been! Your patience was truly amazing.

And the veritable zoo. The gerbils, chameleons, dogs, and cats. On and on and on. You taught me the value of taking good care of my pets, even though my choice in creatures was not always similar to yours!

Remember when I had to feed the chameleons the first time? We had to buy those ugly maggot-like worms from the pet store and keep them in the fridge! Ahhhh! It grossed me out so badly that I lost weight from not being able to eat out of the fridge, while the chameleons got fat! I made you feed them the first time, too. You put up with my choice of pets and you had to feed them!

I am also grateful for the way our love has grown through the years. Particularly those years when I was moving into adulthood and not doing a very good job of it. I know that I have been an unloving person on many occasions, but still, you stood by me and loved me anyway. The devotion you have for me and the whole family can't be touched by others.

When Don and I announced our engagement, you were so happy and excited. That joy carried me through, especially when the planning was getting difficult. And then, the big wedding day. How about that veil, huh? And the steamer! I figured everyone would walk out on me that morning! . . . I was so proud and pleased to have you walk me down the aisle and give me away. That was a very special moment that I will never forget. Thank you for persevering with me through that difficult but joyous day.

Mom, you are a woman of strength and devotion. Your determination is a beautiful gift from the Lord. Your perseverance, tolerance, patience, honesty, integrity, and ethics are not to be surpassed. Words like *kind, thoughtful, caring,* and *gentle* were created to describe you. You are loving, giving, compassionate, and generous.

Like God, you gave us a free will to live our lives the way we choose. But unlike so many parents, you gave us a solid foundation based on your attributes that has affected us tremendously, and I thank you from the bottom of my heart for teaching us well.

Thank you for being Mom in labor on July 19, 1960. I never would have known the depths that love could go to had it been someone else.

CHAPTER 9

The Gift of Compassion

Once an adult. Twice a child.
—A grandfather's proverb

In August 1992 I was enjoying the Barcelona Olympics on television when I observed a scene of compassion I will never forget. The story was repeated many times around the world, but I most like the account written by Ivan Maisel of the *Dallas Morning News*:

BARCELONA, SPAIN—Jim Redmond did what any father would do. His child needed help. It was that simple. The Olympic Games have the kind of security that thousands of policemen and metal detectors can offer. But no venue is safe when a father sees his son's dream drifting away.

"One minute I was running," Derek Redmond of Great Britain said. "The next thing was a pop. I went down."

Derek, 26, had waited for this 400-meter semifinal for at least four years. In Seoul, he had an Achilles tendon problem. He waited until a minute-and-a-half before the race began before he would admit he couldn't run.

In November 1990, Derek underwent operations

126

on both Achilles tendons. He has had five surgeries in all. But he came back. In the first two rounds he had run 45.02 and 45.03, his fastest times in five years.

"I really wanted to compete in my first Olympics," Redmond said. "I was feeling great. It just came out of the blue."

Halfway around the track, Redmond lay sprawled across lane 5, his right hamstring gone bad.

"It dawned on me I was out of the Olympic final," he said. "I just wanted to finish that race."

Redmond struggled to his feet and began hobbling around the track. The winner of the heat, defending Olympic champion Steve Lewis, had finished and headed toward the tunnel. So had the other six runners. But the last runner in the heat hadn't finished. He continued to run.

Jim Redmond (Derek's dad), sitting high in the stands at Olympic Stadium, saw Derek collapse.

"You don't need accreditation in an emergency," Redmond said.

So Redmond, a 49-year-old machine shop owner in Northampton, ran down the steps and onto the track.

"I was thinking," Jim Redmond said, "I had to get him there so he could say he finished the semifinal."

The crowd realized that Derek Redmond was running the race of his life. Around the stands, from around the world, the fans stood and honored him with cheers.

At the final turn, Jim Redmond caught up to his son and put his arm around him. Derek leaned on his dad's right shoulder and sobbed. But they kept going. An usher attempted to intercede and escort Jim Redmond off the track. If ever a futile mission had been undertaken. . . .

They crossed the finish line, father and son, arm in arm.[1]

What a beautiful picture of a parent's compassion for a child. Even now I can picture Derek bursting into tears when he realized his father had come out of the stands to embrace him and help him finish the race.

As I consider how we need to give honor to our parents, I realize that many adults now find themselves in a somewhat similar position—only they need to *help their parents finish the race.* They need to show the same type of compassion toward their parents that they received as children.

Feelings Accompanied by Action

For many adult children, understanding their parents leads directly to compassion. By considering them as people who have experienced pain and disappointment and struggles in life, adult children begin to feel for them and with them.

But true compassion, taught by and embodied in Jesus Christ, means more than just *feeling* for another person. Biblical compassion always results in *action.*

The gospel of Matthew records several telling examples of Jesus' compassion. Matthew 9:35-36 describes how Jesus visited cities and villages, "teaching in their synagogues, and proclaiming the gospel of the kingdom, and healing every kind of disease and every kind of sickness. And seeing the multitudes, He felt compassion for them, because they were distressed and downcast like sheep without a shepherd."

Jesus understood the spiritual and emotional condition of people. And he took action as a result. Matthew 14:14 notes, "And when He went ashore, He saw a great multitude, and felt compassion for them, and *healed their sick*" (emphasis mine).

Matthew 20:29-34 describes an encounter Jesus had with two blind men: "They said to Him, 'Lord, we want our eyes to be opened.' And moved with compassion, Jesus *touched their eyes*; and immediately they regained their sight and followed Him" (emphasis mine).

Matthew 15:32 records Jesus' words to the disciples, "I feel compassion for the multitude, because they have remained with Me now three days and have nothing to eat; and *I do not wish to send them away hungry*, lest they faint on the way" (emphasis mine).

In each case, Jesus' feelings of compassion developed from seeing and understanding people's circumstances. And this compassion then led Him to take steps to help.

I think of the television specials I've watched about world hunger. I may be moved emotionally by viewing children with bloated stomachs in the last phase of starvation. But I have not truly shown compassion toward them until I've pulled out my checkbook or knelt in prayer—until I've sought to help meet their needs.

In the same way, understanding our parents should lead us to "put on a heart of compassion" (Col. 3:12) and take specific steps to demonstrate that compassion to them. Rather than focus on finding fault with them, we should treat them as we wish they would treat us.

This does not mean just feeling sorry for our parents. Compassion is love in action. If understanding means looking at your parents through the eyes of Christ, then compassion involves responding with the heart of Christ.

Three Reasons for Being Compassionate Toward Parents

To help us to "put on a heart of compassion" toward our parents, we need to look at them from a different vantage point. Let me suggest three reasons why adult children should have compassion on parents:

1. Parents need compassion because raising children is an exhausting and painful process. Barbara and I are glad we did not have a smaller family. On the other hand, our children may never know the price it is costing their mother and me. In general, being a parent is demanding if it's done right. And 99 percent of the energy expended in the process will never be remembered by children.

Did your parents ever say something like this to you: "If you ever get married and have kids, I hope God gives you one just like you!'' My mom said this to me when I was a teenager of less than model behavior.

She always made it clear she loved me and thought it was a privilege to be my mom. But her statement was meant to send me a message: "You'll never know the challenges, the worries, and the emotional stretches I went through in being your mom. And just so you feel some of it, I hope you get at least one child who's like you!"

(Her prayers have been answered—numerous times. Barbara and I have six children, and I won't tell you how many are like me!)

Simply put, Mom was saying, "I want you to be a fellow feeler with me in the process of being a parent and experience some of what it demanded from me. I want you to have compassion on me for the pain you caused me."

2. *Some parents need compassion because their children have brought great and deep pain to their lives.* I have watched parents who have a rebellious child—they age at an accelerated rate. The child rejects them and their values and does his or her best to hurt them. They can do this through open immorality. Illegal acts. Disrespectful attitudes. All resulting in public shame and dishonor to parents.

In a recent interview on "FamilyLife Today," author and speaker Josh McDowell told of his older brother's rebellion against his parents and how it affected his mother: "I came home from a date when I was a senior in high school and Mom was crying. Weeping. I asked her, 'What's wrong?' She said, 'Your father and your brother have broken my heart. All I want to do is live until you graduate, then I just want to die.' " Two months later Josh graduated; his mother died two weeks later. "I blamed my brother," Josh commented. "Mom died of a broken heart."[2]

3. *Parents need compassion because, as they grow older, they are increasingly unable to meet all their own needs.* They just cannot do what they used to be able to do. And that is a significant adjustment to make.

Your parents may grieve over their limitations. They may

become angry over their aging. And they need your compassion and friendship to ease the pain of their deterioration.

Barbara Grady Castle of Little Rock wrote me that she and her mother "did not have a good relationship for years, and even up to her death there were unresolved issues." But as Barbara wrote in her Tribute to her mother, she felt a genuine compassion as she began to understand her mom by walking in her footsteps:

> As a married woman, I understand my mother more all the time. For in almost every action, both good and bad, I see where I am very much like her. I hope I have the good-natured concern for others that she has. I wish I could care for my husband's needs the way she did Dad's by having dinner on the table every night. I wish I could be waiting for my children each afternoon when they get home from school, the way she did.
>
> I also can understand my mother's frustrations with her family. Trying to comprehend the needs and wants of a strong-willed daughter is something I pray I never face. But if I do, it would serve me right!
>
> I feel my mother's hurts, too. They say that unresolved pain, resentments, and regrets are carried down from generation to generation. True though it may be, when we recognize our imperfections and those of people around us, we can work for change.

Do you understand what your parents' needs are? Do you know where they are hurting? Finding out may take some careful analysis—or it may simply take asking them.

How to Be Compassionate

The final years of a parent's life constitute a terrible and wonderful irony. He or she is an adult, full of experience and wisdom. Yet with each passing year, this adult—once strong and vibrant—becomes steadily more dependent on others. He feels helplessly trapped as he watches his body deteriorate. If he lives long enough, he may become totally unable to care for himself.

Then there is the child, who came into the world totally dependent on this parent for every need. When the aging parent enters his final years, the child discovers that the roles are now reversed—the parent now is totally dependent on the child. If that child lacks compassion, he will resent this new responsibility, and may become bitter at how he is forced to rearrange his life to meet the needs of this parent.

Let's look at three practical ways we can give our parents the gift of compassion:

1. The gift of compassion means meeting your parents at their point of need.

Ralph Kinney Bennett and his twin brother, Roger, grew up in a magical world of heroes and villains, of thrilling adventures and strange, foreign lands. It was a world created by their mother and the books she read to them each night:

> We had no idea whom we'd meet on those wonderful nights. It might be the mysterious horseman galloping in the ominous cadences of Robert Louis Stevenson's poem; the strange Rumpelstiltskin or the humble Abou Ben Adhem; the courageous David poised before Goliath or the serene Jesus standing before Pilate. It might be Paul Revere riding for freedom or Ichabod Crane riding for his life.

Ralph eventually developed into a writer and his brother became an English professor. Many years later their mother contracted diabetes and suffered several strokes. She was nearly blind, could hardly talk, and was confined to her bed and chair.

Reliving fond memories of being read to as a child, Ralph brought a pile of books whenever he visited her. After they'd talked awhile, his mother would always ask, "What did you bring?" Then her son read to her as she had to him and his brother:

> There is nothing quite so pleasurable as to hear my mother laugh at stories that amused us more than forty years ago. So we trot out Thurber again or Benchley. She sits, eyes closed, hands clasped, nodding as the words smile, and cry, and thump us on the forehead . . .
>
> Sometimes, on my way home, I think back to nights when Mom's old Plymouth pulled into the driveway. She'd be weary from the thirty-mile trip from her job, but never so tired that she could not open a book and share it with us. And as I drive, I thank God for words and books, and for the exquisite pleasure of returning the precious gift of a mother who read to me.[3]

Rich Skinner of Holt, Michigan, also had the opportunity to care for his mother in the last days of her life. "I have a lot of memories of my mother during the early years," he said at her memorial service. "She would tuck me into bed with a prayer and a kiss. When I was in grade school, I would try to duck under the covers when the kiss was coming.

"Last week I was so glad I had five days to spend with her as she lay in the hospital. I had the chance to pray with her, read Bible passages, and give her good-night kisses. She took care of me when I was sick. Now I was able to give back to her in those last days when she was in need. A cool washcloth on the forehead and holding her hand were ways I could show her I cared."

Real compassion may extract a sacrifice—but that's the very reason it's so valuable. Sacrifice involves giving your time —time to help out, time to talk, time to listen without any agenda.

My dad modeled this beautifully with his own mother. As a boy I used to go with him to her house after dinner. We'd sit in our chairs, sometimes talking, sometimes not. I remember how impatient I became when nobody said anything. The only sounds were the ticks of an old clock and the creaks of Grandma's rocking chair.

I realize now that Dad was being compassionate. One of my problems is I'm an active person, and even today when I visit my mom I have problems sitting still. But I'm learning to go and just be there with her.

What are your parents' needs right now? Are they emotional? Spiritual? Physical? Are they about needing to go to the doctor? Having a dripping faucet repaired, or a lawn mowed? Their needs may require simply writing them a letter. Or they may require the complex task of bringing them into your home during the final years of their lives.

The needs of our aging parents can change. And we need to be flexible and available to them, just as they tried to be for us.

2. The gift of compassion means giving your parents a blessing instead of an insult.

Over the years I've heard a number of adult children talk about how difficult it is whenever they visit their parents. Sometimes they seem to be describing a prize fight.

In one corner of the ring: parents who can't stop being parents. They see our mistakes and jab us, still trying to help us finish growing up.

In the other corner: adult children who come out swinging emotionally and verbally because "parental corrections" have hit them in the gut.

The result: three days of sparring, feinting, dodging, and slugs to the heart. And as both sides retreat to their corners after yet another stalemate, they wonder how the fight began in the first place.

Your life is so intertwined with those of your parents, and you know them so well, it's easy for you to judge them harshly. The natural reaction to any insult is to return it with something similar. But Peter spoke to our need to return good for evil when he wrote, "not returning evil for evil, or insult for insult, but giving a blessing instead; for you were called for the very purpose that you might inherit a blessing" (1 Peter 3:9).

We need to take off our boxing gloves and stop the prize fight by giving our parents a blessing!

Here is my challenge to you: On the next visit with your parents, try to be the one who gives the first blessing. Rather than reacting negatively to your dad for being critical, pointing out your mistakes, or yelling at you, compliment him for what he does right.

If your mom spends too much time fussing over how you're raising your children, make a conscious choice not to react to her motherly advice. Even if you vehemently disagree, thank her for her insight—she's most likely giving the advice because she cares. It won't come naturally to do this, but bless her by walking up, putting your arm around her, and giving her a big hug.

You may need to pray for grace to give these "blessings." But if you are not on the offensive by giving a blessing, you soon may find yourself angrily lacing up your boxing gloves.

3. The gift of compassion means praying for your parents' spiritual needs and being available with the right words when the time comes.

Perhaps you're rightly concerned with the spiritual needs of your parents and want to do all you can to reach out and help them. It could be that writing a Tribute may not only bust up the logjam in your relationship but also open a stream of communication to discuss their relationship with God.

It all begins with prayer. Pray God will soften their hearts to receive and feel the words of love in your Tribute. Pray for an opportunity to share God's love and forgiveness that is found only in His Son, Jesus Christ. Then, when the time comes, present a clear explanation of the gospel through a booklet such as "The Four Spiritual Laws" or "How to Know God Personally." Josh McDowell's book, *More than a Carpenter*, contains an excellent presentation of the gospel of Christ.

It is very difficult for parents to receive spiritual direction from their children. In many cases this is pride—but often it is only because they know us too well. It's important to move slowly with your parents. Be careful not to shove Christianity down their throats. Many have tried to do this and have failed, paying the price for their insensitivity for years afterward.

At the right time and in the right place, God can move in unusual ways to give you the opportunity to reach out to your parents and help them consider their spiritual needs.

I know of a son who found God's forgiveness through Jesus Christ. He began praying for his father, a drunkard who had abused him for much of his life. Then the son was critically injured in an automobile accident.

The son was near death and his father went to visit him. There in the hospital, the son told his dad he wanted to forgive him for all he'd done to him. The father broke and began to weep. "How can you forgive me for all I've done to you?" he sobbed.

That opened the door for the son to share with him how he had recently found God's forgiveness through His Son, Jesus Christ. Later that day, the father became a Christian.

Someday you may find yourself in the same situation—suddenly reaching out to your parents and seeking to meet their needs. Eventually your once-strong and independent dad and mom will find themselves limping, running the race of their lives. And perhaps they will need you to come out of the stands and onto the track to help them finish the race.

Maybe the most compassionate act you can give your parents is the act of forgiving them. We'll take a careful look at this challenging subject in the next chapter.

"I count it a privilege to take care of your needs."

A Tribute from Betty Dillon to her mother, Alice McCollum, of North Little Rock, Ark.

Betty Dillon's father died while she was in high school. He left behind a wife, three children at home . . . and no life insurance. "I know this must have been a very difficult time for Mom," Betty says, "but being a self-centered teen I was not sensitive to her needs. She has always just loved us and never offered her opinion about things unless we asked."

Today Betty has the opportunity to return that love and care to her mother, Alice, now eighty-two years old. "She deserves the very best of care and I hope I can always give her all that she needs," Betty says.

Alice suffered from cancer a few years ago, and Betty and her sister, Muriel, assumed major responsibilities in caring for her. Now Alice lives in her own apartment in a retirement complex. "She enjoys doing a lot of things—playing cards, eating out, going to movies—and she has a lot of friends to do them with."

Betty and Muriel see their mother several times a week to ensure that particular needs are met. Because Alice has some problems remembering things, Betty continually checks to make sure her mother is taking the correct medications. They also monitor her health and usually have to hospitalize her for various problems every few months.

Betty feels fortunate to have a sister who can help (her other siblings live out of town). "It never fails that the times I get most frustrated with Mom are the times that Muriel has the most patience and tolerance. Because we do this together, and we both know the demands and struggles, we are more able to encourage one another." She doesn't look forward to the day her mother cannot live alone. "I think she will get very depressed if this happens. I know my sister and I will have to again shift our thinking in how to deal with her and help her to maintain a good attitude and proper perspective. We will have

*to care for her completely differently than we do now. I think
that anyone who gives care to an elderly person has to be constantly open to new methods when they change."*

*The following Tribute that Betty wrote to her mother is
different from the others in this book. Betty says she has expressed her gratitude to her mother many times in the past, and
when she wrote this piece, she wanted it to reflect the stage in
life that both women find themselves in.*

**Mom, you are at a special time in your life. You had a
traumatic change in lifestyle last fall as you moved
from your home of thirty-two years into Parkstone
Place. You have always been independent and self-reli-
ant (more than anyone I know who does not drive). Since
you sometimes struggle with asking us for help, on this
Mother's Day I just want to share the reasons why I
count it a privilege to care for your needs. I know that
each of your children could write the same things.**

**One of the reasons that I care for your needs is that
God tells me to. In the Bible, God says we are to honor
our parents. If we do this, then the Scripture says we will
receive a blessing. Everyone likes a blessing, so why not
do as God says?**

**Is that the only reason I care for you? Of course not!
My main motivation is that I love you.**

**Sometimes I have to disrupt my schedule to take
care of a need you have. Sometimes it's not convenient.
When this happens, I think of all the many times you
probably did the same thing when I was growing up.
How many times (probably uncountable) did you change
your plans, goals, desires because your children needed
you at the time, or they were demanding so much of
your time that you could not do what you really wanted
to do?**

**You will never disrupt my schedule as often as I have
disrupted yours over the years. When Jon was little you
were always there to babysit. I remember one time when
I was not a very good mother and left him sick with you.**

He ran a high fever and finally I came home and took him to the doctor. Mom, thanks for always being there. For giving up your plans, many times, so that you might satisfy the demands of your children. You are never a bother, and I count it a privilege to be able to pay you back for your many sacrifices for me.

I know, Mom, that many times I overstep the boundaries in helping you make decisions. When I do this, please let me know so that I can step back. I know how difficult it is for you at your age to make lots of decisions. When I step in to help, it's only because I want to take some of your burden away. Please forgive me when I go too far.

Another thing I know I do is to expect you to stay the same. I don't know why, because everyone is always changing. I have changed tremendously over the years. But, Mom, you're not supposed to change. You are always supposed to be the same. As the young people say, *"Not!"* The Lord has shown me I need to accept you just the way you are, not expect you to act, think, or react as you did when you were younger.

What I really want to tell you, Mom, is that I count it a privilege and blessing to be able to take care of your needs. I will never be able to repay you for the care, love, and sacrifice you have given to me over the years. Please don't ever feel bad about asking for my help.

You are a special lady. Your life has been good but not easy. I look back to when Dad died and only now as an adult do I realize exactly what you went through then. Three kids to raise and no financial help. God was faithful and we never did without. I praise you for your strength and character that kept you going on our behalf.

My prayer for you is that you will be able to maintain your present level of independence until the Lord takes you home. But whatever happens, don't ever think that you are a burden. You are my mother!

10

The Gift of Forgiveness

*Children begin by loving their parents. After a time, they
judge them. Rarely, if ever, do they forgive them.*
—Oscar Wilde

Captain Joseph Hazelwood was not unlike most sea captains of old in his love of brew. It had cost him his driver's license when he was found guilty of driving while intoxicated. But he still retained his license to command a ship—a big ship.

On March 24, 1989, under Capt. Hazelwood's command, the Exxon oil tanker *Valdez* impaled itself on a reef in Prince William Sound, Alaska, ripping a hole in the ship fifteen feet wide. Ten million gallons of Alaskan crude oil gushed out and covered some 2,500 square miles of the ocean.

That infamous oil spill exhausted over a billion dollars and thousands of men and women—scrubbing and swabbing rocks and birds on oil-drenched beaches—in a massive cleanup effort. The environment and wildlife in the area are still recovering. It has been impossible to contain the deadly effects of that man-made disaster.

In the same way, some parents have steered their family ships onto damaging reefs. Habitually intoxicated parents, for example, have abused children by spewing anger and disruption throughout the home. The residue of mistrust now stains miles of shoreline in their children's hearts.

Cleanup campaigns in the heart are costly and can take years of effort. Yet even then the impact can't be overcome fully. The damage is felt for a lifetime—even for generations to come.

Some adult children become "environmental extremists," blaming their parents for everything. They want to litigate every parental mistake and error. And in the courtroom of their minds, they replay, testify, and find fresh ways to bring charges against these parental polluters.

In reality parents *are* guilty; some or many of their actions and mistakes are indefensible. Parents are indeed responsible for their failures and evil abuses. But at some point children have to stop prosecuting and persecuting them for their mistakes.

Once you've given your parents the gift of understanding and the gift of compassion, one more gift remains: the gift of forgiveness.

The Scripture is clear: A failure to forgive and seek forgiveness results in an angry heart, resentment, and bitterness. Left to run their course, these emotions will destroy a relationship.

But it's forgiveness that makes long-term relationships possible. Reconciling and restoring relationships, forgiveness gives us the hope that we can move beyond our hurt and honor our parents.

A Terrible Tragedy

It was a mistake any five-year-old could've made in 1959 or even now. Nonetheless, it was childish disobedience that resulted in a tragedy. A triple tragedy.

Cindy was a chubby-cheeked, blond-haired five-year-old who loved being with her younger brother Andy, age two. They were buddies. They played together. Ate together. Enjoyed just being together. So, when their mom left them alone at the house for "just a few minutes" to run an errand it was only natural that Cindy, being the older child, should seize the moment.

She knew it was wrong. She had been warned never to do it. But she did it anyway. Cindy played with the matches.

The house caught fire and burned down.

Cindy escaped. Andy didn't.

Those two tragedies—the loss of life and the loss of a home—were not the only results, however. After the fire, Cindy's mother couldn't look at her daughter without being reminded of what she'd done. The pain in her mother's heart grew so intense that one day she announced to Cindy, "I don't want you any more. It's just too painful. Every time I look at you I'm reminded of your horrible mistake."

She gave Cindy up for adoption. And she moved away, refusing ever to see her daughter again.

Cindy's aunt intervened, quickly taking her in, adopting her, and raising her. This aunt led Cindy to faith in Christ at a young age.

Through the years Cindy's faith deepened and grew, though her struggles through the teenage years were intense. And as she grew into adulthood, Cindy had to confront her feelings about her mother: Yes, Cindy realized she had made a terrible mistake. But how could her mother have disowned her?

Cindy realized she couldn't continue to harbor bitterness in her heart. So she chose to forgive her mother.

When Cindy turned thirty, she searched out her mother and asked if they could meet just once. She wanted to show her mom she had turned out all right—that she was a good, Christian woman leading a productive life. And indeed she was, for she had become a woman with a countenance of peace that never revealed her deep hurt.

To Cindy's surprise, her mother accepted the invitation to meet her for dinner. Cindy was thrilled and hopeful. It had been twenty-five years.

Finally, the day came. Cindy cautiously opened up about her life as they ate their meal. Her mom's growing silence was a signal that all was not well. At the end of the meal, she told Cindy that seeing her had brought back all those terrible memories. She asked her daughter never to contact her again.

Cindy continues to pray for her mom.

We Hurt Them, They Hurt Us

Hurt, disappointment, pain—it's the nature of relationships. We fail one another. Punish each other. Our parents damage us and we injure them. That's the tragedy of what Cindy and her mom experienced.

But each dealt with it differently. By forgiving her mother, Cindy felt free to attempt to reconcile with her. She had peace. But by choosing not to forgive Cindy, her mother exiled her daughter and committed herself to a path that can only lead to a life distorted and decayed by anger and bitterness.

Perhaps for you, forgiving your parents is the most critical step to take in trying to establish a new relationship with them. It may be the only thing that can free you to move away from the past and move ahead with your life.

Joan Hemingway, a Christian counselor in Little Rock, told me, "Not one person enters my office and leaves without discussing his or her parents. Most people have unresolved issues, especially the abused." *Forgiveness is always at the core of healing.*

Your pain may not go as deep as Cindy's, but the impact of an injury caused by parents can still be felt decades later. The critical question is, how will we respond to our parents' failures and mistakes? There are many reasons—or, more accurately, excuses—why children do not forgive their parents:

Excuse Number One: "They need to be punished."

The desire for revenge is a natural, human response. Sigmund Freud revealed a slice of mankind's decayed heart when he said, "One must forgive one's enemies, but not before they have been hanged."

We sometimes respond to our parents' neglect of us as a child by saying, in effect, "When I had needs as a child, you weren't there. Now that you have needs, I'm not going to be there for you, either."

Often, the only way you can take revenge on someone is by the way you treat that person. "Sometimes our hate is the only ace we have left in our deck," wrote Lewis Smedes. "Our contempt is our only weapon. Our plan to get even is our only consolation. Why should we forgive?"[1]

So we punish our parents. We punish them because when we needed advice about the opposite sex, they remained silent.

We punish them for withholding acceptance and giving it only when we performed to their standards.

We punish them for yelling and screaming at us when we were formative children.

We punish them because when we played ball, they were absent.

We punish them because when we wanted to talk about problems we were facing at school, they didn't have time to listen.

We punish them for laughing at us when they should have understood us.

We punish them for dividing our family by bringing divorce to our home.

We punish them because we have been hurt deeply. We are angry. And we want them to feel personally some of the white-hot heat.

The desire for revenge, however, chains you to the past. It traps you in a deadly loop in which you are destined to repeat the events of the past again and again. Consider the story of Sandy, who struggled for years with her mother's selfish and controlling behavior. Sandy lived several hours from her parents and usually visited them three times a year. But each visit was a strain, especially after Sandy and her husband began having children.

On a recent Thanksgiving visit, Sandy experienced the usual frustrations and pressure. From the moment her family arrived at her parents' home, she had to devote all her time to watching her toddler, who loved to pick up small objects. She tried to convince her mother to put anything fragile and expensive out of reach, but her mother replied, "This is my home and I'm going to keep it the way I like it. That child should know by now that he shouldn't touch anything."

For the next few hours, that comment stewed in Sandy's mind. *Who does she think she is, telling me I'm not a good mother? Has she forgotten what it's like to take care of a toddler?*

Sandy hardly spoke to her mother for the entire visit. Naturally her mother noticed, and naturally that made her angry in turn. *Here I am having to cook the Thanksgiving meal for everyone, and I'm not getting any help at all!*

When Sandy finally put her child down for a nap, she decided to lie down herself. That didn't last long, however, because soon she looked up to find her mother glowering in the doorway. "Are you planning to give me any help in the kitchen, or do you plan on lying around all day? I can't do it all, you know."

"Mom," Sandy replied, "do you realize that not everybody in this world jumps up to attention when you give orders? I'm tired of you always telling me what to do! I'm twenty-eight years old, and I'm doing a good job as a mother. And if you want to see me more often, you need to loosen up."

Can you see how the cycle worked? Sandy's mother angered her, so Sandy retaliated by maintaining a wall of silence. This behavior increased the tension so that the mother responded by hurting Sandy again. That, in turn, sparked additional anger in Sandy, which caused her to make a critical comment.

Trying to punish a parent is a no-win option.

Excuse Number Two: "They need to earn it."

There are two problems with having a parent earn forgiveness. First, the parent who wounded you may never be able to repay you for the damage caused. And second, why should you give this person control over the situation? A writer named Hannah More once wrote, "Forgiveness saves the expense of anger, the cost of hatred, the waste of spirits." You may suffer for years—emotionally and physically—waiting for repentance that may never happen.

Someone has said, "The longer you carry a grudge, the heavier it becomes." Many things can exhaust a person's resources over a lifetime, but none is more draining than anger.

Excuse Number Three: *"They'll use my forgiveness to manipulate and control me."*

Fear is the motivator here. It is a big reason why people don't work through issues. We feel so fragile we cannot face the possibility of being hurt again. And we so fear rejection that we would rather live in its grip than go to those who have offended us.

Being controlled by fear results in a failure to love. First John 4:18 says, "There is no fear in love; but perfect love casts out fear, because fear involves punishment, and the one who fears is not perfected in love."

The pain of avoidance is no substitute for the peace that comes only from doing what is right.

Forgiveness Frees

Forgiveness is a choice you can make to break free from the cycle of hurt and anger. It gives you the freedom to begin creating a new future. "Forgiving creates a new possibility of fairness by releasing us from the unfair past," Smedes wrote. "A moment of unfair wrong has been done; it is in the inevitable past. If we choose, we can stick with that past. And we can multiply its wrongness. If we do not forgive, our only recourse is revenge. But revenge glues us to the past. And it dooms us to repeat it."[2]

By breaking the cycle of bitterness and unresolved conflict through forgiveness, you can allow your relationships to start afresh. This does not mean you are required to instantly trust the person you forgive; but it does give both of you hope for a bright future. Philip Yancey writes, "Forgiveness . . . does not settle all questions of blame and justice and fairness; to the contrary, often it evades those questions. But it does allow relationships to start over."[3]

A friend who read an early version of this book wrote to tell me about the time he offered forgiveness to his father. "A month after I became a Christian, God impressed on me to forgive my father for abusing me as a child. I called him to do just that, but his response was, 'Just forgive yourself.' I felt so angry and betrayed—and for an instant I wanted to curse. But in the next instant God reminded me that I had done all He had asked me to do. I was obedient and I was free."

During the next few years, God used that act of obedience to build a stronger relationship between father and son.

If you harbor bitterness and anger toward your parents, you will feel hindered in any attempt to honor them. Honor and love can be in shackles—imprisoned by anger, cemented by disappointment, incarcerated by unmet expectations. I'm convinced one of God's reasons for the fifth commandment is to help succeeding generations be at peace by cleaning out any anger we may feel toward our parents. True honor demands that we deal honestly with how we feel about our parents.

Forgiveness Is Not . . .

For some the very thought of forgiving their parents brings an uneasy feeling. They wonder why God would ever call them to do something that seems so unfair.

One reason many people never seek to move through the process of forgiving their parents is that they have several misconceptions about forgiveness.

Misconception Number One: Forgiveness means excusing or condoning someone's sin. No, it does not mean smoothing things over. However, saying "I could never forgive my parents," could be purely a willful act of defiance and a refusal to grant them forgiveness. Saying "I can't forgive you" may really mean "I refuse to forgive you."

Misconception Number Two: Forgiveness means forgetting a person's sin. According to Lewis Smedes, "We do the miracle when we remember and then forgive."[4] Forgiveness means

that when we remember the offense of another, we choose
to give up the right to punish that person. It is as we practice
this discipline over a lifetime that the memories and pain
lessen.

*Misconception Number Three: Forgiveness means denying you
have felt pain, hurt, and anger.* It is not hypocritical to feel like
not forgiving another person. Forgiveness is an act of faith that
begins as an act of the will. It takes time for your feelings to
catch up and begin to fall in line with your decision to choose
to forgive your parents.

*Misconception Number Four: Forgiveness means stuffing your
grief.* As you look honestly at your family relationships, you
need to express grief. You may need to admit the pain that is
there and begin to process that pain openly with another person. If you're single, you might need to find a good friend to
help you work through this; if you're married, the obvious person to do this with is your spouse. In severe cases, however, it
may be necessary to seek a professional counselor who can
assist you in the process. (We'll look at this further in chapter
15 when I discuss abusive situations.)

*Misconception Number Five: Forgiveness means instant, full
reconciliation.* Reconciliation is possible only over time and with
effort by both parties to restore trust. However, the process
requires maturity and humility that may not be present in your
parents (or you). Some parents simply have too much baggage
of their own ever to humble themselves to the degree that
would allow a reconciliation.

Looking at God's Example

Now that we've discussed what forgiveness is not, let's
take a look at what Scripture says it is. In Ephesians 4:31-32,
the apostle Paul commands Christians, "Let all bitterness and
wrath and anger and clamor and slander be put away from
you, along with all malice." Instead, Paul says, "Be kind to
one another, tender-hearted, forgiving each other, just as God
in Christ also has forgiven you."

John Wesley, founder of Methodism, was talking once

with Gen. James Oglethorpe. The general remarked, "I never forgive." Wesley replied, "Then I hope, sir, that you never sin." In other words, if we can't forgive others, how can we expect God to forgive us?

Look again at Paul's instruction to forgive others "just as God in Christ also has forgiven you." This simple phrase raises two very important questions: Why did you need forgiveness? And what did God in Christ do to forgive you?

To answer these questions, I'd like to take you to a pivotal moment in human history—the crucifixion of Jesus Christ as described in Luke 23. It's a story rich in significance.

After Christ was betrayed; after He was tried and convicted unfairly; after He was humiliated and scourged and jeered and spat upon, He finally suffered the cruelest indignity. The only perfect man who ever lived was hung on a cross alongside two criminals. Below Him, soldiers mocked Him and stripped Him of His clothing. People sneered, "He saved others; let Him save Himself if this is the Christ of God, His Chosen One" (Luke 23:35).

Yet Christ's response was incredible. Even as He was suffering the most terrible abuse, He said, "Father, forgive them; for they do not know what they are doing" (v. 34).

Here are four powerful truths about forgiveness:

Forgiveness embraces the offenders. The first crucial lesson from this story is that Christ offered forgiveness to the very people who hurt Him most. But that's not all—He offered it to them *while they were still hurting Him.* They did not earn His forgiveness.

In the same way, your sins are a direct affront and an obscenity to a holy God—and yet He forgives you.

Forgiveness initiates. God desired your fellowship so much He took the initiative to forgive you. He did not wait for you to earn forgiveness—because you never could. Romans 5:8 reads, "But God demonstrates His own love toward us, in that while we were yet sinners, Christ died for us."

Forgiveness gives up all rights to punish. God canceled your debt against Him. You deserve to die as the penalty for your sins—but God, knowing it was absolutely impossible for you to pay that debt, had Christ pay the penalty as a substitution for you. Colossians 2:13-14 says:

> And when you were dead in your transgressions and the uncircumcision of your flesh, He made you alive together with Him, having forgiven us all our transgressions, having canceled out the certificate of debt consisting of decrees against us and which was hostile to us; and He has taken it out of the way, having nailed it to the cross.

Forgiveness is based on reality. The final lesson of the crucifixion is found later in Luke 23. One of the criminals hanging next to Christ recognized He was the Son of God and called out, "Jesus, remember me when You come in Your kingdom!" Christ replied, "Truly I say to you, today you shall be with Me in Paradise" (vv. 42-43).

Jesus forgave this criminal of his debt to God. But there is one thing Christ did not do. He did not deliver the man from the earthly penalty for his sins.

Forgiving your parents means canceling their debt against you—but it does not mean absolving them of other responsibilities. Your parents may need to work hard to regain your trust. In fact, you may need to confront them with their sin at some point and possibly set requirements for them to meet in order to restore a relationship with you.

You have chosen to release them of their debt to you personally. But, for their good, they will need to make choices of their own in order to rebuild their lives and their relationship with you.

Just as *understanding* means seeing a person through the eyes of Christ; and just as *compassion* means feeling with the heart of Christ, *forgiveness* means releasing someone from his debt—as Christ did for you.

Steps to Forgiveness

Having worked through the previous two chapters, you may have found that seeking to understand your parents and having compassion on them inevitably has led to your need to forgive them.

One writer told of the way this new understanding allowed her to forgive her father. He was a domineering man who had ruled his household harshly, not allowing anyone to discuss religion because "churches are full of hypocrites."

After she became a Christian, however, "God allowed me to see my earthly father as a boy in an aging body; a boy who, like most of us, wants his own way. Once I saw beneath his facade, I realized I might not have liked his actions but that I truly loved him. To my joy and amazement, that revelation enabled me to forgive him."[5]

If you still struggle with forgiving a parent, try the following eight steps. They are not a magic potion—but they can move you closer to the point of being willing to forgive your parent as God has forgiven you:

1. *Get alone.* Spend a day alone with your Bible in prayer. I suggest setting aside several hours, because often it can take more than an hour just to clear your mind of other distractions. That way you can truly focus on the process of prayer God may have for you.

2. *Thank God for your parents.* Faith pleases God (Heb. 11:6). Thanking God for your parents—for who they were and who they were not; for what they did right and what they did wrong—demonstrates faith in God. It does not mean you have to *feel* thankful; rather, it means only that as an act of faith you can say to God, "Thank You for my parents."

A friend of mine shared how giving thanks to God for his parents was important. He told me, "I thank God for my mom and dad. I can say, 'Thank You, God,' for my alcoholic father, because God says in Romans 8:28, 'And we know that God causes all things to work together for good to those who love God. . . .' "

My friend concluded, "I believe I have become a better

dad, a better husband, and a better man because of my mom and dad. He will cause all things to work together for good.''

3. *Write out a list of offenses.* It is helpful to some people to take a sheet of paper and write out how their parents have failed them. If you choose to do this, I encourage you to begin such a time in prayer. Ask God to help you call to mind those things you specifically need to deal with—and for the grace to face them.

4. *In prayer, yield your rights to punish your parents for their offenses.* Write across the top of your list of offenses: "I choose today to relinquish all rights to punish. I give them up. I release them from their debt." Rereading Ephesians 4:31-32 will help to give you some needed perspective.

The process does not end there, however. For many, the act of forgiveness needs to continue over a period of time until their feelings begin to change. Here are some further suggestions:

5. *Share the process with a close friend.* After you have spent your day alone, you may find it helpful to discuss everything with your spouse or a trusted friend. Talk about the process, your feelings, and your conclusions.

6. *When the temptation to punish your parents arises in the future, admit those feelings—and again give up the right to punish them.* Forgiving another person is a process that continues each time you are reminded of an offense or hurt. We have to choose to forgive an infinite number of times—as Jesus said, "Seventy times seven" times (Matt. 18:22).

7. *If you believe it is necessary to confront your parents, then seek wise counsel before doing it.* A wise pastor, gifted Christian counselor, or mature Christian needs to be consulted before venturing into a potentially damaging situation. You need people around you who can help you to make wise decisions to protect you from further harm. (Dan Allender's book, *Bold Love*, is helpful reading on this subject.)

8. *Replace bad memories with good ones.* At some point, you will need to choose consciously not to think of negative memories. I believe the process of writing a Tribute, which I'll describe in chapter 13, will help you to focus on good memories.

"Anger Was Eating Away at Me"

Your role in this is to deal with your response to your parents, not their response to you. Romans 12:18 admonishes us: "If possible, so far as it depends on you, be at peace with all men." You do not have total responsibility for the relationship. Yet the phrase, "so far as it depends on you," is not meant to give us an escape clause but a balanced perspective. You may do everything 100 percent right and still not experience complete healing in the relationship.

Melissa is one woman who squarely faced her responsibility to forgive her mother. While Melissa was growing up, her mother ruled the house as a strict disciplinarian. She was an extreme perfectionist: There was one way to do things, and that was her way. For example, before Melissa came downstairs for breakfast, her room had to be perfectly clean. Even the socks and shirts in her drawers had to be perfectly folded and arranged *by color*. "I always knew if the President ever gave an award for the cleanest home, we would win," Melissa says.

Melissa grew up with a lot of insecurity because she never felt she could please her mother. "We were told to say, 'Yes ma'am,' or 'Yes sir.' If we had another opinion, we were never allowed to voice that. We were just supposed to obey absolutely.

"I knew she cared for me, but I thought I wasn't a good kid because I could never do anything well enough to please her. I wanted her to like me and love me. But I never heard her say she loved me as I grew up."

Melissa rarely received any approval. "I got an award in high school that I was really excited about. I called home to tell Mom, and she just said, 'Well, it will make me happy if you can make straight A's on your report card again.'"

After Melissa matured into an adult, it took many years to change the relationship. She recalls a time when she was about twenty-one and was sitting on the patio with her mother. She said, "Mom, what I really wish is that we could get to the point where we could be friends. I'm just about on my own now. I know I could never have been here without you and Daddy, but I was wondering if someday we could step out of our roles as mother and daughter and try to be more like friends?"

"We will never be friends," her mother replied. "As long as you live, my job will be to be your mother."

Melissa has struggled through the years with anger. Her mother continues to criticize her and offer her opinions on everything from marriage to finances to which clothes she should wear. But Melissa says her relationship with Christ has given her great freedom, because being assured of His love has helped release her from the need for her mother's approval.

Her relationship with God also has given her the ability to forgive her mother. "The key has been understanding how much God has forgiven me for things and feeling His grace in my life," she says. "I realized that anger was just eating away at me. And the only way I could get rid of that was to give it to God in prayer and give Mom the grace He had given me."

Melissa has seen her mother begin to change during the past few years. "She tells me she loves me now, and she never did that before. Lately her actions have shown me she wants to be more like friends. She talks to me more the way she does to her friends, about things going on in her life. I can tell our relationship has really evolved."

Hope and Healing for "Human Environmental Catastrophes"

Oil spills: a parent's habitual caustic comments, pattern of neglect, or a damaging choice such as divorce.

Environmental impact: hurt, confusion, mistrust, isolation, anger, and bitterness.

All are caused by human error. All demand cleanup campaigns. All need forgiveness.

Yet, before we leave the subject of forgiveness, I must point out another issue you may need to confront: children are just as capable as parents of polluting the home. In addition to forgiving your parents, you may need to approach your mother and father to ask forgiveness for your own failures.

That's the subject of our next chapter.

11

Removing the Offense

Forgiveness is the fragrance the violet sheds on the heel that crushed it.
—Mark Twain

hen Elizabeth became a Christian, she learned how to love others with the love of God. Except for her father. She'd consider God's commandment to honor her parents and think, "Surely God has not met my dad. Surely He would not ask me to do that."

This went on for several years, until the day she heard a speaker say, "If you have bitterness in your heart toward anyone, you need to ask him or her to forgive you." This simple line began an interesting conversation between Elizabeth and her Lord:

God: "You need to ask your dad to forgive you."

Elizabeth: "In the first place, I don't talk to my dad. In the second place, we don't talk about forgiveness. In the third place, I never see him. And in the fourth place, I don't want to do this!"

God: "You need to ask your dad to forgive you."

Elizabeth: "I'll tell You what, God. I'll ask Daddy to forgive me if You bring him here."

She thought she was safe with this prayer, because her father never came to the city where she lived. The very next day, however, her mother called and said, "Elizabeth, your cousin is sick, and we are here in town at the hospital."

Even as she drove to the hospital, Elizabeth kept "bargaining" with God; "Lord, surely You don't want me to ask Daddy to forgive me. But if You do, God, I pray that he'd be alone in the hospital."

She walked into the hospital and there sat her father in the lobby all by himself.

Reluctantly, she dragged herself over to him and said, "Daddy, may I speak to you?"

"Yes, Elizabeth."

"Daddy, God has convicted me that I've been bitter and sarcastic and that I've not honored you. I wonder if you can find it in your heart to forgive me?"

To her complete astonishment, her unemotional father began to cry. "Thanks for saying that. It's broken my heart." Elizabeth realized God wanted to work through her to make a difference. "He can take things that the world says never can happen, or never would happen, and He can make them happen," she says. "He wants us to believe Him."

That event marked the beginning of a true healing in Elizabeth's relationship with her father.

Cracking the Rusty Hinge

If forgiveness helps to free people to experience deeper relationships, then we as children need to realize we hurt our parents just as they hurt us. And, therefore, we may need to approach them and ask for their forgiveness. For some people, like Elizabeth, this act of humility can help crack open the rusty hinge that prevents them from opening the heavy door of separation.

Have you ever thought your parents may have legitimate complaints about how you've treated them? Sometimes the offenses are small, sometimes major—but you can bet they're remembered.

On my wedding day, I was staying at Barbara's house. Her father tried to coax me out of their house that morning because he thought it was "bad luck" for a groom to see the bride. "I don't believe in bad luck," I replied, undoubtedly very piously. "There's no theological basis for that."

Boy, was that a stupid comment! Totally unnecessary. It smacked of "spiritual pharisaism"—something I hate. My father-in-law never said anything about it, but I know what I said must have hurt. What I should have done was defer to his tradition, rather than try to correct what I deemed "a theological inaccuracy."

Children of All Ages Hurt Parents

It's easy to understand how children can be oblivious in parceling out hurt to parents. Especially teenagers.

I'll never forget the time when Barbara and I were working on our book, *Building Your Mate's Self-Esteem*, and we interviewed a mom with teenage boys. She spoke of how her boys hammered her, taking out their frustrations on her because they thought they could get away with it. She was a damaged mom.

The nature of children is self-centeredness to the tenth power. The intensity of their selfishness and how it affects their parents may not always be the same throughout the different stages of their growth—but it hurts just the same.

As a five-year-old I embarrassed my parents by announcing that my mom had "tied me up for three months." It actually had been only thirty minutes, and I had deserved the penalty. That story later became a joke in our home, a sort of classic memory.

But things changed when puberty hit. Gone was the little boy with his front teeth missing. In his place was an expressive, impulsive, emotionally explosive teenager.

My parents' rules made me angry. Like a little prosecutor, I gave them all the reasons why I ought to be able to do what "everybody else does." When my dad told me I couldn't drive more than five miles on my first night with the car, I unhooked the speedometer cable.

I lied to them. And got caught. I stole from them (pocket

change). And didn't get caught. Just to think of it now—well, it had to have hurt them.

That was when I was a child, so you probably would expect some of that. But as adult children we can continue hurting our parents as well. By disregarding their feelings and needs we continue to dishonor them. And hurt them deeply.

Common Ways Adult Children Offend Their Parents

Recently I gathered some comments from adults who described some of the ways they've bruised their parents. Here's what they said:

> "I'm adopted, and I remember once in an argument telling my parents that they weren't my parents. It really hurt them and I have regretted it to this day."

> "While arguing with my Mom about abortion and homosexuality, I said that someone who professed to be a Christian wouldn't hold such views. She felt judged."

> "I didn't go to see my father in the hospital when he had a broken hip. I was waiting for another month when I would see him on a planned Christmas vacation. He died unexpectedly."

> "I told them (my parents) if my wife and I died, we would not want them to raise our children, for religious reasons. They were hurt deeply and offended."

> "I tried to force my newfound faith in Jesus Christ down my parents' throats. I was very judgmental and full of a preachy attitude."

"My mother had planned to stay several weeks with me. I don't like anyone smoking in my house. I told her this. She smokes, so she went home."

"I got married in spite of the fact that my father tried to tell me I should reconsider the person."

"I forgot my dad's birthday because I was wildly infatuated with a guy at the time. I apologized, but I think it really hurt his feelings because the next year he didn't call me on my birthday."

Now I'll add one of my own. A few months after Barbara and I were married, her brothers called to say they were planning a special twenty-fifth wedding anniversary party for their parents. Barbara wanted to go, but I came up with all kinds of reasons not to make the trip: We lived in Boulder, Colorado, at the time, and Houston was a full, two-day drive. We didn't have any vacation days left. And I thought we shouldn't spend our hard-earned savings on expensive airplane tickets. Besides, in my family, anniversaries were celebrated only on two occasions: golden (fifty years) and platinum (seventy-five years).

So I said, "No." Pretty firmly, as I recall. In my youthful insecurity and selfishness I was trying to establish myself as the leader of this new unit of two, and I simply didn't think the trip was a good idea.

Well, I found out that the twenty-fifth anniversary of your new in-laws was not an event to be missed.

I blew it.

Five years later I helped Barbara and her brothers organize a surprise thirtieth anniversary party. And my stock rose a little. (When you've been through a stock market crash, the only way to go is up!)

She Could Be Your Mother

The offense that may hurt parents most, though, is *ignoring* them.

Sue lives in a small town on the edge of the urban sprawl of Chicago. She's eighty-two, and five days a week she walks three miles inside a mall near her house. She's active in the small church she has attended for more than fifty years. She has a ministry with young mothers, mentoring them in the care of their children and love for their husbands. Her life is full of people and relationships.

When I asked her how her sons and daughter honor or dishonor her, her vivid and honest answer gripped me. I didn't sense an ounce of anger in her words, only tons of regret.

As you read Sue's words, ask yourself: "Could this be my mom?"

When my husband died ten years ago, that was a shock. But an even greater shock has been the reaction of my four grown children to me. I had hoped I would get my relationship restored with them. There was no hope of my getting my husband back, but I kept hoping I would have a good relationship with my children.

I don't require all that much from my daughter and sons. Just a little bit of communication. Just a phone call. But I can go six weeks at a time and never hear from a member of my family—four children and eight grandchildren. Isn't that unusual?

I notice when they do call it's always for some reason. It's never, "Mother, are you all right?" I have Parkinson's Disease, and I'm a diabetic. I go to a cardiologist and an eye doctor. It's not that they don't know I'm under different kinds of treatment, but they never want to hear anything about it.

I think that's because they don't want to be responsible for me. I really can't think of another reason why they wouldn't call.

I called my son at his office last fall to tell him something real funny that happened to me. I opened the conversation by saying, "Well, I know you're busy, but I just wanted to call and hear your voice and see if you are okay."

He responded by saying, "Yes, I've been busy." I said, "You know that old piece of property that your dad bought back before he died?" He didn't answer me. I went on, "You know he bought it when it was outside the city limits and he paid $500 for that one-acre lot. Well a real estate agent came by and said it's worth $12,000! Isn't that hilarious?"

He said, "Mother, you may live five or ten more years, and if you start selling everything you have there won't be anything left to take care of you!" I responded, "Oh, honey, I've got enough. I'll be taken care of."

His voice went tense: "Well, I want you to know that I can't work any harder than I am and I just can't take care of you." And I said, "You won't have to. Please don't worry about that." I finally just said, "Honey, I called to hear your voice and I have, and I'm going to hang up now."

He can't share any of my joys.

My dining room table will seat forty people. It's been used one time since my husband died. My children used to come here often until he died. And that's the thing that has multiplied the pain: they're ignoring me, and now their children have, too. My grandchildren have cars, but I never see them either.

There are so many things about me they don't know.

You may be thinking, "Is she just another bitter old woman, sitting around complaining about her kids in her last years?" Definitely not! If you knew Sue, you'd find her to be an incredibly optimistic, upbeat, life-changing woman. She's not bitter—she's honest, and is willing to say how she feels in a way most adult children do not want to hear from their parents.

How to Seek Forgiveness from Your Parents

It might not be necessary to go to your parents and ask for forgiveness. Your Tribute will be all that's needed.

If you come from an abusive or otherwise evil situation, going to your parents to seek forgiveness might be dangerous. You'll need to seek counsel before going.

The fact is, some parents will find it difficult to hear the words in a Tribute if their child has failed to take responsibility for his or her wrong actions and attitudes. Asking for their forgiveness may be the first step toward making your relationship the "two-lane highway" I described earlier.

Here are some suggestions on how to do it:

1. Ask God for direction as you go through this process. The Bible compares us to sheep. We need to be prodded occasionally to keep us going in the right direction. Some sheep want to be told, step-by-step, exactly what to do. But only the Good Shepherd knows the intimate details of you, your parents, and your family. He will guide you as you go through the process.

Ask the Lord to search your heart and point out where you have offended your parents. The psalmist prayed, "Search me, O God, and know my heart; try me and know my anxious thoughts; and see if there be any hurtful way in me, and lead me in the everlasting way" (Psalm 139:23).

If nothing comes to mind, don't feel guilty and try to manufacture some meaningless or insignificant offense.

2. Go to your parents and ask them to forgive you. I would not recommend going to your parents with a long grocery list of things you've done wrong, asking for forgiveness for each specific item. That kind of confession often isn't necessary—in fact, restating and reliving deeply damaging events can sometimes do more harm than good.

Instead, go to them with an attitude of humility and honor that says, "I've been wrong in my attitude toward you; I love you and want to honor you. Will you forgive me for not being the son or daughter I should've been?" Confessing an ungrateful heart, a rebellious attitude, or selfishness is appropriate and can bring healing (James 5:16).

Two other suggestions should help you prepare to ask forgiveness of your parents:

▶ Don't ask them to seek your forgiveness for anything they've done wrong. If that's necessary, do it at another time.

▶ If you're planning to write a Tribute for them, make sure you ask their forgiveness beforehand. You could consider doing that through a letter or phone call if appropriate. If not, ask their forgiveness face to face on a day other than the one you've planned for the Tribute.

3. *Leave the results—including your parents' response—to God.* You are not responsible for their response or lack of it.

The vast majority of parents stand ready to forgive and move on. They do not want to further punish you, only to love you. First Peter 4:8 is a passage that describes how parents have had to handle their sons' and daughters' imperfections: "Love covers a multitude of sins."

Still, that's no guarantee. Seeking forgiveness can be risky. Some parents may not be healthy enough spiritually or emotionally to grant forgiveness. Some simply may not be willing. The currents of mistrust may run so deep in your family that you may have to prove you are sincere (which you may not be able to do). Still others may not want to forgive because that means they will have to deal with their responsibility toward you as well.

So, as you go to your parents, keep your expectations in check. Having heard a number of stories of adult children who went to their parents for forgiveness, I'm amazed at how stoic most parents are in these situations. Some are too reserved to express how meaningful it is to have a son or daughter approach them for forgiveness and pursue a relationship with them. I know of one father who called his daughter two months after their meeting and said, simply and finally, "Thank you."

The Blessing of Obedience

There are other benefits for those who keep their slate clean with their parents, as the following story illustrates.

A friend of mine, Ney Bailey, once described how she became convicted of her need to honor her dad. As she began to think about how she would do this, she realized she needed to ask her father's forgiveness for her wrong response to him.

Ney was emotionally abandoned by her father when she was three years old. Hurt gave way to anger. Anger grew into an intense resentment. As a teenager Ney sometimes went into her parents' bedroom and opened a drawer that contained her dad's revolver. "I used to stand there beside the bed he slept in, hold that revolver in my hands, and think about murdering my dad."

As an adult, Ney began to look at her father through God's eyes. Up to that point she had resented her father, not understanding his apparent lack of love for her. Now as a single woman, she began to learn things about the family *he* grew up in. And she began to understand. Soon she sensed she was beginning to accept him, becoming free of judging and criticizing him.

Ney decided to go to her parents' home for vacation. "I remember one day in particular," she says. "We were sitting in the living room together. I was on the couch and Daddy was in his reclining chair in front of the TV. Soon he fell asleep. I looked over at him in his chair for a long time and then said in a soft whisper, 'Daddy, I love you and I accept you just like you are . . . sitting there in your chair.'"

Their relationship began to change because Ney's attitude toward her dad had changed.

Some months later Ney realized she needed to honor her dad by asking his advice on a career decision she was facing—and by asking forgiveness for her wrong response to him all those years.

"One Sunday afternoon when I was visiting, Dad and I were at home alone watching a football game together. I mustered up all the courage I could. Then I asked him for counsel on my career decision. He was extremely helpful, and it went much easier than I'd expected.

"Then I said, 'Daddy, there's something else I've been thinking about. I harbored a lot of bad attitudes when I was growing up, attitudes of ungratefulness and lack of love. I realize how wrong I was, and I'd like to ask you to forgive me. Will you forgive me?'

"He turned in his great, overstuffed reclining chair and looked at me with a slight twinkle in his eyes.

" 'No.' Then he paused. 'I don't remember all those things . . . except for the time . . . ' He named an instance and laughed.

"I thought for a moment and said, 'Well, will you forgive me for the things you can remember?'

" 'Yes,' he answered."

The ball game continued.

Ney went on to tell of the thaw that continued in their relationship. Before Ney left home on that visit, her father expressed interest in her work schedule, and when she'd be home again. All were things he'd never shown the slightest bit of interest in before.

A couple of days later Ney received a phone call from her mom. Ney asked her, "Did Daddy say anything to you about our visit?"

"Yes," her mom replied. "He said, 'Ney must be losing her mind! She asked me for some advice.' "[1]

Ney later shared her love for her parents further by writing a five-page Tribute to them on their wedding anniversary.

Later, when her father died, she was at peace with him.

Ney learned that parents need to know that they have great worth and value in their children's eyes, we appreciate them as human beings for who they are, and that their feelings matter to us. When they begin to sense this kind of grateful spirit, their hearts can more easily respond.

When a person dares to obey God, great things can hap-

pen. I cannot guarantee your parents will respond the way
Ney's father did. But God can take your obedience and use it
in ways you never dreamed. He has always been the God of
"all things . . . possible."

12

The Power of Public Honor

*All that I am or hope to be I owe to my angel mother. I
remember my mother's prayers and they have always followed
me. They have clung to me all my life.*
—Abraham Lincoln

When the members of the
Continental Congress met
to form the United States of America in 1776, why did they
have to send Thomas Jefferson away to craft a special document? Why didn't they just say, "We declare our independence!"? Why did they go to the trouble to hand-letter his
declaration and formalize it through a ceremonial signing?

It was all because they had a vision for our nation and felt
the nation was worth it. Those leaders understood the power
and permanence of the printed word. They knew a written
"Declaration of Independence" could inspire and arouse their
fellow colonists to join them in the cause. It also would be a
public statement of their cause, a formal declaration of their
desire to break free from England's rule.

The Information Age

Most of us are aware of how greatly technology has affected our lives and our family relationships during this century. Each new invention—the telephone, radio, movies, and

television—seems to move us to a more verbal, superficial, image-conscious, and feeling-oriented society.

We live in the age of information, when a flood of communication overwhelms us and trivializes many of the important things in our lives. The influence of images and music have made us much more pathos- or feeling-related. Advertisers often do not want us to think about decisions—they want us to act on our feelings and be seduced by our emotions, not our judgment.

In our culture, a written document can carry special power. That's why I encourage you to put together a written Tribute. It can be an island of intimate appreciation in a sea of form letters and impersonal communications.

What if the apostle Paul had just "reached out and touched" Timothy by direct dialing instead of writing First and Second Timothy? Instead, we have a document that has been preserved and has eternal value. I think the same is true for us today: Those things we value most need to be formally preserved in writing.

A Public Declaration

Janelle grew up in the rural South, in a farming family with four brothers and three sisters. Her father worked a large farm, growing cotton and soybeans, and raising cattle. And her mother supervised the children in keeping up a garden that provided part of the family's food.

She had a happy family, and she didn't recall many family problems growing up. But the one ingredient that seemed to be missing was the ability to express love and intimate feelings to one another.

Janelle attended a FamilyLife Marriage Conference in the spring of 1992 and felt her heart stirring when she was challenged to write a Tribute to her parents. A few months later, her parents briefly separated. Some of the siblings divided, each taking the side of one parent. It caused some unnecessary things to be said. Bad feelings lingered, leaving some of them not speaking to one another.

Three weeks before Christmas, her mother called and said, "You're the only ones who won't be here for Christmas this year." That's when Janelle knew the time had come to write her Tribute. She and her husband rearranged their plans.

Now Janelle had to write the Tribute she had prayed about for many months. One night as she sat down to write Christmas cards, she began recalling many episodes from her childhood. "As I jotted them down, it all began to come together. In just a short time, there was the Tribute I had prayed about."

The stakes were different now. Her family needed healing. On Christmas Day, they gathered together. After all the Christmas gifts had been opened, Janelle stood up to present the Tribute. "I had prayed that the Lord would allow me to read it aloud because I knew it wouldn't be the same if I had my husband read it," she says. "The Lord granted me the ability to do that. I would read a verse, and then emotions would take over. Then I'd regroup and start again."

All the grandkids sat spellbound as Janelle presented the Tribute. And when Janelle finished, everyone sat silent. It seemed almost like a sacred moment. Even after a brother-in-law broke the silence with a funny remark, the emotion remained.

Janelle's parents expressed their appreciation and love. But she was especially pleased by the way her siblings began to talk again as the day progressed. "I can't say the Tribute was totally responsible, but I think it brought everyone to a point of softness. It was as if that day had been a turning point."

Janelle says that during the past year "there have been a lot of changes in all of us. God knew what was going to happen during the year to come, and He placed a desire in me ahead of time so I could pray. Our heavenly Father desires to restore broken lives and families. I praise Him for bringing our family together that day to begin healing."

A Tribute Is Special

I've heard many stories like this one during the past few years. And they've given me the confidence to challenge you to create a formal, public document honoring your parents.

Yet I can hear your questions forming now: "Won't a letter be enough? Isn't it enough just to stay in touch and spend time with them?"

Those are all great ways of honoring your parents. And I have included a number of other ideas for you in chapter 17. But there is something special about a Tribute.

A public document makes a statement that a letter does not. A letter is a personal form of communication that can be stuffed into an envelope and put into a drawer. Over a lifetime an individual may receive several hundred letters. Letters are common. Formal tributes are not. A document such as a Tribute—crafted through hours of writing and then typeset or put into calligraphy, matted, and framed—adds an exponential sense of weight and value to the words.

A framed Tribute on a wall in your parents' home can turn an ordinary hall into a museum of grand memories.

Let's say you call your parents one day and say, "I've been thinking today about all you did for me as I grew up. I just wanted to call and say thanks for all of that." You could even recall some special memories. That could be a very meaningful phone call for your parents.

But now consider the special significance of taking weeks to put together a formal document. The fact that you put so much work into it, then dress it up and put it in a frame, means you want others to read it and know what you believe about your parents. Think of how it must feel to a parent to be praised in public by his or her children. In a way, it doubles the honor for parents; they're proud not only for what their child has said, but also for the fact that the child wanted others to see it.

People Love to Be Praised—Privately and Publicly

You might argue, "I know what will happen. I'll go to all this work, get it typeset, matted, put it in a frame, and it'll wind up in the attic."

Yes, that could occur. But it is not likely. I have heard dozens of stories about Tributes given to parents who could be characterized as derelict in their responsibilities—and I've been amazed to hear how many responded with a tenderness of heart never before seen.

People love to be praised. A formal document, hung in a place of honor in the home, gives your parents something to show off to their friends—and to take encouragement in.

A woman approached me at a FamilyLife Parenting Conference and told me about the Tribute she had written for her parents. "They live in a very, very nice home and everything on their walls is artwork," she said. "The thing that showed me it was meaningful to them was that they put up my Tribute in their house. My husband and I joke that they put it up only when we come over. But we've been over there a couple of times when they weren't expecting us, and there it was, up on the wall.

"I sometimes say to my husband 'I hope my kids do that for me when I'm older.' If I were to get up in the morning and read something like that, it would make my day."

Tributes sometimes take on a life of their own. People often ask for copies of the Tributes I wrote to my parents to use as a creative spark and give them ideas as they write their own. People have asked to purchase copies of the "We Will Be a Family" Tribute that Jeff Schulte and his brothers and sisters put together for their mother. It's as if a Tribute strikes a hidden chord within the soul, and people feel better when they read about parents who are worthy of honor—even when they are directed toward *other* parents.

The Power of the Spoken Word

Not everyone is able to read a Tribute aloud to a parent or to do it in front of the rest of the family as Janelle did. But the rewards are worth the risks, because a public ceremony seems to take a family beyond just surface relationships in a way few other things can. I can't tell you how many times family members have ended up in tears as a Tribute is read aloud. I have seen videos in which I could hardly hear the sound of the person reading because of the sheer volume of the sound of sniffles and blowing noses!

Somehow a Tribute conveys a message from one heart to another. So many people seem to live their lives on a tasteless plane of repetition and superficiality. But by recalling shared experiences and happy memories, a Tribute can peel back the veneer and allow people to be vulnerable and truly connect emotionally, even if just for a few minutes. Yet those few moments can be permanently life- and relationship-changing. How many moments like those do we experience with our parents in a lifetime?

If you come from a family who buried their emotions, the idea of writing a Tribute and reading it to your parents may unnerve you. I understand some of the risk and vulnerability involved in this kind of presentation. But I strongly encourage you to do it anyway. It could help you all to get beneath the surface—just once—to deepen your relationship.

Of course, some parents (mostly men) simply don't want to show their emotions. In these cases, reading a Tribute may actually dishonor them by causing them to feel uncomfortable. Todd, a single man in his late twenties, wrote Tributes to his mother and father who divorced late in life. He read his mother's aloud to her, but his dad wouldn't allow him to do the same for him. "I think it made him feel too vulnerable, hearing about things from the past," Todd says. "He didn't want to show any emotion."

Todd left the Tribute for his father to read and promised to mat and frame it. A year later he learned how much the Tribute had meant to his father when he asked his dad what he wanted for Christmas. His dad reminded him, "Remember, you said you would put that thing you wrote in a frame?"

Try to present your Tribute at an important family gathering—a holiday, an anniversary, a birth, a Mother's or Father's Day. Your parents will probably consider it one of the greatest gifts they have ever received. And you will have the privilege of engraving a memory on your parents' hearts they will never forget.

A Document to Pass On

I imagine that whenever my mother goes to be with the Lord, the Tribute now hanging in her home will come back to me. I'll hang it in a new place of honor in our home. And at that point it will serve an additional purpose—to remind my children and grandchildren of the family legacy and what my mom was like.

What if your children and grandchildren maintained the Tribute tradition in this way? In one hundred years your descendants might even have a "Wall of Tributes" or a "Book of Tributes." A hall really could become a family museum. It is not hard to imagine that happening. Think of the impact upon a great-grandchild who reads and is reminded of what his grandparents and great-grandparents stood for. A formal document can be like the Declaration of Independence, reminding subsequent generations of their heritage, values, and spiritual moorings.

It could be that your values not only will be written on the hearts of your children, but will be passed on by your children in Tributes and read to succeeding generations. These Tributes might be read aloud at family gatherings. What a way for a family to honor its parents and truly connect with their past!

Marble Tributes

London's Westminster Abbey is a grand structure in which thousands of people are memorialized in marble tributes and buried in the floors and walls. Recently I had the privilege of wandering through that massive abbey and reading the tributes to prominent leaders, politicians, artists, and literary giants. Some had been enshrined for more than five hundred years.

It was fascinating to see such famous lives described in two dozen words—words that often were quite profound. Kings were honored for their leadership, warriors acclaimed for their courage, statesmen and writers for their contributions to England.

The gravestones of some of the most famous men and women reminded me of the impact of one life upon a nation and world, and of spiritual values that are vitally important.

As I walked among those marble tributes, I couldn't help wondering why our burial stones here in the United States rarely say anything about a person's life, about what they lived for, about their values and impact. A gravestone simply bears the name of the deceased and the date of his or her death. I think of what my friend Crawford Loritts says about inscriptions on gravestones: "An entire life is summarized by a dash between two dates."

Isn't a life worth more than a dash? Perhaps a portion of your Tribute may someday make it onto your parents' gravestones to remind descendants and succeeding generations of how to invest their lives. And even if your Tribute is never etched on marble or granite, but is simply a framed, public document hanging in a home, it always will be a reminder to all who read it of an important legacy.

"A Christmas Tribute"

A Tribute from Barbara Rainey to her parents, Bob and Jean Peterson of Camden, Arkansas.

My wife, Barbara, took special care in preparing her Tribute to her parents, matting it with lace and ribbons intertwined and presenting it to them as a Christmas gift. She knew God's desire for her to honor her parents, and she wanted to show them her appreciation in a tangible way.

On Christmas Day in 1987, after all the regular gifts were unwrapped, I took our kids into another room so Barbara could be alone for a few moments with her parents. I could barely hear her as she read it, and I could tell she was nervous—I've never heard her read anything so fast!

By the time Barbara was finished, all three were crying. It was a holy and unforgettable moment. The three of them embraced and shared a tender time of tears, gratefulness, and appreciation.

Barbara's parents immediately hung the Tribute in their kitchen, where it remains today. Since then, Barbara has seen that honoring her parents has helped to dismantle miscommunications that had occurred in the past. It also has opened up opportunities for Barbara to enjoy her relationship with her parents even more and to see them grow together in a solid friendship.

As a side benefit, my relationship with my in-laws has benefited as well. When Barbara honored them, I think they felt like I was honoring them as well. And I did . . . I was part of it.

One of my most vivid and pleasant memories is of us kids watching you both work and working with you. As I look back, much of the work I remember was seasonal. With Mom I remember weeding, working, and planting flower beds in the spring. Dad supervised us when he took down storm windows, and we kids got the screens, lined them up against tree trunks to be washed, rinsed, and hung in anticipation of the warm summer days to come. In the summer, there was flower-bed maintenance and lawn work to do. I remember my job was to trim the edges of the driveway and sidewalks with the hand clippers. When fall arrived there were leaves to be raked and storm windows to be returned to their protective duty. And then, as the snows came, our shovels kept the sidewalks and driveway clean.

There were inside duties as well—such as cleaning sinks and learning to wash dishes the right way. Mom taught me to sew, iron, embroider, and to finish what I started. I remember being told more than once, "Anything worth doing is worth doing well." Thank you for the gift of a strong work ethic from both experience and your example.

The gifts of character and common sense are now mine because of your model. I learned to value honesty, respect for my elders, and good manners. You taught me to be conservative and not wasteful, and to value quality because it would endure.

I'm thankful to you both for the gift of self-confidence. Though my self-esteem faltered during my teen years, you demonstrated that you trusted me, and I always knew you believed in me. I remember your allowing me to do a lot with Jimmy when he was a baby and toddler. I felt at times like he was mine as I fed him, rocked him, talked and played with him, and took him to a carnival with my date when he was only three.

You also expressed trust by allowing me to express my creativity—at your expense! You let me decorate the house at Christmas, arrange flowers in the summer, and fix my room up the way I wanted. But the one that took the cake was when you let me paint the bathroom fire-engine red with white-and-black trim—a thing I don't think I'd let my kids do. But I'm very grateful for that expression of trust, because it gave me a greater sense of self-confidence.

Another priceless gift was the gift of a good spiritual

foundation. As we faithfully attended church and Sunday school as a family, and as I was encouraged to attend Vacation Bible School in the summers and youth group in the teen years, I learned the central importance of God in my life. Because we were always there, I memorized many of the great Christian hymns which I love to this day.

Because you loved me, you corrected my grammar, picked up my Kleenexes, and you let me go: to France, to college, and to Dennis. Though many of the details are long since forgotten, I'll always remember how proud I felt as I walked down the aisle with Dad, and you both gave me away in marriage.

The last gift I mention is in no way the least. In fact, it is probably the greatest because it is foundational to all the others: it is the example of your marriage. I cannot recall a single argument or disagreement between you. It was apparent that you loved each other, cared for each other, and liked each other. I never felt insecure or fearful that you would leave one another or get a divorce. I treasure that gift of your good, solid, happy marriage. I attribute a great deal of the success of my marriage to the example I saw in yours.

And so, in this season of giving, some thirty-eight years after you gave me the gift of life, I give you this tribute. With a heart of gratitude, I give you my appreciation, my admiration, and my love.

Your daughter, Barbara
Christmas 1987

13

Writing a Tribute

God gave us memories so we could have roses in December.
—*Unknown*

Perhaps you are intrigued with this idea of writing a Tribute to your parents. And possibly, at this point, you feel a growing conviction that you need to do this.

Maybe you have no problem putting words onto paper. Or maybe you're asking yourself questions such as:

▶ "How can I write something like this when I don't know what to say?"
▶ "How can I write a Tribute if I can't remember much about my childhood?"
▶ "How can I do this if I'm not a good writer?"
▶ "My grammar and spelling are not the best."

I've discovered that parents don't care if you're a gifted writer, grammarian, or spelling bee champion. They feel honored by the fact that you're speaking from your heart. And to be effective, a Tribute must include emotion and a piece of your heart. You can accomplish this as you include special memories—those times of happiness, joy, celebration, and even pain and sadness that recapture how you felt as a child.

In a way, these shared memories tell the story of your

family. And as the following excerpts from Tributes show, memories can create a sort of time warp, transporting your family decades into the past. Notice how each of these portions of actual Tributes mentions specific places and events:

> Dad, your life and concern were also modeled to your extended family and neighbors. I can still picture you outside shoveling sidewalks heaped with snow and helping others dig out their snowbound cars in the UpperEnd. You were only a phone call away to help!
> The many times you gave of your time to Aunt Lela, Aunt Ethel, Uncle Harry, and Aunt Ada, and your cousin Ethel Webb illustrated a deep commitment to family. I'll never forget those late spring visits to Hookstown Cemetery to plant geraniums at loved ones' graves to honor those who were dearest to you and Mom. And your friendship with Tom Marett, which prompted your overnight drives to Georgia for rolls of carpet, taught me about sacrificial giving and love. Dad, I wish I had your energy and servant's heart.

> Growing up on the farm provided many adventures for this skinny kid who always wished he was as big as his little brother. There were tunnels and paths through the hay barn and a board pile along with a hammer and nails for building projects like a tree house. There was fishing in the ponds, homemade ice cream and even a few episodes of skinny dippin'. We went mushroom hunting in the spring, and Mom, I remember when you packed picnic lunches for Dad and we all went to check on him over at the Wolfe Place.
> At least you never traded me in, even though you had plenty of reason to. There was the time we

greased the slide in the basement with lard to make it
go faster and ended up with the whole basement floor
coated. Another time I wore out a pair of new blue
jeans on a mud slide and came back covered head to
toe and had to take off all my clothes outside and get
hosed down before being allowed back inside.

Of course, your love was expressed to me in
many other ways. Growing up, you were always there
with Bactine, Band-Aids, heating pads, aspirin, hot
tea with honey, and a dozen other remedies to "fix"
a sick or hurt little boy.

You taught me how to swim in the concrete
"pond" in our backyard; wrote me letters while I was
away at summer camp; were a den mother in my Cub
Scout pack; allowed Tamara and me to have three
dogs, one bird, some fish, turtles, and a cat, even
when you weren't crazy about pets; and you were
always there to calm my fears whenever the coat rack
in my bedroom would turn into a hideous monster at
night, once the lights were turned off.

They started out their lives together very
humbly. Too poor to own a farm of their own, they
had to live with his mom and dad for a year. It was
hard, but they persevered. Soon they had a little
homestead of their own, but it needed a lot of fixing
up. One winter morning they woke up to snow on
the foot of their bed. But they worked hard, fixed up
the house, even put in a bathroom, got some cows,
and began their family.

You always give of yourself so unselfishly and in
so many different ways. . . . I recall wanting to go to

the state fair as a seventh grader. I was irresponsible and had saved no money, but you bailed me out with the five dollars you had been saving to buy yourself a new hat. In a larger way, you helped me buy my first car. That red VW Bug still stands as the best car I've ever owned.

My Christmas memories are mainly of you—not only the one hundred different kinds of chocolate candy you made every year. But you would wake us up at four in the morning to open presents because you were just as excited about giving to your children as receiving gifts yourself.

She suffered a parent's most bitter pain, seeing one of her children face death too soon. All her heartache from years spent trying to guide a young life could not compare to the ache in her heart when that life ended suddenly one October day. She wept and prayed that her daughter's troubled spirit might at last have found its rest.

Can you sense the emotion in these statements, even in the simplest memories? This is why a Tribute often takes family relationships beyond the surface, even if it is for just a few, magical moments.

When I advise people on how to create Tributes like these, I usually suggest a few simple steps. These approaches seem to work well in unlocking a flood of memories and even an occasional surprising burst of creativity.

Step One: *Prepare your heart.*

Once you decide to write a Tribute for your parents, you should spend some time examining your heart. Take an afternoon to be alone with God. Talk with Him, read His Word, and allow Him to search your heart. As Psalm 139:23-24 says, "Search me, O God, and know my heart; try me and know my anxious thoughts; and see if there be any hurtful way in me, and lead me in the everlasting way."

Here are a few questions to help you get started:

▶ Are you willing to look at your parents through the eyes of Christ?

▶ Are you looking to God rather than to your parents for approval?

▶ Are your motives pure? Are you seeking to manipulate your parents through this gesture in any way? Is giving them honor your goal?

▶ Are you prepared to honor them regardless of their response?

▶ Do you need to ask for their forgiveness for anything?

▶ Are you willing to forgive them for how they have hurt you?

Let me remind you not to become morbidly introspective over these questions. Work through any issues that arise if you need to, but do not "stall out" in this step. The goal is to honor your parents, not manufacture additional, unnecessary guilt in your life.

Step Two: *Create a memory list.*

Your goal here is to collect as many memories as you can. Write down the good memories you have about your childhood—memorable events, happy occasions, interesting experiences with your family, things your parents taught you, and more. Don't be selective at this point—just pull memories out of your mind and put them on paper.

You might want to start with an hour alone, simply writing down anything you can remember. Then, over the next few weeks, carry around a notepad or some small cards and write down anything that comes to mind. You will be surprised,

once you start, how many little things will spark memories—
smells, sights, things people say, things your kids do.

When I sat down to write my Tribute, I had memories
written on church bulletins, water bill envelopes, and little
scraps of paper. In preparing her Tribute, Barbara found that a
pad of paper in the kitchen and on her nightstand proved helpful. The point is, we collected memories no matter when they
came.

As I've read the Tributes people have sent me, it is interesting to note how often they write about kitchens and favorite
foods. I like the comment made by Gary Allen Sledge in an
article he wrote about his mother in *Reader's Digest*:

> It's difficult to know what counts in this world.
> Most of us count credits, honors, dollars. But at the
> bulging center of mid-life, I am beginning to see that
> the things that really matter take place not in the
> boardrooms, but in the kitchens of the world.
> Memory, imagination, love are some of those things.
> Service to God and the ones we love is another.[1]

My mother always used to complain about how small our
kitchen was, but I remember it only as the warm center of the
household. In my Tribute to her, I wrote, "A warm kitchen
was her trademark—the most secure place in the home—a
shelter in the storm. Her narrow but tidy kitchen always attracted a crowd. It was the place where food and friends were
made!"

Questions to Help You Unlock Your Memories

When I was a young boy, I enjoyed pumping water out of
a cistern next to my Grandma and Grandpa Rhea's house.
One day, I grabbed hold of the rusty, old handle and pumped
with all my might. Not as much as a gurgle came out of that
old spigot. And just as I felt hopeless and about to die from
exhaustion, my Grandpa's huge hand wrapped around mine;
his other hand poured a cup of water into the top of the old

hand pump. As the water came gushing out, he explained that what he had done was simply prime the pump.

If you have trouble remembering what happened in your childhood or what you can thank your parents for, you may need a little help priming the pump. The following list is divided into several categories, and it contains the equivalent of several gallons of pump primers so you'll be assured of an ample supply of memories. Not all of these questions will apply to you, but probably quite a few will. (Be sure to jot your thoughts down on a pad of paper.)

Memory Pump Primers

- ▶ What school projects did they help you with? What was your favorite gift your dad or mom ever got you? What memorable conversations do you remember having with your parents?
- ▶ Where did you go on vacations? What did you do?
- ▶ What was your favorite vacation?
- ▶ What was your happiest moment as a child?
- ▶ What did you enjoy doing with your dad?
- ▶ What did you enjoy doing with your mom?
- ▶ What was your favorite moment with your dad?
- ▶ What was your favorite moment with your mom?
- ▶ What smells remind you of your dad? Your mom?
- ▶ What sounds accompanied your home growing up?
- ▶ Where was the warmest spot in your house (not physically, but emotionally)?
- ▶ What was your favorite room in your house?
- ▶ What was the first movie you ever remember seeing?
- ▶ What TV shows did you watch regularly as a family?
- ▶ What was your favorite book your parents read to you?
- ▶ What songs did you sing together?
- ▶ What was your favorite restaurant?
- ▶ Who was your favorite relative to visit with your family?
- ▶ What do you remember about your dad's office or place of work?

- What hobbies did they enjoy?
- What holiday traditions did your family observe?
- What were weekends like in your home?
- What was your favorite tradition?
- Did you ever climb in bed with your parents?
- If you woke up scared from a nightmare, what did you do? How did your mom or dad respond to you?
- What problems did they help you with as a child? As a teenager?
- What pets did they get for you?
- What "dates" did you go on together?
- What activities did they encourage you to be involved in?
- What activities did they participate in with you (as your coach, teacher, etc.)?

Family Funnies

- What were the family jokes?
- What was the funniest moment you experienced with your dad? Your mom? Your family when everyone was there?
- What special phrases did your family invent?
- What nicknames did people in your family have, and how did they earn them?

Holidays and Celebrations

- What was your favorite holiday? Why?
- What costumes did you wear on Halloween? Where did you get them?
- What was your favorite Christmas present?
- What was your favorite birthday?

Character Qualities

▶ What did other people think of your parents? How did they react to them? How did they treat your father and/ or mother at work?

▶ What did you admire about your parents?

▶ How did your parents display affection for you?

▶ How did they display affection for one another?

▶ What's one thing you appreciate that your dad often did for your mother? And vice versa?

▶ How did they treat other people?

▶ Do you remember seeing your parents cry?

▶ What character qualities did they model that have stuck with you?

▶ What sacrifices did they make for you?

The Legacy They Passed on to Me

▶ What hobbies or skills or interests did they pass on to you?

▶ What else did they teach you how to do?

▶ What did you learn from your parents about work?

▶ What did they teach you about life?

▶ What values did they pass on to you?

▶ What advice did they give you that you are grateful for?

▶ What was the greatest lesson you ever learned from your mom? From your dad?

▶ What did they teach you about being a parent?

▶ In what ways are you like them in your personality, skills, habits, etc.?

▶ What values that you learned from them are now being passed on to your children?

Unlocking Memories

As you review these questions you should be able to recall at least ten or fifteen specific, good things about your parents, unless you had a parent who deserted you at a young age or an evil parent. (If you had an evil parent, I will address that in chapter 15, "When the Damage Goes Deep.") It may take a weekend or a year, but usually those memories are stuffed in your brain—it's just a matter of bringing them out.

Often a simple question can unlock a long-buried memory. My cohost on "FamilyLife Today," Bob Lepine, helped me brainstorm the list I just presented. One question—"What activities did they participate in with you?"—led him to say, "This reminds me of when I was in eighth or ninth grade and I spent a week at Boy Scout camp with my dad. He was there as the Scoutmaster more than he was there as my dad, and I don't remember that we got any emotional closeness or bonding or anything out of that. But I just now realized he took a week of vacation to do that. That's a sacrifice."

Bob's recollection shows how a parent's actions can make a special statement to a child. I heard of a young man who was selected to be a varsity cheerleader in college. When his father heard of his son's achievement, he commented sarcastically to him, "So, where's your skirt?" But his father later traveled to games and tournaments just to watch his son perform. In the end, his actions meant more than his words. The words still hurt, but that father ultimately came to appreciate his son's achievement.

As you reclaim memories, you might try talking with other people. By telling stories to your spouse or your children, you may recall additional details. Or they may ask questions that spark further memories.

If you're still stumped and the "memory well" seems empty, a phone call to a brother, sister, aunt, or uncle may help prime the pump.

Some people fear they won't have anything to remember. One woman in her late thirties found her notepad nearly empty after several months of trying to remember things. Her family didn't have fun when she was growing up and didn't encourage family members to share openly. Two things, however, helped her prime the pump of memories. First, her husband interviewed her by asking probing questions about her childhood. And second, she ended up taking an entire Saturday at a park to try to focus. One by one the memories came, and eventually she captured enough to write a Tribute. It was a powerful, emotional experience for her and her parents.

Step Three: *Organize your material.*

If you are writing a Tribute for two parents, you'll need to decide up front whether you want to write two individual Tributes or one Tribute to both your dad and mom. There's no right or wrong way to do it. It all depends on the occasion and what you feel more comfortable doing.

There are many formats you can use to present your material, including a scrapbook, a book, a notebook, or a framed picture. The format you choose will help determine the length and look of your written material. For the rest of this chapter, I am going to concentrate on the format I think works especially well—a framed, typeset document.

After you have finished your "Memory List," you may end up with dozens of items. You'll need to reduce its length to fit the size you choose for your framed picture, so now it is time to prioritize.

Go through the list and select the memories you feel are most important to include in the Tribute. You don't need to include every memory that pops into your head, such as, "I remember going to the grocery store with you one time when I was a small boy and you bought green beans." Some memories simply have no meaning. Like picking only the freshest blooming flowers for a bouquet, choose only those memories that are the most meaningful and vivid emotionally to you.

Concentrate on those items your parents would appreciate most. Include the memories that will carry the most meaning to them, such as specific things they did for you or the lessons you learned from them. Include tender emotions, possibly even a sad moment or two, and include humor if it is appropriate.

Step Four: Write the Tribute.

Now it's time to do your writing. Don't worry about being fancy here—just tell the story as if you're talking to a friend.

You might want to start with a statement *telling why you have written this Tribute.* For example: "Too often we let our lives go by and we fail to let the ones who are most important to us know just how special they are. You are special. There are so many reasons I am thankful that you are my daddy."

Then try to *turn each memory you have selected into a sentence or paragraph.* The following examples show how you can turn a single phrase or memory into a sentence or paragraph just by telling the story.

Memories	Tribute Phrases
Good provider . . . hard worker . . . went to work even when he was sick or when it was icy outside . . . paid my way through college . . . always got me cars . . .	I never, ever worried that I wouldn't have the things I needed or wanted, because you are such a hard worker. I can remember days you went to work even when you didn't feel well and a few times you had to walk to work because of icy roads. And, unlike many parents, you paid my way through college. Even provided a car. I can never remember hearing you complain about the drain it probably put on your pocketbook.
Always loved me, was proud of me . . . tour through Nabisco . . .	I never doubted you were proud that I was your daughter —and that has helped me be confident in who I am today because I have been assured of your love. I remember taking a tour through the Nabisco plant, and I had people point-

	ing to me, saying, "That's Jim's daughter," because you let everyone know that I was coming through.
Football games, driving through downtown, honking horns . . .	We had lots of fun together. Remember when we would go to football games? You would let us scream for our team out of the car window and blow the horn as we drove through downtown Atlanta. Of course, you were enjoying it too, because you have always been a kid at heart anyway.
Love for people . . . never met a stranger . . .	Your love for people and your lack of fear of strangers has been passed down to me. I find that quality so useful in reaching out to others for Christ.
Great grandfather . . . girls love "Papa" . . .	I also am thankful that you are the papa to Bethany and Missy. They love the attention and love you give them, and I'm sure that is a big part in helping to shape them into secure girls.

Finally, *conclude the Tribute with a special note of thanksgiving and appreciation.* For example:

Thank You, Lord, for giving Thomas M. (Jim) Dodd as a daddy to me and a papa to my children. You knew what You were doing when You gave him to us. I love you, Dad.

Your youngest daughter,
Merry

After you have written this first draft, read through it several times, looking for ways to improve it. Does everything make sense? Is the writing clear enough to understand what you are describing?

It also helps to have another person—a friend or your mate —read through your Tribute because he or she may be able to spot some problems you haven't thought of. This is especially true if you are concerned about grammar and spelling.

At this point, count your words to see if they'll fit within the limit for the format you've chosen. Here are some suggested word limits, corresponding to different sizes of format and type (allowing for a one-inch margin on all sizes, plus matting on the two larger sizes):

Frame Size	Type Size	Word limit
8½ × 11	14 pt.	350–500
	11 pt.	500–700
8½ × 14	14 pt.	500–600
	11 pt.	600–750
11 × 17	14 pt.	900–1100
	11 pt.	1350–1500
18 × 24	18 pt.	850–975
	14 pt.	900–1200

Step Five: *Frame the Tribute.*

Now that you've finished writing your Tribute, it's time to design the gift for your parents. First, you'll need to *create a clean version of the document, suitable for framing.* Here are a few options:

▶ If you have access to a computer with good word-processing or desktop-publishing software, set your document in the style and size you desire and then print it on a high-quality laser printer.
▶ Have your document typeset at a local typesetter.
▶ Hire someone to put the document in calligraphy and

on parchment to give it an elegant look. Make sure the words are large and clear. This approach doesn't usually work well with longer documents unless a very large size of paper is used. Calligraphy can be difficult to read otherwise.

▶ Decide if you want to add any photos, artwork, or other mementos to the document and plan accordingly. Barbara used ribbon and lace threaded through a mat to add a personal touch to her Tribute for her parents. Some creative Tributes I have seen included line drawings corresponding to the theme of the document. For example, one Tribute began with a drawing of a twig on a tree next to the opening sentence, which read, "AS THE TWIG IS BENT and as a young child is led, so determines the direction of that life. . . ."

Step Six: *Present the Tribute to your parents.*

Don't just *give* your parents your Tribute. *Present* it to them.

Have you ever eaten at someone's house or a great restaurant that knew how to present a meal? If you have, you've probably never forgotten it. And as is true with an outstanding meal, presentation can set your Tribute apart from the myriad of gifts you've given your parents over the years.

Here are three ways to present your Tribute to your parents:

1. *Do it publicly.* As I mentioned in the previous chapter, this is the most effective way to make the Tribute memorable. I suggest doing it at a special occasion—a family reunion, anniversary party, a birthday, Mother's or Father's Day, or a time when the family gathers together around a holiday, such as Thanksgiving or Christmas.

2. *Do it privately.* You may want to steal away with your dad or mom for a private reading of your Tribute. A trip home for no other reason might etch the message on their hearts

permanently. You may need to pull them aside at a family gathering, such as Christmas, and read it to them.

3. *Do it with your children listening.* Some of the most profound scenes painted in my mind are of an adult son or a daughter and his or her children gathered round the feet of honored parents during the reading of the Tribute. What better picture could we give the next generation of the power of obeying God's commandments?

Does It Work?

Dave Boehi assisted me in innumerable ways in crafting this book, but he had not actually written a Tribute for his own parents until the manuscript was nearly finished. Dave and his sister, Denise, went home and honored their parents on their fortieth wedding anniversary with Tributes. They prepared a special meal, gave them cards and gifts, and led them into the living room. Then they brought their kids in to listen as they read the Tributes to their parents.

I couldn't wait to hear what happened, so I called Dave soon after he returned home. Dave is a reserved man, and he was surprised at how he reacted as he read the Tribute. "I tried to express things in the Tribute that I'd never said before, and I got more and more emotional as I read it," he told me. "I don't think anyone expected me to cry the way I did. My wife and my daughters didn't know what to do—they'd never seen me cry like that! My youngest daughter, Missy, sat on my lap and kept looking up at me with surprise on her face. Then she hugged me, wanting me to know everything was okay."

Dave could tell his parents were deeply touched, but they didn't say anything about the Tributes during the following day. But then his mom later told him in a private moment that the evening had been the "most memorable experience of my life."

Frogs on a Log

One of my favorite parables I love to tell at our FamilyLife Marriage Conference has to do with frogs and a log. Read carefully—and answer honestly:

If you had five frogs on a log and three of them decide to jump, then how many frogs would you have left on the log?

The answer is *five*.

Why? Because there is a difference between deciding to jump and jumping.

Will you decide to write a Tribute?

Or will you do it?

"To the Mom and Dad I've Taken for Granted"

A Tribute by John to his parents, Jack and Peggy Hailey of Nashville, Tenn.

While attending a FamilyLife Marriage Conference in Birmingham, Alabama, John and Debbie Hailey heard my message on honoring parents, and both decided to write Tributes. For each the experience had a special meaning.

In a letter John wrote to me, he says he was struck by a sense of "ungratefulness" in himself, realizing that for many years he had taken his parents for granted. "I had a good childhood and have always had a good relationship with my parents," he writes. "My family is loving but does not tend to be very warm or expressive of emotion."

John decided to address both his parents in one Tribute. "The process wasn't easy. Trying to put down in writing the feelings I have inside was difficult. The exercise was good for me, though, since it forced me to examine what my parents mean to me and how blessed I am to have them.

"The presentation of the Tribute was not really what I had expected but, in retrospect, what I should have anticipated. On Christmas morning, after they unwrapped the framed Tribute, I read it to them. I hurried through the reading, feeling somewhat embarrassed that I thought something that I had written was worth framing! After I finished they hugged me and thanked me for such a nice gift. The moment lacked the powerful, emotional 'oomph' I had envisioned. The excitement of the morning and my own hurried reading dampened it. Nevertheless, I know my parents were touched by the moment and will cherish the memory."

Debbie, meanwhile, wrote separate Tributes for her parents. Her mother's was easy for her to write—but it was different with her father's. "Debbie has always had a great respect for her father, but finding words to communicate honor and gratitude to him didn't come as easily," John writes. "The exercise forced her to examine the positive impact he has had on her life. Now that she has, she has a much greater appreciation for him!"

Debbie wasn't able to present the Tributes to her parents in person, so she mailed them. Shortly after they had been opened, she and John received a phone call from her mom and dad. "Mom was crying, and Dad was bragging about what a fine piece Debbie had written," John says. "They were definitely touched!"

John concluded his letter by saying, "Our parents were honored by the Tributes they received. Debbie and I were the ones who received the blessing, though. Now that we are parents we can better understand what our moms and dads went through to raise us. Just being able to recount the input they had into our lives at a time in our life when we can appreciate it was worth the effort."

Mom, I can still remember coming home from school to the smell of homemade cookies. As I sat down to snack on a warm snickerdoodle, I probably thought, "Everybody does this—everybody's got a mom at home who's able to make cookies for her kids, who's always there when her son needs her, and who's able to give him an example of self-sacrifice."

Dad, I can still remember afternoons in our backyard pitching baseball, passing the football, shooting hoops, or doing whatever sport the season called for. As I hauled in a long pass, I probably thought, "Every boy does this—every boy's got a dad who comes home and plays ball with him, who's always at his games, who's able to teach him a strong work ethic without putting his job above his family."

I can still remember those trips home from Bruceton, riding in the backseat of our family car. Margaret was in the seat next to me, and you, Mom and Dad, were in the front. We had enjoyed a big dinner at Momo's and then a lazy afternoon of playing catch with Uncle Frankie, watching a game on TV, and just visiting with the family. As we traveled home I was a little tired but very satisfied and carefree. If I had thought about it, I probably would have reasoned that every child has a mom and dad "in the front seat" making sure his world is under control.

I can still remember the time you decided to put me in Brentwood Academy. I wasn't getting much of an education at the school I was in, at least not the kind I was supposed to be there for. I know now what a financial sacrifice that must have been. I'm sure I thought at the time, though, "Big deal, every parent would do this for their child."

When I went to college the same scene was replayed. You could have insisted that I go to a local school to save money. You let me go to Georgia Tech, though, recognizing that it would be an asset to me down the road. Again, I probably thought you did what every parent would do. There are some things I can't remember. I can't remember a time when you didn't accept me. I was always okay. My performance was okay, too, as long as I tried my hardest. I can't remember a time that there wasn't harmony in the home. The two of you may have had disagreements, but I don't remember them. I guess the atmosphere of love you provided overshadowed any conflicts there may have been. I can't remember a time when faith in God was not stressed. I grew up knowing a real God, a God who created me, a God who loved me and cared for me enough to send His Son to die for me.

Mom and Dad, words are so empty, so inadequate, to really express what I know and feel now. I know I have been blessed to be able to call *you* Mom and Dad. I know also that you love me and that I love you, too.

"They Rise Up and Call Her Blessed"

A Tribute by Debbie Hailey to her mother, Jane Weas of Elizabethtown, Ky.

Titus 2:2-5 says, "Older women are to be temperate, dignified, sensible, sound in their behavior, not malicious gossips, nor enslaved to much wine, teaching what is good, that they may encourage the young women to love their husbands, to love their children, to be sensible, pure, workers at home, kind, being subject to their own husbands, that the Word of God may not be dishonored" (paraphrased).

God has given me such a woman to be a role model for my life. I would like to pay tribute to this woman and share a few things I have learned from her. Most of the things she has taught me have been from the things I have observed in her life over the years. Her name is Mom.

Mom was born in a small town in Kentucky. She was married in the middle of her senior year in high school. Two years after that I was born. Mom didn't go to college and pursue a glamorous career. She did something much greater—she raised four children who now rise up and call her blessed.

The Titus 2 passage sums up my Mom.

I. Mom showed me what it was to have faith in God. She taught me how to love God and worship Him and serve Him.

II. Mom showed me what generosity and sacrificial giving were all about.

III. Mom taught me what it meant to be appreciative and grateful. She taught me about being honest. She taught me manners.

IV. Mom showed me what it was to love your

husband. She has loved him now in marriage for thirty-eight years!

V. Mom loved us kids. She was always doing special things for us. She gave us the best birthday parties. She was always the Room Mother.

VI. Mom took care of herself. She was so beautiful and I was always so proud of her. I wanted to grow up and be a mother just like her.

VII. Mom loved working around the house. She loved to cook and gave me a love for cooking also.

VIII. Mom showed me that the most important thing a woman can do is to serve her family by staying at home with her children.

Mom is now reaping the rewards of being a grandmother. My children are blessed to have her for one. I know that God has called me to be a mother. I am proud to be one and proud to have a mother like the one I have. I pray that I can take what she has given me and pass it down to my daughters.

Thank you, Mom, I love you.

"How to Be a Mean Father"

A Tribute by Debbie Hailey to her father, Ken Weas.

A mean father never allows candy or sweets to take the place of a well-balanced meal.

A mean father insists on knowing where his children are at all times, who their friends are, and what they are doing.

A mean father breaks the child-labor law by making his children work—washing dishes, making beds, learning to cook, and doing other cruel and unpleasant chores.

A mean father makes life miserable for his offspring by insisting that they always tell the truth.

A mean father produces teenagers who are wiser and more sensible.

A mean father can smile with secret delight and pride as he hears his own grandchildren call their parents "mean."

Dad, I want to thank you for caring enough to stand firm in doing what you thought was best for us. I know people said that you were too hard on us kids, but you can be proud that your four children are now adults who are mature, responsible, and able to raise their own families.

I thank you for teaching me how to make it on my own and not having to be dependent on you and Mom. I thank you for teaching me that honesty and being truthful are the ways to a successful life. I thank you for showing me that common sense is the way to think.

I thank you for all the wonderful childhood memories: of playing in the sprinkler after a hard day's work in the yard; of going to Playland Amusement Park and riding the roller coaster and shooting darts; of all the wonderful camping trips and waterskiing until we dropped; of riding around at Christmas looking at all the pretty lights. Thank you for all the delicious barbecue. And of course the memories would not be complete without remembering how we listened to Kentucky Wildcat basketball games on the radio!

I thank you for accepting John as a part of the family as if he were your own son. I thank you for loving my children and being a wonderful grandfather, helping them create special memories of their own. I thank you the most for loving Mom and staying together for thirty-eight years.

Thank you, Dad, I love you.

14

No Regrets

*Even now, twenty-one years after my father died, not a week
goes by that I don't find myself thinking I should call him.*
—Herb Gardner

Terry and Carol Murphy are true family champions. They once served as leaders for one of our West Coast FamilyLife Marriage Conferences and left an impact on hundreds of marriages and families.

In the spring of 1992 they invited Carol's sister, Cathy, and her husband, Frank, to the Los Angeles conference. A few months later the Murphys wrote me to tell what had happened as a result. Carol Murphy's letter tells the story:

> Frank was a wonderful man, but he also was stern and stoic—he taught his three boys to be strong, tough, no more tears, no more hugs, and only manly handshakes at bedtimes. He liked things done his way. He was not a good listener. But, of course, he did give lots of logical advice.
>
> Then the last weekend of May they attended the FamilyLife Marriage Conference in Woodland Hills. Frank went home a changed man, a changed husband, and a changed dad. He thanked us over

and over for inviting him and encouraging him to attend.

You see, Frank had an incurable form of cancer that spread from his legs to his lungs, spleen, and various parts of his body. He was forty-three years old when he found out how numbered his days were. The doctors gave him a two-year prognosis. God gave him three and a half years.

Within days of learning he had cancer, he gave his life to Jesus—something his wife and sons had prayed years for. So Frank began to trust in Jesus Christ and go to Him for strength and courage. I think this is how God had begun to change Frank so that on Sunday evening when the conference was over he was ready to change any way God wanted him to.

Hugging and loving his sons became commonplace in their lives. He shared from his heart with the boys, cried with them, told them how proud he was of them and how very much he loved them. He became the listening, loving husband every wife dreams of. He realized that his life on earth was only in preparation for the ultimate goal of heaven.

His last four months here on earth were filled with laughter and good times with his family. Even though the cancer was taking over his body, God gave him a quality life to the end. As a family they had a two-week summer vacation they will never forget. They also spent lots of time together in prayer and in conversation. Frank prepared his family for his death and for the task ahead of them, so that they, too, would one day reach the goal and stand before God's throne.

Terry counseled the boys about three weeks before Frank died to each write their dad a letter of love, so they would be sure they told him everything they wanted to say. He also encouraged them to read it to their dad even though it would be difficult. Well, they wrote the letters and read them to their dad and, together, sons and father wept for the blessing they were to each other.

With the family's permission, here are the letters written by Frank Lynn's three teenage sons—Russ, Brian, and Kevin:

Dad,

You are and always will be the best Dad. You taught me a lot; you taught me to be a man. Thank you. Right now I'm thinking of you. You will always be in my heart and soul.

I'll always remember a home volleyball game when I killed a ball, and looked over at you. You had a big smile and were cheering. I will never forget that. I hope that I made you proud, because I am so proud of you. Thanks for the two weeks of vacation with you. It definitely made me feel closer to you.

I will take care of the house, Mom, and the boys the best that I can. I will always love you, Dad.

Bye.

Love, Russ

P.S. See you up in heaven!

Dear Dad:

I'm writing this to you because sometimes it's easier to write things down than to try to say them.

I know that I never really told you how I felt about you. When I think of Frank Lynn, a lot of things pop into my mind. You are a person I look up to, the way you pushed yourself in track and then college. I think the best thing is how strong you have been through all those operations and chemotherapy. I really think of you, as I grow up, as the one person I most want to be like. I also believe that you brought all three of us up to become mature adults.

You don't always realize all that your dad does for you. I was thinking of all the good times we had, and if I had to do it all over again I wouldn't change a thing. I would want you right there beside me.

If God decides to take the best dad from this earth, I want to let you know when I meet you in heaven we will have to race. So instead of saying good-bye, I'd like to say, "See you in heaven."

Love, your son, Brian

P.S. Dad, keep on fighting. You and God can beat this. Hang in there.

Dear Dad:

I'm writing this letter to you to say thank you for all the things you have done for me. You changed my diapers for me when I was a baby, and as I grew up, whenever I wanted to play you always played with me. You taught me how to ride a bike, and you taught me how to be a man.

You showed me how to save money and buy what I really wanted and not junk. You showed me how to fix things around the house and how to use tools.

You took me to the ocean and the lake, and taught me to fish and water ski. You also watched TV with me, and we enjoyed it together.

Thank you for being there with me. Thank you for everything you have done for me now and in the future.

Love, Kevin

In the final hour of Frank's life, he was barely coherent, but Terry sensed he wanted his sons near him. Russ decided to read his letter one last time to his father, and when he was finished he and Terry saw a tear rolling down Frank's cheek. Frank died ten minutes later.

At the memorial service, the three boys further honored their dad through the following statement:

> Before our dad died he told us that he didn't want anyone to be sad. He said he wanted his passing to be a celebration. He said he couldn't wait to see his dad and his heavenly Father. He told us that the hardest part was leaving his family and friends behind. But we would like to share with you now his last hours with us.
>
> On Monday we were called home about noon. We had a great time talking and being with Dad. We even played his favorite song for him. At about two o'clock, our mom sat on our dad's bed with him and put her arms around him, hugging him. Our Aunt Carol wrapped Dad's arms around Mom, because she knew that was what he wanted but was too weak to do.
>
> Mom told Dad so much in those last minutes. She told him how very much she loved him, and that she was so proud of him, and thanked him for giving her their three wonderful sons. Soon she asked him if he could hear the angels singing or the bells ringing, and his breathing slowed. She said, "Jesus is there for you, with His arms out. Can you see Him, can you hear the bells?" She said, "I want you to go from my arms into Jesus' arms."
>
> At that very moment, our dad took his last breath and we knew he went to be with Jesus.

"The Living Takes It to Heart"

Three sons. No regrets.

Ecclesiastes 7:2 reminds us, "It is better to go to a house of mourning than to go to a house of feasting, because that is the end of every man, and the living takes it to heart."

Frank Lynn's story is a stirring reminder that we need to do the important things while we still have time. There's nothing like visiting a "house of mourning" to jerk us to a halt and consider how we've spent our lives.

Recently, I read a quote that jolted me into reality. After recovering from his third bout with cancer, former U.S. Sen. Paul Tsongas said, "It's the dread of being removed from the scene that makes you appreciate being on the scene. If you presume endless days, then no day has particular value.

"I think of all the fathers who have young children and play golf all day Saturday and Sunday. They've never had cancer. I think of the husbands who never voice their affection for their wives. They've never had cancer."[1]

As I consider those words, I think about adult children who have never expressed their thankfulness to their parents. They know their parents will die—someday. They know they need to make an effort to honor them. But they procrastinate, thinking they can always do it "later."

No Words Left Unsaid

During the early 1980s, when I first began to speak on honoring parents, I received a letter from a student that put this issue in perspective:

Dear Dennis:

Your lecture today brought to mind the importance of phone calls to parents. My mother died about one year prior to my enlistment in the Air Force. As I departed New York City bound for San Antonio, Texas, my father took a day off work to see me off on my new adventure. To my knowledge, it was the only day off work he ever took, other than at my mother's funeral, and the only time I saw him cry.

I left with a promise that I would call him every Sunday at 2 p.m. and was faithful to that promise. One Sunday the phone rang for a long time and when Dad finally answered, I was truly concerned that something had gone wrong. Dad assured me all was well.

He seemed to have a lot to talk about that day. He expressed his sorrow at not having been able to spend more time with me as I grew up. I assured him that I understood, and that all the times we did have together were memorable and meaningful. His closing words were, "I love you and I miss you."

Those were the last words he spoke to me. Two days later I received a phone call and the voice on the other end said, "Pops is dead." It was later determined that Dad suffered two heart attacks, one conceivably on the day that I had called.

I pray that you will continue to emphasize contact with parents. However that contact is made, it could be the last opportunity to share your heart with someone who loved you and for you to express that the love was mutual.

(signed)

A student thankful for being reminded of a two-way blessing.

I like that last phrase—"a two-way blessing." That's what honoring your parents is—a blessing to the parent in finally receiving thanks for what he or she did right, and a blessing to the child who can grow old knowing no words were left unsaid. I know how it feels to have a parent die with words unsaid.

My dad died of a heart attack a few days short of his sixty-sixth birthday. I never had the chance to say good-bye to him. For a decade prior to his death, I had sought to honor him—but I'll always regret that I never expressed it in the same way I did to Mom, with a Tribute.

Two Questions to Ponder

I'd like to challenge you to consider two questions: The first is:

Would you have any regrets if your parents were to die tomorrow?

I know how it is for many adults—especially those in their twenties, thirties, and forties. They feel consumed by responsibilities at work, in their marriages, with children, at church. And it's easy in the midst of a busy and hectic schedule to leave parents in the dust. They reason, *They'll always be there, won't they? Once I get past that next deadline . . . once we finish this vacation . . . once the kids grow a little older . . . then I'll spend some time with my parents.*

If your relationship with your parents is difficult—or if anything with your parents remains unresolved—it is even easier to shove the problem into a corner of your mind. *I'll have the chance to talk with them someday. But I'm just not ready now.*

I know of one man who was motivated to honor his dad even though he'd only seen him twice since he was ten years old—at his sister's graduation and at her wedding. "I'd seen him two times since then, but I didn't want to live with the regret that the last time I would see him would be standing over his casket at his funeral. I knew Christ and he didn't. My responsibility to love him began to grow within me. God has forgiven him. I might be the only one in my family to share with him God's love and forgiveness in Christ."

This man has sought to honor his father through numerous visits. And he calls and writes to him regularly. Today that man has no regrets.

Others offer rationalizations: "I've done all I can do." A friend of mine has a good relationship with his father but is concerned his sister does not. He has asked her, "Would you have any regrets if Dad were to die tomorrow? Are you content with it ending this way? If not, why not do something about it?"

She responded that she was content, that she'd done all she could do. But the real problem seems to be that she doesn't want to go through the process of reconciling. She'd rather deny the pain than face it.

I believe she has a false sense of security. And when her

father dies she may struggle with guilt that she hadn't made more of an effort. She may deeply regret not having tried.

The second question I want to challenge you with is:

Why wait for the eulogy to praise your parents?

As wonderful as a funeral eulogy can be, I wish I could start a new tradition. It would be this: "Say those words of praise to your loved one *before* he or she dies as well as after." We need to say these things when our words can still be nourishment to an old soul, when it will be most encouraging. I often wonder how many eulogies are delivered with the hope that parents can somehow hear the words that were never spoken during their lifetime.

Dan Eichenbaum, a Jewish convert to Christianity, told my sixth-grade Sunday school class a wonderful story about a lesson his father had taught him:

> I recall how as a child, after Sunday school, my father would take me to the cemetery. He would take my hand and we'd walk around and I would ask him, "Daddy, what are you doing?"
>
> He'd say, "Well, I want to go see where my mother and my father were buried."
>
> He would stand there and cry, and I turned to him one day and I said, "Daddy, when I get big, I'll come out and see you in the cemetery."
>
> He turned to me and he said something really outstanding, and it stuck with me all these years. He said, "I don't want you to do that."
>
> I said, "Why?" And he said, "Well, I would rather you give flowers to the living, because when I am dead and gone and I'm out there in the cemetery, I won't be able to smell the flowers you bring me. So I would rather you do nice things to please me while I'm alive."
>
> If nothing else, my father left me a legacy of seeking to honor parents while they are alive. Instead

of going through life thinking about what we can get from our parents, what our parents can do for us, and how our parents can help us, we have to—before they die—say, "What can I do for you?" How can I please my parents who have nurtured, raised, cared for, disciplined, and loved me?

No matter what kind of bridges have been burned or doors have been closed, if your parents are still alive, it is your responsibility as children to make the step forward. We must make the move because our parents are sometimes set in their ways. *We* are the ones who must come forward and bring a bouquet of flowers while they are still living. We owe it to them and we owe it to God.

If a Parent Already Has Died

If you are feeling regret for not having honored a parent before he or she died, this chapter may unearth some difficult emotions for you. As I know personally, you may never be able to erase those feelings. But I can offer you two suggestions:

First, *allow yourself to grieve—over the loss of your parent and over your failure to honor.* I can still remember sitting at my dad's funeral with deep grief—but also with immense pride in a man who truly had been the bedrock of my early years.

According to an old woodman's proverb, "A tree is best measured when it's down." It wasn't until after my Dad was gone that I truly began to measure the man. Twenty years later I continue to take measurements, and the magnitude of what he left me looms even larger in my mind.

Second, *make a special effort to honor the living parent—as a way of honoring the one who is deceased.* By praising the man my mother chose to spend her life with, I was telling her, "Not only was your husband worthy of honor, but you are worthy as well because you made such a wise choice."

Finally, *look for ways to honor your deceased parent.* Consider that your children will benefit from knowing the legacy their grandfather or grandmother left them. A Tribute can be a permanent milestone for your kids as they begin their pilgrimage through life.

Chapter 17 includes many ideas on how to honor your parents. Some may be appropriate for a deceased parent.

I wrote a Tribute to my father nearly ten years after he died, which I think not only honored him but also brought healing to me. I have no idea whether those in heaven are able to see what happens here on earth, but I do know he would have been pleased had he been here to hear it. And I'm certain of this: *God sees*, and He is pleased with the Tribute I wrote because it honors my dad.

The only thing better would have been to give it to him in person. Here it is:

"A Tribute to 'Hook' Rainey"

"**D**ad's home," I used to yell as the back door slammed shut.

Our small, two-story frame house would shudder whenever the back door slammed shut. The sound of the slamming door was especially loud when one man came through its threshold—my dad. I can recall, as a little boy, playing in my room and hearing that door send a series of quakes that rippled through the walls and rattled the windows. It was my dad's signature and his signal that a day of work was completed and a man was now home.

I would yell, "Dad's home!" and then dash through the hall and kitchen to greet him with a well-deserved hug. I would then follow him like a little puppy to the washroom where he washed his grimy, calloused hands like a "real man." Everything about him signaled he was a "real man"— from the gritty Lava soap to the Vitalis hair tonic and Old Spice after-shave.

My dad was a unique blend of no-nonsense and discipline with a subtle sense of humor. He was a quiet and private man. He was a man of few words who didn't seem to need many words to get the job done. His countenance commanded respect. In fact, several boys had a personality and discipline transformation when they graduated from the third-grade Sunday school class to my dad's fourth-grade class. Miraculously, discipline problems dried up along with dozens of paper spitwads. In the twelve months that followed, paper airplanes were grounded and eight boys sat up straight in their chairs dutifully listening to the lesson.

"Hook" Rainey, they used to call him. The tall lefty got his nickname from his curve ball—a pitch so crooked it mystified batters. I got the feeling he was on his way to becoming a legend in his day—he even pitched a game against Dizzy Dean. Funny thing, he never could remember the score of that memorable game! (I used to accuse him of convenient amnesia!)

I recall the easy chair that used to carry the shape of his exhausted form. It was as he read the evening paper that I usually planned my assault on him. I'm certain I nearly pestered him to death on more than one occasion while asking my weary dad to play catch. And play catch he did. Night after night, "Hook" taught me how to throw a curve, slider, and knuckleball. He used to claim you could count the stitches on his knuckle-ball—and when he threw that patented knuckler the entire front yard was filled with laughter—his and mine. I always loved to hear him laugh. Somehow it told me everything was secure.

When I was three or so, he went hunting in Colorado and "bagged" a fierce teddy bear. He staged the "action" on film and brought the fierce beast back to me. My kids now play with that worn-out, thirty-five-year-old, black-and-white bear.

I watched him look after the needs of his mother

—he used to visit his mom three or four times a week. He modeled what it meant to "honor one's parents." From him I learned about integrity, trust, and how to be a man of my word. His example taught me the importance of perseverance, for he stuck with his job for nearly forty-five years. He leaves me an indelible imprint of sinking roots down deep—and living among the same people with whom he did business.

When I was in high school, I won a magazine sales contest because I introduced myself as Hook Rainey's son. That was good enough for an instant sale for nearly 100 percent of my "customers." My dad had helped so many people that being his son gave me immeasurable credibility. (For a while I actually thought I was a great salesman!)

His reputation was untarnished in the community. His funeral was attended by nearly a third of the small, southwest Missouri community. He lived and did his work all within five miles of where he was born. One man was able to say about my father, "In all my years I never heard a negative word about Hook Rainey."

He gave me imperishable memories instead of just things: memories of Little League baseball (he was coach); fishing trips where he netted my fish, so small they went through the holes in the net; and a clipped collection of all the baseball and basketball scores from my games, not one of which he ever missed. There are memories of watching him through the frosted window of our old pickup truck delivering hams at Christmas. Memories of the feel of his whiskers when he wrestled with me on the floor of the living room, and memories of him whispering to me—an extroverted, impetuous boy—not to bother people while they work. And finally, memories of snuggling close to him as we watched the game of the week with Dizzy Dean as the announcer.

As an impressionable young boy, my radar caught more of his life than he ever knew. He was the model and hero I needed during some perilous teenage years—and you know what? He still is. He taught me the importance of hard work and completing a task. I learned about lasting commitment from him—I never feared my parents would divorce. My dad was absolutely committed to my mom. I felt secure and protected.

But most importantly he taught me about character. He did what was right, even when no one was looking. I never heard him talk about cheating on taxes—he paid them and didn't grumble. His integrity was impeccable. I never heard him lie, and his eyes always demanded the same truth in return. The mental snapshot I have of his character still fuels and energizes my life today.

"Dad's home!" I can still hear the door slam and the house quake. This morning as I write this, Dad truly is "home"—in heaven. I look forward to seeing him again someday and saying thanks for the legacy he gave me. And mostly for being "my dad."

But right now, you'll have to pardon me—I miss him.

15

When the Damage Goes Deep

*My father was frightened of his father, I was frightened of my
father, and I am damned well going to see to it that my
children are frightened of me.*
—King George V

If you have had abusive parents, or if a parent abandoned you, nothing I could say would adequately capture what you've felt as you've made your way this far in the book. The idea of honoring your parents and making the relationship a "two-lane highway" seems nearly impossible. Maybe your heartache is so intense you feel I've been insensitive to your situation.

I want to assure you that my encouraging you to honor your parents comes after numerous encounters I've had with victims of abuse. I've counseled, cried, and agonized with both youngsters and adults who feel a pain I can hardly imagine.

I remember a teenage girl who slept with her legs crossed because her dad assaulted her almost every night for six years. I've heard the stories of a dad who used to whack his sons on the face and hands with a two-by-four he kept by his dinner table. I've been to sexual abuse seminars. I've interacted pro-

fessionally with numerous counselors. The damage goes deep
—much deeper than I could ever fathom.

I realize not everyone comes from a home like the one I
grew up in. Some parents are evil. Wickedness personified.

I realize too that not everyone who reads these pages is
ready to face his or her abuser, let alone entertain thoughts of
somehow honoring such a parent. And I realize some parents
might mock any effort to honor them. I cannot promise you a
happy ending. This is not a chapter about an instant, superficial cure for a deep wound caused by an abusive parent. Writing a Tribute will not magically solve your problems with your
parents.

Yet for the adult child who was abandoned or abused by
his or her parents, the process of honoring parents—even in
small ways—*may* be a critical step of healing and perhaps reconciliation.

Gently, I want to encourage you to progress—by God's
grace—in the pursuit of healing through the honest admission
of abuse, thoughtful forgiveness, and honor of your parent.
The important thing is not that you have arrived, but that you
are on the road to healing. Oliver Wendell Holmes said: "I find
the great thing in this world is not where we stand, but in what
direction we are moving."

Moving Toward Honor

Why is moving toward honoring a parent an important
process for a child who is abused or abandoned? I can think of
several reasons:

1. *We need to be obedient to God regardless of our pain.*

Humanly speaking, it doesn't seem fair or even logical
that God would command victims of emotional, physical, or
sexual abuse to honor the parents who abused them. This is
hard to understand and often painful to accept, but because
the Bible is God's truth and shows us how to live, we are wise
to obey Him and follow His direction.

Many abuse victims are led to believe—often by the very

people who harm them—that they deserve the abuse and are somehow at fault. Nothing could be farther from the truth. But the victim *is* responsible for something else: how he or she lives the rest of life. Bitterness and rage are certainly understandable in an abuse victim, but ultimately that victim must make a decision whether to allow God to bring comfort and healing.

Fortunately, the God of truth is also the God of grace (John 1:14-17). He is the giver of mercy and grace and is patient with us as we go through life's processes.

In fact, God has built a track record of taking things that were meant for evil and turning them into something good. Joseph's brothers, for example, sold him as a slave. But Joseph believed God wanted to use his circumstances for His purposes. Joseph saw God's fingerprints all over his life. Later, after God used him to save His people by bringing them to Egypt, Joseph told his brothers, "You meant evil against me, but God meant it for good in order to bring about this present result, to preserve many people alive" (Gen. 50:20).

In the same way, God can use your limitations and your circumstances in an evil world to bring His good to your life. God would never want anyone to be abused by evil. He doesn't cause evil, but He does allow it. And somehow He mysteriously weaves His purposes into our lives through people—like us—who are fallen, depraved creatures.

2. We may experience healing by going through the process of honoring our parents.

As we've seen, the process of honoring our parents can help move us from rage and anger, denial and ambivalence to an honest assessment of what was their fault and our responsibility. And ultimately it moves us to a trust in a sovereign God.

If we are faithful to deal honestly and honorably with the parent who has abused us, God will reward us "that it may be well with [us]" (Eph. 6:3). The command of God to honor our parents may be exactly what it takes to move us out of denial and toward forgiveness—and toward pursuing a parent who has damaged our lives. Masquerading behind a facade of Christian slogans and catchphrases, an abuse victim can "spiritualize" his or her problem and deny its very existence.

Tom Barrett has counseled for more than a decade in the Washington, D.C., area. Tom, who specializes in family therapy and has counseled numerous abuse victims, makes this point: "Parents have no idea how powerful they are in a child's life, for good or for evil. Yet, I have seen that God has put it in the heart of a child never to want to give up on having a relationship with his parents. He wants to give his parents every benefit of the doubt he can. He has an innate desire that never goes away to love his parents and have a healthy relationship with them."

Pursuing the Mother Who Left Her

Between the ages of eleven and twenty-five, Christy saw her mother only twice—for a total of fifteen minutes. Her mom couldn't handle the resulting guilt of having walked out of her marriage, leaving her husband alone to care for Christy and her two brothers. So she dropped out of their lives.

Her mom missed report cards, scraped knees, cheerleading, graduation, a college scholarship, a life-threatening auto accident, marriage, and the birth of a baby. Her only response to cards, letters, and phone calls was a heart-piercing silence.

Yet Christy had a compelling desire to honor her mom by establishing a relationship with her. The command of Exodus 20:12 moved Christy over a two-year period to summon up all the courage and faith she could muster. Finally, she decided to spend a few days with her and honor her in some small way.

Christy's brothers quietly questioned the idea. They thought Christy was a "glutton for punishment." They didn't understand, because their mother had physically and emotionally abandoned them. They thought she didn't deserve this kind of attention.

But Christy called her mother anyway. And her mom consented to see her.

Christy's feet felt leaden as she walked to the door of her

mom's house. No walk from a car to a house ever seemed longer. Her mind was awash with questions, worries, and the risk of further rejection that this face-to-face meeting represented.

"I knew I could get blown out of the water," Christy recalls. "Emotionally I was a wide-open target. I wanted a lot from Mom, but I had purposed to lower my sights. My expectations were zero. I did not want to dredge up the past. I had forgiven her for all that. I wanted the opportunity to let her know I loved her, and that I regretted not knowing her."

The next few hours with this stranger called "Mom" challenged Christy to the core. Several times she nearly decided to leave because she was bored stiff and had nothing in common with this woman. Her mom said some things Christy disagreed with. But finally Christy decided she was there to establish a relationship. "I went in there to begin to win the war with my mom, so I had to give up trying to win some little battles along the way."

Finally, as she prepared to leave, Christy's eyes met her mother's. She choked back the overwhelming emotion of the moment and said, "Mom, I want you to know that even though I don't agree with what you did, I still love you. You're still my mother, and no matter what has happened I think it would be good for us to get to know each other better. Would you like that?"

Her mom began to cry and said, "I thought you hated me all these years after what I did to you. I've missed you so much."

A lot of healing took place at that point, Christy says. "I felt like a ten-year-old girl with her mom. I just wanted to know if she loved me. And she did."

Now a decade later, Christy has seen the relationship blossom with her mom. She admits that she has had to initiate 90 percent of the calls. Each call is a white-knuckle time of anxiety and knots in the stomach because of the fear of rejection. Yet, each call is emotionally satisfying.

Her mom is learning to love. And she's showing a growing interest in Christy's faith in a God whom she's always disliked.

"It feels good to have swept that area of my life out. I'm clean," Christy says. "I feel whole. I've dealt with a tragedy in my life. I'm no longer controlled by my anger toward my mom."

Christy says she ranks four events in her life as the most "life-changing": coming to know Christ, marrying her husband, and honoring each of her parents. "Honoring my parents has freed me to love, to forgive, to be forgiven, to love my husband, and to be a mom to my kids."

Christy's story demonstrates how a child's heart can move toward healing when she honors her parents. But it also illustrates the next reason why it's important for abuse victims to honor parents.

3. We need to do everything we can to reconcile a parent to God.

Perhaps the idea of honoring your parents is almost laughable. You may have a parent who seems to have no redeeming value. Or you realize that in order to have a relationship with a parent, you need to painfully confront him or her about past abuse.

Many books written by counselors detail the steps an abuse victim needs to take in order to confront the abuser. But few, even in the evangelical culture, seem to acknowledge the responsibility to "honor" such parents.

I have no problem with the concept of confronting parents when such confrontation is necessary. But it should be done with the right attitude. I believe honoring parents demands that as you confront them you do it with the desire to help them know Christ as Savior. Rather than demand revenge, a child has to offer love and support. As Dan Allender writes in his book, *The Wounded Heart*, "The objective must be to bless the other person rather than to make sure we are not abused again."[1]

In the same book, Allender tells the story of a young man who confronted his father about past sexual abuse. The father denied it, and eventually the son chose to break off the relationship. You might think this is the opposite of honoring, but it isn't. The son also had made it clear he was willing to begin again if the father would repent. He had forgiven his father—but he wouldn't allow his dad to continue sinning by denying the abuse.

This is what Allender calls "bold love"—making the effort to restore a person to full life. "He honored his father," Allender writes, "by giving him the opportunity to repent and taste the restoration of relationship with the righteous Father. The door to relationship was closed, but not locked."[2]

Suggestions for Honoring an Abusive Parent

There are no simple solutions for such a deep and diverse topic as honoring abusive parents. Writing a Tribute, for example, will demand prayerful consideration. It may take years before you can write it. But if it does take you several years to write one, that's okay. You need to realize God isn't forcing you to do this; it is something you must *want* to do.

If you are at that point, you'll need to commit to wrestling honestly with your past—the good and the bad, the joyful and the painful. Denial of reality is a very real enemy. You must wrestle with the feelings of mistrust, betrayal, and anger.

Following are some suggestions to consider as you begin. I encourage you to talk to your pastor or a mature Christian counselor who can guide you through the process of healing and help protect you from further abuse.

First, *acknowledge any emotional shock, fear, and anger you may have at the thought of having to honor your parents.* You may be adamantly against this outrageous thought, thinking, "He's crazy if he thinks I'm going to risk more rejection to try to honor them!" Or, you may think, "I've already been damaged enough. The safest way to live out my life is to keep my distance from my parents and to protect my heart."

These are real feelings. Fair feelings. But God calls us to live by faith, not by feelings. He also calls us out of our self-protection and preservation and into self-denial and self-sacrifice in relationships.

Real meaning in life is found in a real relationship with God and with people. It does not mean living with a layer of insulation around your heart to protect you from further abuse. True relationships demand risk and authenticity. I'm not speaking of going back and placing your life under your parents' control. I'm talking about developing an attitude so that you're able to approach them with an open heart, receptive to both love and pain.

The second step is to *take an honest inventory of the extent of your abuse.* It's interesting how often most of us want to avoid reality. Some abuse victims pretend their families are perfect and are unwilling to admit or confront past abuse. Others focus solely on the negative and refuse to acknowledge that their parents may have done even a few things well.

Dan Allender summarizes eight truths that a sexual abuse victim must admit. Most apply to those who have suffered other forms of abuse as well:

1. I have been abused.
2. I am a victim of a crime against my body and soul.
3. As a victim, I am not in any way responsible for the crime, no matter what I might have experienced or gained as a result of the abuse. [Note: While this point is true for sexual abuse victims, I believe it may not be completely true for some other forms of abuse. For example, if a teenager provokes a parent to anger, and that parent beats the child, both individuals have made mistakes. The parent should be held accountable for the physical abuse, but the child should not have goaded the parent. I'm not saying the beating was the child's fault—just that he needs to acknowledge his own responsibility in how he treats his parents.]
4. Abuse has damaged my soul.
5. The damage is due to the interweaving dynamics of powerlessness, betrayal, and ambivalence.
6. My damage is different from others' in extent, intensity, and consequences, but it is worthy to be addressed and worked through no matter what occurred.
7. It will take time to deal with the internal wounds; the process must not be hurried.

8. I must not keep a veil of secrecy and shame over my past, but I am not required to share my past with anyone I feel is untrustworthy or insensitive.[3]

The third step is to *choose, as an act of your will, to forgive your parents for all the damage they've done to you.*

Brian's dad had done an average job of providing but a poor job of loving. And after Brian became a Christian, he began to realize he needed to give up the anger he felt toward his father. Over a period of months Brian moved from the murky waters of bitterness and anger to a clear, honest assessment of what his dad had done right and wrong. Finally, Brian was able to forgive his dad and let go of all the negative feelings he had for him.

Brian embarked on an adventure to honor his father—and their relationship began to germinate. Some years later, his dad died. Brian stood by his father's casket, put his hand on his dad's hand, and prayed with a genuine heart, "Thank you, God, for who Dad was and for who he wasn't."

The fourth step is to *thank God by faith for who your parents were in your life.* First Thessalonians 5:18 commands us to give thanks in all things. By doing this in faith, we acknowledge that God never stopped loving us, that He is intimately aware of who we had as parents, and that He knows what He is doing.

This is not an easy concept for many to grasp. In a recent interview on our daily radio program "FamilyLife Today," Josh McDowell spoke frankly to our listening audience about how he had to come to the point of thanking God for his dad. "Dad was well known as the town drunk," Josh said. "As a teenager I was ashamed of him. I hardly knew him sober until I was almost twenty years old."

Late one night when Josh was in his early thirties, more than a dozen years after he had become a Christian, he forgave his mom and his dad—even though his parents were no longer living. Josh said, "It was the first time I thanked God for my parents. I had grown up envying other people's parents. It was as if God said, 'Josh, who do you think I have used most in your life, whether good or bad, to make you who you are?' I had to admit it was my mother and father.

"God says in Romans 8:28 He will cause all things to work together for good to those who love Him and are called according to His name," Josh concluded. "I believe I have become a better dad and husband because of my mom and dad. He will cause—and has caused—all things to work together for good."[4]

The fifth step is, *when you are ready, go to your parents to honor them.* For some this will be the ultimate test. I still wonder how the command to honor parents is worked out in many difficult, dark situations. When I hear some people talk about what they experienced in the past, I wonder if I would be able to forgive "seventy times seven," as Jesus commanded us.

But if you do attempt to honor your parents with a written document such as a Tribute, keep your expectations in check. Go with an obedient heart, but beware of expecting a positive response. If your parents respond positively to your Tribute, then healing can begin. But if they don't, ask God to enable you to fulfill the command of Romans 12:18: "If possible, so far as it depends on you, be at peace with all men."

Keep on laying aside the desire to be the avenger of your wounds. Let God handle it. In the same chapter of Romans 12 Paul warns and promises, "Never take your own revenge, beloved, but leave room for the wrath of God, for it is written, 'Vengeance is Mine, I will repay,' says the Lord" (v. 19).

God is bigger than your parents. You may never see how He handles it, but He will settle all accounts. It's His promise.

An Optional Step

At this point I'd like to recommend an optional step in the process which some abuse victims may find achievable.

Maybe you just can't bring yourself to write a Tribute and give it to your parents. I'd like to suggest that you go through the process of writing a Tribute that will be only for you to read. Use the process of writing the Tribute as a way of expressing yourself and your faith to God. You may even want to write a Tribute to God, giving thanks for the parents He gave you. Perhaps the expression of forgiveness, love, and honor that come through this private Tribute will promote healing in your soul . . . and bring you one step closer to actually presenting the Tribute to your parents.

A Few Cautions

For victims of abuse, the process of honoring parents won't be simple. It will involve prayer, immersion in the promises of Scripture, counsel, and sacrificial obedience—all occurring over a long period of time.

Relationships are risky. Period. The process of knowing and being known by another person demands the costly currency of a transparent human heart.

Indeed, the rewards can be great. But for the abuse victim, cautions worth noting are:

1. *Do not make writing a Tribute the ultimate test for your relationship with your parents.* Be careful not to view it as a make-it-or-break-it venture. When you're ready, let it be simply what it is—one step toward honoring your parents and restoring your relationship.

Most important is what happens in your heart. Some people will write Tributes to their parents and never work through the feelings they have toward them. Prayerfully take your time in moving through the process, rather than rushing ahead only to be disappointed by your parents' response or lack of it.

2. *Be patient as you work to reclaim positive memories.* Perhaps as you've read this book you've traversed the landscape of your mind in search of good memories with your parents only to find a parched, barren wilderness. You may have looked far and wide to come up with enough pleasant memories to fill a Tribute—but as hard as you try, you can't come up with any.

Good memories are like roses—fragrant and alive, vivid and lingering in our minds. You may go in search of a field of roses, only to find you couldn't gather enough to fill a vase. If this is so, then admit your disappointment and anger.

You may have to acknowledge the possibility that your

parents may have planted some roses but you just can't remember them. Those roses may be surrounded by a thicket of thorn bushes that have to be uprooted to reveal the flowers.

3. *Realize that your parents may refuse to be reconnected.* For some adult children, the process of doing a Tribute results in a joyous connection with parents for the first time ever. But some parents don't want to take responsibility for their failures. At this point in their lives they may not be able to assume that responsibility. And at your gesture, they may become (or remain) mean, evil, hardened people—resisting your love.

4. *Realize God commands us to honor our parents, not the abuse.* We honor the person who has been given the position, not the evil, degrading acts. Not their wrong choices. Not their damaging, wounding acts against us.

5. *Avoid comparison to others.* For some people, one baby step can demand as much faith and courage as another person who is walking a mile to honor his parents. A phone call to your parents may represent a small but high-risk venture. And a Tribute may be out of the question right now. Simply be obedient to take the steps God sets before you.

6. *Use extreme caution as you seek to build a relationship with abusive parents.* If your case is severe—such as habitual sexual abuse or extreme emotional trauma—it may be wise for you to avoid personal contact. You also may need to protect your children. And, in cases like these, it's important to seek counsel.

To Whom Will You Turn?

The tragedy of so many abuse victims is that they seek to cope in their own way and end up causing more damage to themselves. Recently I read a story told by professional speaker Bobbie Gee of her encounter with a young woman in 1981. After a speech, Bobbie was resting in a lounge, and a twenty-four-year-old woman with extremely short hair walked in. Bobbie complimented the woman on how her hair looked and was surprised at the reply: "Are you kidding?"

The woman proceeded to tell Bobbie that her hair was

just growing back after being shaved for the removal of a brain tumor. She also was recovering from an extreme case of anorexia, which her doctors felt had helped cause the tumor.

And what circumstances led to the anorexia? "When I was eighteen years old, I came home from my high school graduation to find my bags packed and waiting on the front porch with a note from my dad that said I was now responsible for taking care of myself. It seems that all my dad lived for was getting us kids out of the house at eighteen."

Determined to somehow reach her unfeeling father, she got herself arrested for shoplifting. That didn't work, so she stopped eating.

It wasn't until she lay in the hospital, near death from the anorexia, that her father finally came to see her. When he got up to leave, she began screaming, "You just can't say it, can you? I'm going to die and you still can't say it!"

"Say what?" he asked.

" 'I love you.' You never have, and I guess you never will."

These words finally shook the father. "My father returned to my hospital bed and began to cry like a baby when he realized that I had almost died and was willing to risk my life just to hear him tell me he loved me. At that very moment I began to recover from my anorexia—but I had already begun to form a brain tumor."

The woman's final comment was, "It's amazing the length some kids will go to try and get their parents to say, 'I love you.' "[5]

I can't help but think there is a better way to cope with such tragedy. And God offers it—through a relationship with Him. He is the One who can heal a "wounded heart"—and even cause it to reach out to the one who wounded it.

"Instead of just blaming you for the past, it is now time for me to give you honor."

A Tribute from Stan Harrison to his father, Ed Harrison of Tacoma, Wash.

To appreciate the Tribute that Stan Harrison wrote for his father, Ed, you need to know a little of that family's history. As Stan says, "I grew up hating my father."

Ed Harrison was an alcoholic and physically abused his wife. "We always walked on eggshells, waiting to see how Dad would respond to us when he walked in."

In alcoholic homes, the children often adopt certain roles. Stan became the "hero," the one who felt the responsibility to care for his mother and little brother. His experiences and personality probably contributed to the profession he pursued—a high school substance abuse counselor.

After Stan married and had children, he felt a greater desire to improve his relationship with his dad. "I felt that part of my relationship needed to be to help my dad with his alcoholism rather than blaming him," he explains. "I think part of the reason I wanted to develop a relationship with dad was having my own son. All of a sudden I realized I wasn't a perfect father, either."

He still recalls the day his five-year-old son, Danny, asked him, "Dad, are there any alcoholics in our family?" Surprised at the question, Stan asked Danny, "What do you think an alcoholic is?"

"Someone who is sick and can't stop drinking," Danny replied. "Is anyone in our family an alcoholic?"

"What do you think?"

"I think Grandpa is, because he always smells like alcohol."

"Wait—we've told Grandpa that he can't drink around you," Stan said.

"Yes, but sometimes he goes off by himself for a walk, and when he comes back, he smells."

Then Danny asked the question that pinned Stan to the

ground: "*Dad, you help all these kids go to treatment so they can know the Lord and get back on track. Why don't you help Grandpa?*"

"*That's the day,*" Stan says, "*when I decided I really needed to help my own father, and get to know him.*"

A few months later, Stan was able, through an informal intervention, to convince Ed he needed to seek treatment. It's now been over four years since Ed took a drink.

After Stan attended a FamilyLife Marriage Conference and heard about honoring parents, he decided he needed to thank his parents for the good he had seen in the family. "*My mom was dying with cancer at the time. When we had gone through family therapy during the treatment for dad's alcoholism, a lot of negative things about the family came out, and I wanted to let her know there were a lot of positive things in our childhood, too. I never had a chance to actually write one to her, but one time when I was with her in the hospital I was able to verbally tell her a lot of the things I would have written had she lived longer. She was hardly even able to open her eyes at the time, but she cried as I talked with her.*"

His father was more difficult. Stan had a good relationship with Ed by this time, but he kept putting off writing a Tribute to him—until, as he says, "*God kept convicting me that I needed to do it.*"

On Christmas Day, after all the gifts had been opened, Stan had his son give one last package to Ed. "*Dad opened it up and said, 'What's this?' I told him that I had written something to him that I'd like to read to him.*"

In front of his brothers and their families, Stan read through the Tribute. It was one of the few times he saw his father cry. When he was finished, Ed gave him a hug and said, "*That's the most wonderful gift I've ever received in my whole life.*"

A few days later, Stan visited his father and was surprised to find the Tribute hanging on the wall in his home. "*That's what impressed me the most. For a sixty-year-old man to put a picture on a wall so quickly showed that it was very valuable to him.*"

This Tribute is different from many others in that Stan begins by briefly acknowledging the problems the family had experienced. "I wanted to write only positive stuff, but I just couldn't. I talked to Dad about that, and he understands. 'Stan, if you had started with the positive, it would not have been real.' I didn't dwell on the negative, and I think I was able to say what I did because we aren't there anymore—we have a good relationship now."

Stan now works at FamilyLife, helping promote the FamilyLife Marriage Conference. As part of his responsibilities, he shows conferees the same message on honoring parents that helped him. "A lot of the people come to the conferences and think, 'I should do this, but I can't. They don't understand my situation.' But Stan understands the situations many adult children face because he's experienced them himself. "I believe that 95 percent of the people in the United States need to write a Tribute," he says. "There may be some people who need to get some good counseling first, but after that they still need to do it."

"Mr. Ed" . . . My Dad

I remember, as a child, watching you at work as you would skillfully fit shoes on the feet of children of all ages, sizes, and colors. They all adored you, like Santa Claus, as you made them feel loved and important when you played with them and "squeaked" their noses or toes and gave them a gentle hug. You were a master salesman. I loved to hear them affectionately call you "Mr. Ed" at the store. But as I grew older, I began to resent you and emotionally started to pull away from you, mostly out of selfishness, immaturity, confusion, anger, and fear.

We have had many opportunities in the past few years to discuss these feelings that were created by your alcoholism, abuse, and emotional neglect, but very few words were ever spoken about my *positive* childhood memories. Instead of just blaming you for the past, it is now time for me to *thank you* and give you *honor*, because it was *all* of my past, both the positive and negative moments, that molded together to make me the person I am today.

I fondly remember numerous predawn fishing trips to Silver Lake. I loved climbing into the rowboat and using the black fishing pole with the red stripes as you would row us around the lake all morning. I loved seeing the mist rise from the water's glass-like surface, the majestic view of the mountains at daybreak, and drinking hot cocoa back at the dock's cafe that had a red fox as a pet. We always caught our limits, with the help of "triple teasers" and "dick nights."

I now appreciate the sacrifices you made, both financially and in the lack of sleep, to always ensure a magical Christmas morning. We never went without— "Santa" was always very generous! The thought of you making red and green pancakes still makes me laugh inside.

I get dizzy just thinking about the space-capsule ride you brought home from Trovani's. It looked like a huge orange donut. Steve and I would get inside that thing and spin around all day. It's a miracle we survived!

You were (and still are) my favorite "Golf Pro." I remember caddying for you and Ralph Trovani many Saturday mornings. I was more proud of you after each tournament you won; each trophy seemed so tall to "little" me.

I remember the time you came to Lakewood General Hospital after I had an accident and almost ripped off my left arm. I felt safe having you and Mom by my side. I needed you, and you were there!

I can vividly recall the pride in your eyes when I shot my first buck. That was indeed a very special day for both of us. Thanks for sacrificing your Remington 6.5. It is one of my most prized possessions, and it contains many special memories of being up in the hills with you.

You gave me a special appreciation for the outdoors

—more than just hunting and fishing, but the ability to enjoy a beautiful view, the sound of a river, the breeze blowing through the trees, or the colors of autumn. Whether we were at the Hamma Hamma River, Silver Lake, National, Bay Lake, or "The Rocks" on Lightning Ridge, you helped me take the time and really see the great gift God created for our enjoyment.

You taught me through example to honor and respect my elders, to establish a strong work ethic, and to complete a task with excellence. You are a man of your word. Many of these qualities are best exemplified by your ongoing recovery since your stay at Sundown M Ranch.

I want to thank you for never divorcing Mom. The thirty-nine years that you stayed together were tough on both of you. This set an example that is priceless in our world of "easy outs." Thanks for staying committed to her until the end of her life. I know that you both really did love each other, even though it seemed impossible at times.

I am proud of how you have grown spiritually and emotionally in the past few years. You are now developing a positive legacy for your four sons and ten grandchildren. I have recently enjoyed developing a healthy one-on-one relationship with you that I pray will continue to develop even more with time.

You are a fantastic "Grampie," and I rejoice to see my kids love and adore you. You make them feel loved and important just as you did other people's children when you were "Mr. Ed" years ago.

I love you, Dad!

Stan

16

Helping Others Honor Their Parents

Nobody's family can hang out the sign, "Nothing the matter here."
—Chinese proverb

Afew years ago I was teaching my Sunday school class of approximately sixty-five sixth-graders about the importance of loving someone who seems unlovable. For many of those preteens, their unlovable someone may have been a pesky little brother or sister or a cruel classmate at school.

Nina Cameron, one of the parents assisting me, told the class a story that hit us all like an emotional freight train. I'd like to share the story here in Nina's own words. It demonstrates how one person can help another give honor to a needy parent.

Nina embodies how Christ's love can penetrate the surface of even the most crusty individual. Some parents may not seem worthy of any honor, but when you peel away the facade you may find a tender heart—and, in this case, a parent waiting to be loved.

My daughter, Natalie, and I visited a nursing home for several years, and there was one particular lady there who was so offensive and grumpy that no one wanted anything to do with her. But somehow the Lord gave me a genuine burden and love for Mary. I began to try to reach out and be her friend.

Unfortunately, the harder I tried, the more distant Mary became. When we came to visit her, she would make some crude remark and turn her back to us.

Determined not to be discouraged, we continued trying to find a spark of interest that would reveal a way to show love for her. One day I asked Mary, "Isn't there anything you like?"

She looked at me out of the corner of her eyes and mumbled, "I like butterscotch candy . . . and I like to draw." I asked what she liked to draw and she replied, "See for yourself—there's a box under my bed."

We pulled out the dirty box and inside were sheets of notebook paper with some of the most beautiful sketches of flowers and women's clothing designs I had ever seen. Looking through them, I caught a glimpse of the woman she once had been—a talented artist who could take a simple sunflower or bluebird and turn it into a masterpiece. I was intrigued and curious to know what could happen to cause someone with this much warmth and sensitivity to become the surly old woman that the outside world now saw.

When I praised her ability to draw, Mary looked at Natalie, who was about five, and said, "Well, if you could get her to sit still, I'd draw her picture." Natalie agreed and jumped up on her bed. As I watched Mary draw, I could see a talented artist at work, taking note of every detail of my daughter's features. A part of her seemed to come alive, and for a moment she forgot where she was.

During our subsequent visits, we tried to coax her to draw again, but usually she wanted nothing to do with us. She still didn't like anything about us, right down to my name, Nina. She decided to call me "Luke" instead.

Every time we visited, she would ask, "Luke, did you bring me some butterscotch candy?" Then she would begin complaining about the nurses, the food, her roommates, and anything else she could think of.

Her eyes were getting so bad that she could not read very well. So one day I asked if she would like me to bring a Bible and read to her. "Luke, I don't like that religious stuff," she replied. "And I don't want to hear anything about it again."

It seemed that she rejected every word and every attempt of kindness we offered her. But somehow I could tell she was warming up to us, even though she would never admit it.

Several months of these visits went by and then she developed cancer. She was in the hospital for quite a while, and when she returned to the nursing home I realized she would not live much longer. I asked her to tell me about her family, and she told me she had a son in New York whom she had not seen in six years.

As I left the nursing home that day I felt a heaviness of heart that is hard to explain. It was as if Jesus Himself were in the car with me. When I arrived home, I dialed information for New York and got the son's phone number. I called him, introduced myself, and told him I had been visiting his mother in the nursing home.

There was dead silence—I could almost feel the coldness. I silently asked God to penetrate through his pain, and at that moment he began to weep. "Lady, I don't know who you are, but I love my mother," he said.

I asked if he would consider coming out to see her before she died. He said he wanted to, but he didn't have the money. When I hung up the phone, I could tell by the way my heart was aching that it could not end this way. My husband and I decided to pay for the son's plane ticket, plus a hotel room when he arrived in Little Rock.

I called the son back and told him what we were going to do. "Why are you doing this, lady?" he asked.

"Because I'm a Christian, and in the Bible Jesus told us that when we have helped the least of these, 'you did it to Me.' "

A few days later I picked up the son at the airport and drove him to the nursing home. I was not sure what the reunion would be like after all these years and all the pain that had kept them apart. But when he walked into Mary's room, she called his name and they fell into each other's arms, weeping. I quietly left the room, but I was not alone. The look on Mary's face and the joy in her eyes went with me.

While the son was in Little Rock, I was able to tell him about Christ and my life with Him. I also brought him to church on Sunday. He said he could not remember how long it had been since he had been in a church.

As it happened, our pastor spoke about the blood of Christ in the sermon that morning. Afterward the son said he wanted to tell his mother what he had heard.

He spent the next several days sitting by her bedside, talking to her and rubbing lotion onto her dry, wrinkled skin. He bought her a scarf that she wore on her bald head. He drew the way she had taught him to draw many years before, when he was a little boy.

When I took the son to the airport at the end of his visit, he told me, "There are not words in the English language to express how I feel." And when I returned to the nursing home, for the first time I saw a glow of peace on Mary's face. She looked at me, took my hand, and said, "Luke, I love you."

I knew it was the first time in many, many years she had felt love, or at least had let down her guard enough to say it. The next thing she said was, "I want you to bring that Bible and read it to me when you come back."

She died before I had a chance to visit again, but she died with peace in her heart and with her unfinished business resolved. She died knowing that God loved her.

As you've seen by the stories I have told in this book, some special blessings are reserved for those who obey God's commandment to honor their parents. Nina's experience reveals another type of blessing—the joy of helping others to honor their parents.

Encouraging Others to Do What's Right

It may be your spouse, a friend, family members, or perhaps even brothers or sisters who need to honor their parents just as much as you do. I remember Robert Lewis's words in chapter 2 of this book: "God's Word holds unique, special, and powerful experiences for those who will radically grab hold of it and see it through to the end." All that others may need is your prompting and encouragement to help them become doers of the Word rather than merely hearers.

Hebrews 10:24 encourages us to "consider how to stimulate one another to love and good deeds." In some cases, this may mean simply involving your brothers and sisters in your Tribute.

This works especially well for major celebrations, such as a wedding anniversary. Let your siblings or others know in a phone call or a letter that you've had a growing conviction of your responsibility to honor your parents. If appropriate, let them know there may be shortcomings in your parents for which you could reject them, but you nevertheless feel compelled to honor them for the things they did right. Tell them about the process you have gone through in coming to this point, and ask them to write a Tribute, too.

Judy White of Dayton, Ohio, wrote to describe how she involved her siblings in honoring her mother a few years ago:

> When our mother, Ruth Black, [yes, Judy White was Judy Black before she married!] was approaching her seventieth birthday, she was really having a struggle thinking about turning seventy. A couple of weeks before her birthday, I distributed stationery to my three brothers, their wives, and children. Each one was asked to write a letter about "what you mean to me"—relating things she had done specifically for them; funny things we adult kids remembered from childhood; how she impacted our lives, etc. I also took pictures of everyone and put them with their letters in a nice album.
>
> We are a great family for springing surprises, so we also had a surprise party for her, inviting her special, close friends. When it was time for the gifts to be opened, we kept the album until last. The original plan was to have her open it and then take it home and enjoy the letters in private. But as I had read them while putting it together, there were some real funny things; so I asked permission from the various family members to read those parts aloud. They granted it, and everyone had a wonderful time listening to our expressions of love to our mother. She enjoyed it immensely—there were lots of tears (at one point we passed around the Kleenex box) and lots of laughs.
>
> She gracefully slid into her seventies and afterward she said it was the best birthday ever! (Mission accomplished!) She looks through the album now and again and is reminded each time how much her family loves her. (We did the same thing for our father's seventy-fifth birthday two years later.)

If you come from a difficult family, your siblings may resent you for even suggesting they honor your parents. If you face such a situation, clearly explain the reason for your wanting to honor your parents, but let your siblings know you have no desire to place any pressure on them. You may be able to encourage them gently to deal with their bitterness and anger. You also may need to help them understand how they have been hurt—and then show them how to move beyond that pain to compassion and forgiveness.

Help Your Mate—Don't Hinder

If you are married, the one person you probably have the most influence on is your mate. Through your words and actions you can encourage your mate in either direction—toward honoring his or her parents or toward dishonoring them. And I believe you can inspire your spouse to honor them.

Many adults begin to see their parents from a different perspective after they're married. And if they're not careful, a husband and wife can begin focusing exclusively on their parents' negative qualities and spend years bogged down in bad attitudes.

That's what happened to Pat and Terri. Terri's father was a successful lawyer, a powerful man who was accustomed to getting his way. He had provided for his family quite well financially, but during most of Terri's childhood he had been so preoccupied with building a career that he largely neglected his family. He was opinionated, blunt, and bossy. He did not abuse his children physically; but if they failed to meet his standards (and that happened often) he belittled them with cruel and sarcastic remarks.

Once in a while—usually when Terri's father took the family to the beach for vacation—he seemed to loosen up. On these occasions he lavished attention on his children: playing games, swimming, and building sand castles. Terri's mother once remarked that this was the fun-loving man she had married, and she wished she could see that side of him more often.

Terri also wished her father were different. But over the

years she grew accustomed to him and his ways. That began to change, however, when she married Pat. A young insurance salesman, he was a hard driver himself. So it was inevitable he would feel some tension with Terri's father.

Out of respect—and perhaps a little fear—Pat behaved politely during the first few times he spent with Terri's father. Even if the man said something he completely disagreed with, Pat held his tongue. Alone with Terri, however, he expressed his frustration.

"How can you take that man, Terri?" Pat said one night as they drove home after a family dinner. "He treats you like a little kid, he always has to be in control, and he thinks he's right about everything!"

"He's my dad," Terri replied. "I know he's got his faults, but that doesn't mean I shouldn't love him."

"Well, you're always going to stand up for your parents," Pat argued. "But think of the things he says to you . . . He always seems to find some way to let you know you don't measure up to his expectations. And I would especially hate to be your older brother, with the way your dad constantly goads him on."

By the time they reached home, Terri was depressed. Memories she had suppressed for many years—of birthday parties missed, of hugs she'd wanted from her dad but never received—came flooding back.

Over the next few years, this pattern continued. To avoid any conflict, Pat mainly kept to himself whenever they visited Terri's family. But he heard everything that went on and often led a debriefing session while driving home afterward. Meanwhile, Terri felt more resentment and anger toward her father. She wondered why God could not have put her in a different family, with a father who loved her.

Like many adult children, Pat and Terri found themselves feeling increasingly alienated from her parents. On one hand it was easier, because the less time they spent with them, the less tension, pressure, and anger they felt. But deep inside, they wished things were different. When a friend mentioned her father, Terri would say, "I wish I could find a way to break through to my father. But he's so cold."

What Pat did not realize was that *he* was the main problem. By dissecting each family visit during the drive home, he led Terri to focus on her father's negative attributes. He brought confusion and tension into his wife's life because he was encouraging her to alienate herself from a man whom, despite his faults, she loved deeply.

Pat needed to help his wife honor her dad.

Where's Your Focus?

Tensions with parents and in-laws are inevitable in any marriage. But a married couple needs to make a mutual commitment early in their relationship to avoid focusing on the negative. Give your (and your spouse's) parents a lot of grace. Talk about the things they do right.

In many relationships, misunderstandings seem to grow in relation to the distance between the two families and the length of time between visits. When a parent and child live near each other and see each other often, they are more willing to overlook disparaging remarks or actions. In other words, they give each other space and grace.

But if those same people only see each other once a year, they are more likely to take statements out of context. They examine each comment under a high-powered microscope, searching for hidden nuances or motivations. This is a deadly trap. And an adult child needs to avoid it by making a determined choice to honor his or her parents or in-laws even during private conversations.

I know some people who have been so hurt by their in-laws that they actually discouraged their mates from honoring their parents. If this is true of you, helping your mate honor his or her parents may be a crucial step of faith for you. It may require accepting the fact that you may never be considered part of the family. It may mean holding your tongue sometimes at family gatherings. And afterwards with your mate as well.

As difficult as this may sound, another thought should be even more sobering: Do you really want to prevent your spouse from obeying one of the Ten Commandments?

Principles for Helping Others Honor

If you are going to truly help another person seek to honor his or her parents, then these few guidelines may help:

First, *speak the truth.* Your friend or relative may not want to hear about the responsibility to honor parents. But deep inside that person has a desire to do what is right (even if he or she acts otherwise). Sometimes the truth is too painful to hear. Remind that person of God's promise—"that it may be well with you, and that you may live long on the earth."

Second, *be patient.* Each of us tends to look at another person's circumstances through our own personal grid of personality, maturity (or lack of it), and experience. So if you are going to err, do it on the side of giving your friend or family member time to work through the process.

Third, *be available to talk.* It has been said, "He who has a friend needs no mirror." Being a good listener may be one of the most important things you can do for another.

Fourth, *keep encouraging them to cultivate steps in the right direction.* Cheer baby steps. Applaud faithfulness. And caution against trying to recoup twenty lost years in one evening through a Tribute.

Finally, fifth, *encourage them to reduce expectations.* Children of all ages hope they can repair relationships instantly, but usually they take time.

 ## "A Tribute to a Father-in-Law"

One of the best examples I found of someone encouraging her mate to honor his parents was the Tribute written by Shelia Davis of North Augusta, S.C. She wrote it to her father-in-law, Coy Davis, of Little Rock, Ark.

While attending a writer's workshop, Shelia began think-

ing about the wonderful qualities of her husband, Ricardo.
Then she thought of how her father-in-law had helped build
those qualities into Ricardo. The result was the following
poem:

Ricardo is

kind   witty   charming
generous   loyal   faithful   patient
not envious or rude

                              not one who thinks
                                        evil
                              one who rejoices in
                                        truth

He bears
        believes
                hopes
                        endures

                                        all things
He's an epitome of love.
    But how?
                Who shaped him?
                        Of course—God did!
Yes . . . but via what channels?
Oh, Coy, thank you!
Thank you
    for being present in my husband's life,
    for generously providing for your family,
    for being faithful to your wife,
    for patiently enduring Ricardo's adolescent and teen
    eras,
    for not envying,
    for not being rude,
    for diligently keeping the home in order—in your
    way.

Thank you for living a life before him which helped shape his personality—
He's wonderful!
God bless you, Coy!
You're very special!

17

Beyond the Tribute: Twenty Building Blocks that Bring Honor and Build Relationships

Conviction is worthless until it converts itself into conduct.
—Thomas Carlisle

For many people, writing a Tribute helps bring a fresh beginning to the relationship they have with their parents. Yet some have had a head start on the rest of us. They have found other, ingenious ways of honoring their parents. Kim Newlen of Richmond, Virginia, told me a story that has to be one of the most creative I've ever heard. Here is her account:

> Eighteen years ago a thrilling "first letter from home" was sitting in my campus mailbox awaiting my enthusiastic response. It was obvious that Mama had addressed it, but Daddy had scribbled BSSYP in the upper left-hand corner of the envelope. For the life of me, I couldn't figure out its meaning. Out of curiosity and probably homesickness, I immediately

called home. I remember part of our conversation as if it were yesterday:

"Daddy, what is BSSYP?"

"Sugar, it is what I've told you all your life. Be sweet and say your prayers."

All these years, Daddy has never missed leaving his mark on each letter or package that my mama has carefully and lovingly addressed. BSSYP has survived graduation from college, graduate school, marriage, and now, our first baby!

My unique Tribute to Mama and Daddy is a perpetual Virginia license tag with BSSYP on it.

Dennis, God only knows how many people have inquired about its meaning over the years. I've never tired of sharing my Tribute about my special parents, Bo and Maxine Bowman.

I've been teaching for eight years, and an old license plate has always adorned my classroom. The students have inquired about it without fail and for the last few years have been given a little extra credit when they seek out its meaning and tell me the next day. They love it.

The look on my parents' faces when I drove home for the first time donning my "Tribute Tags" was priceless.

This Tribute will be passed on to our new daughter as a Tribute from her special, special grandparents, my mama and daddy.

The Tribute Is Just One Building Block

Have you heard the story of the three bricklayers? An observer asked one of them, "What are you building?" One worker replied, "I'm laying bricks."

He asked the second workman, "What are you building?"

"I'm building a wall," the man answered.

The same question went to the third workman. His reply was, "I'm building a cathedral."

Each of these men played a key role in the construction of that building. But only one had a vision, a lofty goal, in mind.

Much like the first workman, you'll sometimes feel you're just laying bricks or building with blocks. But in reality you are engaging in a much larger construction project. You are building a relationship with your parents that will affect your entire family for decades to come, long after you and your parents are gone. Yet you need to remember that the Tribute is just one block—a very significant block, but still just one block. And you need to continue building with these blocks as long as your parents are alive.

You may spend months crafting a Tribute, but presenting it may take only fifteen minutes. And after all that effort, your mom or dad may respond by saying, "Well, that's really nice!" You're bound to think, "*Really nice? I've poured my life and soul into this, and all they can say is it's really nice?*"

The Tribute may produce dramatic changes in your relationship with your parents—or it may not. It is not a magic wand that will change your relationship with them instantly and forever. Seeing the Tribute as an end in itself can result in missing the big picture, the cathedral. Honoring parents demands that you look at your whole relationship with them and determine how you can honor them as a way of life.

This is particularly important if you're trying to reconnect with your parents after a period of isolation. If you are not writing and calling them regularly, for example, they might see the Tribute as a cynical attempt to manipulate them or gain their favor.

The Tribute is like a cornerstone in the foundation of your relationship. It may never become a fully constructed building—the complete relationship both you and your parents would long for—but the real issue is whether you are loving them and continually laying new bricks.

Twenty Blocks for Building a Better Relationship with Your Parents

Let me suggest some additional blocks you can select from to aid you in honoring your parents and the building of your relationship with them. I have used some of these ideas personally, but many come from people like you. As we prepared this book, we held a contest for those of our FamilyLife Marriage Conference alumni who either had written Tributes to their parents or had honored them in other ways. We received so many great ideas that we've included many in this chapter.

These blocks aren't included to put you under a heavy pile (of blocks!). Just relax and consider choosing one or two you can use in the coming months. Barbara and I would like to implement some of these ideas ourselves.

Got your wheelbarrow ready? Here goes:

Building Block Number One: *Become a student of your parents.*

An essential principle to remember in honoring your parents is to *find out what communicates value, respect, and esteem to them.* Become a student of your parents. For example, do they value phone calls, letters, or visits on family holidays? If so, make those things a priority.

If their birthdays are important to them, make sure you send cards and gifts on time. If you have hurt them by not attending a key family gathering, then make a special effort to be there for the next one.

If they have special skills, you can honor them by asking for their assistance and advice. If your father is good at carpentry, for example, ask him to help you build those new bookshelves you've been wanting to put up in your den.

Pam learned her father thought she preferred talking to her mother when she called home. This was a misunderstanding—her mom was simply more talkative and usually was the one who answered the phone. Pam realized the simple way to show honor to her father was to call him when she knew he was at home alone or to ask for him specifically, even if her mom answered the phone.

In writing your parent's Tribute you may have forgotten to include some of your memories. Or, another memory may have surfaced and you think, "I wish I had included that." Capture thoughts like those on paper and include them in cards, letters, or phone calls.

Building Block Number Two: Give them time.

Most likely, your parents value your time with them more than anything else. If you live far away, however, it may be difficult and expensive to spend much time with them. (Do you find comfort in that distance? It may mean you don't have to struggle with arranging your normal schedule around your parents. Is the distance an excuse so you don't have to go see them?)

Through our own sets of mistakes, Barbara and I have discovered that if we want to honor our parents as a way of life, we have to give up a bit of our independence. It's not always convenient to honor parents.

As you try to determine ways to honor your parents, look for some common interests you can develop. For instance, your father may enjoy fishing or golfing. Arrange for a weekend fishing trip or take him to a local golf course and pay for the green fees.

Many parents feel a special honor when their children name grandchildren after them. We named Benjamin Ward Rainey after my dad. If we had had a third son, he would have been named after Barbara's dad, Robert. We gave our second daughter, Rebecca, the middle name "Jean" to honor Barbara's mother.

Building Block Number Three: Take vacations with them.

In 1990 my family spent a long vacation on a lake in northern Minnesota. Barbara's parents joined us for a few days, and I think it did a lot to cement their relationship with us. One day we ended up with a van full of memories as all ten of us spent some twelve hours together. We toured the port at Duluth, a huge iron-ore mine, and a beautiful high school in Hibbing. We reminisced together as Barbara's dad showed us where he vacationed as a boy with his family. It was loads of fun.

Special times like that one not only build special memories but also create an especially memorable bond of humor. During those few days my father-in-law kept complaining (good-naturedly) about having to transport a "weed" called "baby's breath" all the way back to Arkansas. Barbara and her mom kept picking the stuff, and I've got to admit the back seat of my in-laws' car looked funny as they headed south. For Christmas that year I gave Barbara's father some baby's breath as a gag gift. He enjoyed the attention!

One caution I should mention here is you will need to determine a healthy length of time for you to be together—particularly if you are staying at their home. For many, a three-day stay is often ideal. (Remember the old saying, "fish and company smell at the end of three days"?) You'll have enough time to enjoy each other but not wear out your welcome. But if even that length can present volatile situations, one or two days may be the most you can take.

If you live far away from your parents and are able to visit them only on vacation, it may be difficult to stay less than a week. In this situation, you may need to look for small ways to reduce the possibility of friction. If you sense your parents need a break from your small children, for example, take the family on a picnic for a few hours. I can only imagine what it must be like for my mom to be invaded by all eight of us—her tranquil house transformed instantly into a three-ring circus. It has to be at least a little unnerving.

Building Block Number Four: *Seek their advice*.

If you are about to purchase a home for the first time, for example, let your parents help you by giving you advice. Not only will that allow you to show them respect, but you also might avoid some costly mistakes.

If you feel your parents are too critical of your choices, you'll need to be cautious here. Let them know you are not putting yourself back under their authority, but rather are taking advantage of their experience and wisdom on a major issue.

Your choice of a marriage partner also can be a potential wedge between you and your parents. If you sense they disapprove, question them carefully to find out what bothers them.

I will never forget talking with a friend who told me his daughter was getting a divorce after ten years of marriage. "I regret that I didn't stand stronger as a father before they were married," he said. "I was concerned at the time because of the immaturity I saw in the young man." His daughter hadn't sought his counsel, and he didn't feel the freedom to press the issue.

Sometimes it's risky to seek your parents' counsel because you may choose not to heed it. Your parents may be hurt and you may experience some estrangement as a result. These risks are real. If this could present problems for you, then aggressively seek to honor them in other ways and let time heal the wound.

Building Block Number Five: Write them letters.

I don't want to minimize the importance of regular phone calls (I try to call my mom on a weekly basis). But one of the best things you can do in your relationship with your parents is to resurrect the art of letter-writing. Handwritten, hand-addressed letters. There is something special about sitting down and writing a letter that communicates in a way that a phone call never can.

I think of the "Peanuts" cartoon in which Charlie Brown said, "Nothing echoes like an empty mailbox." If you're like me, you look forward to seeing what comes in each day's mail. You rifle through the pile, set aside the bills and bank statements, and hope that today you'll receive a handwritten letter from a friend or family member.

I remember one cherished letter I received from my

mother. She must have been bored one day in the middle of winter when she wrote a long letter in a circular fashion, starting on the outside and winding smaller and smaller toward the middle of the page. She has always had a great sense of humor.

Letter-writing is quickly becoming a lost art in today's world. In an earlier era, people sent letters much more frequently than they do today. People just don't write letters much anymore, even to those they love the most. Your parents may view letters from you as valuable jewels.

A friend once told me of going through his mother's possessions after she died. He found an old shoe box without a lid, and inside were all the letters he had ever written to her. He noticed many were smudged and frayed from being read so many times. "The thing that astounded me," he said with regret, "was how few letters I had written to her."

Even as I write these words, I realize I'm way overdue on a letter to my mom. I have written her some notes recently, but it's time for a more lengthy letter.

Building Block Number Six: Keep the legacy alive.

In our families we ought to honor our parents not only to their faces but also in their absence after they have passed away. Tell your children about them—about how they lived, what they accomplished, and how they raised you. Tell them the values you learned that are worth imparting to the next generation.

Another way to preserve the family legacy is to maintain collections of photos, films, videos, and other mementos from the past. Your parents may have a box of thirty-year-old home movies in a closet. Have the films transferred to video and give copies to each family member for Christmas. Then watch the videos together as a family.

If you're really ambitious, develop an audio or video history of your family by interviewing your parents, grandparents, and other relatives. People love to talk about the past, and children love hearing the old stories. It gives them a connection with their parents and grandparents. Unfortunately, those family stories will disappear unless you record them.

Building Block Number Seven: Make a special "story album."

When Gene and Jean Nelson of Wichita, Kansas, celebrated their thirty-ninth wedding anniversary several years ago, their children compiled an album titled "Remember When." Each page contained special stories from the past, told in enough detail to make them interesting and entertaining. For example:

> With a pastor's family of twelve kids, it was very rare to find the house empty on any occasion. But on this particular day, there were only three people in the house—Grandpa Albert Nelson, Grandma Esther Nelson, and my dad, who was in high school at the time.
>
> Grandpa told my dad, "Will you come and pray with your mother and me, as we have no money to buy food." They went into the living room and began to pray God would provide somehow.
>
> There was a knock at the door, and Grandpa opened it to find one of the deacons. The deacon had a puzzled look on his face. "I drove by your house and I felt compelled to come back, and I'm wondering why I should be here. Do you have a need?"
>
> Grandpa Nelson said, "We have no money in the house to buy food." And with that the deacon gave the only money he had on him to Grandpa Nelson.
>
> My father Gene was standing there, and he saw and heard this. For the rest of his life he told us that story over and over. He wanted us to know that God was our Provider.

When Gene died in 1987, two of his sons read excerpts from the album at his memorial service. Watching the videotape of the service, I sensed this was a family who lived out the principle of Psalm 78—that parents teach each new generation to put their confidence in God and not forget the works of God.

Building Block Number Eight: Revisit their childhood home.

A couple of years ago I took my mom to visit the house she grew up in, the old homestead.

Mom grew up near a town called Ponce de Leon, Missouri. Nestled in the Ozarks of southwest Missouri, it boasted in its heyday a population of no more than one hundred people. The community was built up around a spring that runs through the heart of the town.

I remember driving to this tiny community with my parents as a young boy. We would visit Mom's parents, who still lived in the small, four-room house where they raised seven children. I played on the feather beds that swallowed me alive. There was a rock porch and steps, barely big enough for two adults to sit beside one another. I used to sit there feeling important as a five-year-old "helping" to hand-crank a burlap-covered ice cream freezer. Mom's family had the recipe for ice cream, friendships, and memories. And they made plenty of all three.

I had not been back to the homestead since my mom's parents died in 1960. So one day my daughter, Ashley, and I put Mom in the car and we drove to see it again.

The house had been abandoned and taken over by cows. We walked inside and talked about what life was like there. She remembered where they used to slaughter hogs and render the lard, and how they made "cracklin's" to eat. We talked about where the barn used to be and how she gathered eggs as a little girl.

We talked about what her mom and dad were like. And about the golden anniversary they celebrated just a few short years before both of them died.

Mom enjoyed the trip. And it was a great way for Ashley to catch a glimpse of her heritage. Looking back, I wish I had asked one of Mom's brothers to join us—we would have found out a whole lot more about her.

Building Block Number Nine: Make a Mother's Day book.

Several weeks before Mother's Day, Edie Andress of Philadelphia purchased an inexpensive blank book, the type used for keeping journals. "On each page I wrote just one message to my mom for something I was thankful to her for: 'Thank you, Mom, for making hundreds and hundreds of school lunches for me. Love, Edie.' 'Thank you, Mom, for helping me when my baby was born. Love, Edie.' "

Edie wrote each message at the top of the page and left the rest blank. After she put one message on each page, she sent the book to her sister, who put one message of her own on each page. Her sister then passed it on to another sibling, and so on, until all had contributed.

"When we were finished, my mom had a tangible Tribute that daily reminds her we haven't forgotten all she does and has done for us," Edie says. "We presented our mom with her Tribute at our Mother's Day dinner. She cried. And we cried as we each read our thanks to her. It reconnected us to her and to each other in a way that was very much unexpected!

"This year it's Dad's turn. Next year, Grandmom's turn."

Building Block Number Ten: Honor parents at your wedding.

Several years ago I was asked to marry a couple in a huge, formal, Southern church. Being somewhat of a creative person, I feared the worst—a purely traditional ceremony. Now, there is nothing wrong with traditions; I have plenty of my own. It's just that traditions can sometimes get in the way of a potentially powerful message or event, such as a wedding.

So, with the permission of the couple getting married, I adapted the ceremony to honor the parents and grandparents. What occurred was a powerful statement of honor that two sets of parents, grandparents, and a couple getting married will never forget. (And in the process it woke up the audience!)

Rather than just have the father "give his daughter's hand in marriage," we paused first to honor the bride's two sets of grandparents for their investments in their children's and grandchildren's lives. We asked them to stand and then addressed them with personal comments written out in advance by the bride (the groom's grandparents were deceased).

I was unprepared emotionally for what happened next. Slowly rising to their feet, the two white-haired couples stood humbly, shoulder to shoulder. I read, "Today in an era in which the marriage covenant is violated repeatedly by divorce, we want to honor you for being married for fifty-two years and fifty-seven years." There were more than a few tears shed when the crowd of some eight hundred erupted in sustained applause. They clapped continuously, honoring these couples who had one hundred and nine years of marriage between them. It felt good and right.

Then, with the groom and bride each facing her and his mom and dad, we honored both sets of parents with some very personal words of memories, appreciation, and honor. More tears. More applause. And even some laughter. That wedding was truly a celebration by the entire family!

Building Block Number Eleven: Honor parents on your anniversary.

If you're married, chances are your wedding ceremony did not include a section honoring your parents. Well, just to show it's never too late, here's another idea you can implement: Joe and Peg Blanchette of Charlotte, Vermont, honored their parents during their own special marriage rededication ceremony on their twentieth anniversary.

The Blanchettes decided to celebrate their twentieth anniversary in a big way rather than wait until the traditional twenty-fifth year. "I was concerned that our parents, all approaching their seventies, might not be around five years from now," Joe explains. "I wanted them to celebrate our marriage success with us, as their influence has played a big role in each of our lives."

During the ceremony, Joe says, "We repeated our vows to one another in God's presence and then paused to draw special attention to our parents in front of family and friends. Peg read her Tribute and I read mine. It was quite an experience. Everyone was moved. It made a wonderful celebration—an especially holy and fulfilling one for our families."

Building Block Number Twelve: *Make an anniversary scrapbook Tribute.*

Ken Barker of Lewisville, Texas, came up with a creative gift for his parents' fortieth wedding anniversary. His father, Dr. Kenneth Barker, was a seminary professor for many years and was general editor of the New International Version Study Bible.

Ken wrote to a number of friends and Christian leaders: "I would like to extend to you, as a highly visible representative of highest family values, the opportunity to participate with us in this celebration. One of the ways in which we would like to honor [them] is to present them with a scrapbook containing letters, photos, and any other memorabilia that would bring a nice memory of the past. Would you please consider making a contribution to this nostalgic book? Could you contribute through sending a letter or a card that simply praises them for reaching this milestone and includes your signature? This would mean a great deal to them, I know!"

I was one of the recipients of this letter, which came as I was working on this book. So, in the card I sent to Dr. Barker, I praised his son for honoring his parents: "Congratulations on your fortieth! Your legacy includes thousands, but none you could be more proud of than your son, Ken!"

Building Block Number Thirteen: *Involve old friends.*

A similar idea to the anniversary scrapbook was submitted by Blaine Strickland of Clearwater, Florida.

As they prepared for their parents' thirty-fifth anniversary, Blaine and his siblings contacted several of their mom's and dad's old friends around the country who they knew would not be able to attend the celebration. Then he bought an ordinary anniversary card and sent it to each friend, one at a time, to inscribe a personal message. "We bathed that card in prayer because we had to count on the friends and the post office to get that one card back to us in one piece—and every time we got it back, it was that much more valuable!" Blaine says.

"My mother in particular enjoyed calling those special friends later with all of the party details. So our Tribute, in the form of an anniversary card, really lasted for months and was a very happy occasion."

Building Block Number Fourteen: Write small notes of honor.

Terri Briggs of Grand Prairie, Texas, has taken advantage of anniversaries, birthdays, and holidays to put together "mini-Tributes" to her parents. Following are some excerpts:

For their twenty-fifth anniversary:

I'm glad that twenty-five years ago you got married. But I'm even happier that you are still married twenty-five years later. I'm glad you didn't give up when things got rough. I'm glad my parents loved the Lord enough, loved each other enough, and loved us enough to stay together through the bad times as well as the good. In a world where "budget" divorces are offered and broken homes are a dime a dozen, I just want to say thanks, Mom and Dad, for giving us the opportunity to grow up with *two* parents who love each other and who love us.

For a church service honoring her mother on Mother's Day:

One day a year is not enough to honor *you*—a woman who gave up any dreams she might have had personally in order to devote her life to raising her children for the Lord. I want you to know I love and appreciate you for that sacrifice. Proverbs 31 says,

"Her children shall rise up and call her blessed," but it's also true that your children have been very *blessed* to have you for our MOTHER.

While many adult children my age are seeking psychiatric therapy to help them overcome their childhoods, all I have are good memories of a mom and dad who loved each other even when times were tough and who loved their children enough to do their best to shield them from the evils of this world we live in. I only hope I can be the mother to my son you have always been to me.

Building Block Number Fifteen: "This Is Your Life."

Karen Brown of Auburn, Washington, and her siblings thought of a creative idea for the eightieth birthday of their father, Ernest Gunnison: a takeoff on the old "This Is Your Life" television show.

"We wrote a dialogue starting out with his birth and continuing to the present," Karen explained. "We divided the script into ten-year segments. As we, his children, finished our description of those years, we asked for anyone present to add their remembrances to our stories. We had given people an opportunity to think ahead as we had told them in their invitations that they would be given the opportunity to share."

The prepared script reveals that the Gunnisons organized a great research effort to capture stories from their father's early days. An excerpt:

During the early 1930s you began attending the First Christian Church of Cheyenne. That's where you met Mom. You were part of a youth group that had a lot of fun activities. We have lots of letters to read from people who were part of your life at that time but who were not able to attend today's event.

We received a letter from Clarice Ellis, who used to be Clarice Hawk. Dad, you will remember her for the time she was in the front of the church telling of her experiences at a conference. A bird flew into the church window and landed on Clarice's head. Uncle Bud Hull, who is here today, just couldn't stop laughing, thinking about a "sparrow landing on a Hawk's head."

Building Block Number Sixteen: Write a note of empathy.

Soon after Gwen Cantwell of Sharon, Wisconsin, gave her parents a Tribute, her mother nearly died of an illness.

"It was a very trying time emotionally and physically. I felt I needed to put feelings into words, so I wrote a piece for my dad on how he must have felt while my mom was in intensive care. My dad was very moved by it."

> He held her hand, not knowing what to say besides, "I love you." She squeezed his hand in reply, "I love you, too." It started as a simple procedure, but then everything was falling apart. The doctors didn't understand, but they kept a silent watch at her bedside.
>
> He remembered years ago making a promise to her—in sickness and health, until death do we part. Was this their parting time come so soon? She was the Lord's, but she was also his life. It seemed like only yesterday she was his young bride, and life was just beginning. Through the years they had become so used to each other. He gave it all to God—the pain, the fear—and God gave His comfort. God said, "Not yet, My child, you do not have to walk alone. I am not ready to take either of you home with Me yet. When that time comes—if it comes—you will be there for each other, holding each other's hands and loving each other until death do you part, and I will embrace you and hold your hand to welcome you home—My beloved child."

Building Block Number Seventeen: Make a "Video Legacy."

This is the story of a wife who went to extraordinary lengths to honor her husband and his entire family. When Henry and Iris Cantu decided to finally sell the family home in San Antonio, Texas, after thirty years, it marked the end of an era for that family. Their son, Eddie, and his wife, Gail, also realized his parents were aging and would not be around forever.

Gail writes that she began to think "about how little my children knew about their grandparents and if I would remember all the stories to tell them. I told my in-laws how important their stories and personal histories were to their children and grandchildren and was able to convince them to allow me to videotape them in their home. We agreed to keep the taping secret—even from my husband—so we could give copies of the tape to each sibling for Christmas."

Gail videotaped her in-laws talking about their past, their courtship and marriage, and the births of their children. Her father-in-law spoke of his childhood, adoption, and World War II years. Her mother-in-law told of her years with her family on the mission field in Mexico.

Then Gail got another brainstorm. "I realized how special it would be to have each of the children, spouses, and grandchildren videotape some of their memories and personal thoughts. I communicated my plan to each family involved and was rewarded with positive responses all around. I think this in itself is a special Tribute to the love and honor we all feel for our parents—and, because of them, for each other."

With five siblings and spouses plus seven grandchildren, and with several families living out of town, the taping took several months to accomplish. "It was interesting to see common themes of appreciation emerge from the children for their parents' particular strengths and attitudes, and especially for the spiritual heritage that was passed down from them to their children," Gail says. "It was also special to hear each of the spouses express appreciation for the love and acceptance offered to them by their in-laws."

Eddie's parents didn't know of this Tribute, and the siblings didn't know Gail had taped the parents. So when Gail organized a special dinner for all the family members in town, each group thought she'd be showing their video.

"My in-laws were surprised when the video came on with the song, 'Love Them While We Can,' followed by Tributes from all seventeen of their children and grandchildren," she says. There was also a segment by the three oldest sisters and brother about their early memories as the only children before the two youngest came along years later. The tape ended with some silent, eight-millimeter footage of a family Christmas about ten years ago, and the song, 'As For Me and My House.'

"Eddie's parents were deeply touched. There were hugs and tears all around and the special camaraderie and joy of having given a very special gift to two people we loved."

But that wasn't all. Gail then began the second videotape on "The Story of Henry and Iris." They couldn't finish the tape that night, Gail says. "But my in-laws were able to witness how highly prized their story was to the rest of their family."

Building Block Number Eighteen: *Make a gift of song*.

Sometimes the best gift of honor and love comes when you attempt something that you feel absolutely powerless to do. That's what happened with Nancy Hicks of Lawrenceville, Georgia, at her church's Mother-Daughter banquet on Mother's Day.

Nancy mentioned to Suzy White that she would attend the banquet with her mother, Kathryn Gerlach, and her ten-year-old daughter, Melissa. The friend, excited to hear that three generations of a family would be there at once, asked Nancy to sing the song "Wind Beneath My Wings" to her mother as a surprise.

Nancy laughed, thinking her friend was joking. "She had never heard me sing, and I'm no singer!" she writes. "But more than that, I have always been one to panic at the thought of having to get up in front of a group and do as much as

introduce myself. Speaking in a group is something I dread
more than just about anything."

But the friend was serious. So Nancy said she'd think
about it—reasoning someone else would be found to sing instead! "But this also gave me time and reason to reflect on
what wonderful Christian parents I was given. I always knew
they loved and encouraged both my brother, Chuck, and me
and always will." When the friend called again, Nancy found
herself agreeing to sing.

Nancy practiced for hours, memorizing the words and
battling her nerves. "I knew in my heart my mother would
truly know without a doubt how much I love and appreciate
her by my doing this for her—more than anything else I could
ever hope to do—because she knows how I feel about getting
up in front of people. It would be even more meaningful for
her because of that."

At the right moment during the banquet, Nancy and Melissa rose and coaxed Kathryn to sit on the rocking chair on the
stage. "I sang with my daughter standing at her grandmother's
side," Nancy says. "We all had tears in our eyes by the end,
and I am thankful to God for allowing me the blessing of honoring my mother in this special way. This is something I was
able to do only through the motivation of love and the power
of God to give me the courage."

Building Block Number Nineteen: Make a hand-sewn quilt of honor.

A friend of mine, Theresa Beck of Boulder, Colorado,
told me about a large quilt she helped make to honor her
grandparents, Leon and Edna Jacobs of Lee's Summit, Missouri, for their sixtieth wedding anniversary in 1983.

All of the children, grandchildren, and great-grandchil-
dren were asked to design their own square of the quilt. Each
piece represented something depicting that person's life. Most
embroidered theirs, but Theresa honored Leon and Edna by
painting a "road" of hills and valleys they had experienced.

The center of the quilt was composed of a large square with the Jacobses' name and wedding date: 6-2-23.

The Jacobses hung the quilt in their family room for many years, until they moved to a smaller home. Theresa remembers that before meals her grandmother would look at the quilt and say, "God bless all of those grandchildren."

(Last June the Jacobses celebrated their seventieth anniversary! They repeated their vows to each other, and this time each of their offspring contributed a page to a scrapbook.)

Building Block Number Twenty: "A good name."

For his father's retirement party, Tommy Woznick decided to pay tribute to his dad with some humorous stories of "growing up with Dad." His most creative idea, though, was a framed picture filled with all the misspellings of "Woznick" he had accumulated over sixteen years. It's a page you must see to appreciate, so I'll conclude this chapter with it:

WOZNICK

A GOOD NAME IS TO BE DESIRED
RATHER THAN GREAT RICHES . .

Prov 22:1

T. J. Wozwick
PO. Box 37 Conoco Inc.
Westlake, LA 70669

Frontier Oil and Refining Co.
2700 E. 5th St.
Cheyenne, Wyoming 82007

Attn: Mr. Tommy Wausnik

TO: Frontier Refining
2700 E. 5th St.
Cheyenne, Wy. 82003

ATTENTION: T. Toznick

Tommy Wasneck
Conoco Refinery
P. O. Box 37
Westlake, LA 70669

MR. TOM WOZNIECK
Frontier Oil and Refining
2700 E. 5th Street
Cheyenne, WY 82007
USA

Dear Mr and Mrs Wozmick,

Mr. Tom Wasner
Frontier Refinery
P.O. Box 1588
Cheyenne, WY 82001

Mr. Tommy Wiznick
P O Box 1588
Cheyenne, WY 82003-1588

FRONTIER REFINERY
ATTN: TOM WOCZIC
P.O. BOX 1588
CHEYENNE, WY 82002

TOMMY WAZNIK
1321 LAURA LANE
SULFUR, LA 70663

MR. TOM WOZNIAK
FRONTIER OIL
P. O. BOX 1588
CHEYENNE, WY 82003*

MR TOMMY WOZNICH
FRONTIER REFINERY
CHIEF ENGINEER
PO BOX 1558
CHEYENNE WY 82003

Frontier Refining Inc
P. O. Box 1588
Cheyenne, Wyoming 82003

ATTN: MR. TOMMY WOZNICK

Conoco, Inc.
P. O. Box 37
Westlake, Louisiana

ATTN: Steve Woznick

Conoco
P.O. Box 37
Westlake, LA 70669

Attn: Tom Woznik

Frontier Oil Corporation
Attn: Tom Wognick
P.O. Box 1588
Cheyenne, WY 82003

Mr. Tommy Wolnick

Frontier Oil
P.O. Box 1588
Cheyenne, WY 82003

CONOCO, INC.
5801 BRIGHTON BLVD.
COMMERCE CITY, COLORADO

Mr. Tommy Woznic
Frontier Refining
Post Office Box 1588
Cheyenne Wyoming 82003

ATTN: TOM WASNICK

Attn: Tommy Wavnich

Conoco, Inc.
P.O. Box 37
Old Spanish Trail
West Lake, LA 70669

Tommy Wasnik
Frontier Refining, Inc.
PO Box 1588
Cheyenne WY 82003-1588

Mr. Tom Wisneck
Conoco, Inc.
P. O. Box 37
Westlake, LA 70669

Attention: Tommy Wosnick

Frontier Oil & Refining
P.O. Box 1588
Cheyenne, WY 82003-1588
ATTN. Tom Warnick

TOMMY WOLSNICK.

Dear Mr. Wazwoznick

DAD,
THANKS FOR THE GOOD NAME

"The farther I go in life, the more grateful I am that you are my mother."

A Tribute to Katherine Lorraine McKnight

In April 1991, Dr. David McKnight of Murfreesboro, Tennessee, attended a FamilyLife Marriage Conference in Atlanta, Georgia. He went with mixed emotions: "On the one hand, I looked forward to the weekend away from a very busy work schedule and a chance to grow closer to my wife, Jennifer, as we explored God's Word together," he writes. "On the other hand, I was burdened by the knowledge that my mother was dying of cancer and would soon be gone."

As conference alumni, the McKnights participated in the "Building Your Mate's Self-Esteem" video conference, which includes a segment on "Putting Your Parents in Perspective." Driving home, David decided to take the following day off from work and spend it with his mother. He also knew he wanted to write her a Tribute while there was still time.

When the McKnights arrived home, they learned David's mother's condition had deteriorated over the weekend and she soon would die. David stayed up Sunday night to write a Tribute and had the chance to read it to her the next morning. "By that time she was in and out of consciousness. But as I read her the Tribute she was totally aware, and we both wept together as we embraced and remembered our times together. Shortly afterward she lapsed into a sleep from which she never again fully awakened and passed away early Wednesday morning surrounded by her family and longtime best friend.

"I am so happy I had the chance to tell my mother good-bye and to say all the things I needed to before it was too late. Soon I will begin working on a Tribute for my dad."

I remember recently looking back through some old photographs and being struck by what a lovely girl you were. What a catch you must have been for my dad! It seems I'm still being struck by your enjoyment and experience of life, even as I find out things I never knew about you. Why is it you never told me that you and your best girlfriend jumped off a moving train together?

The farther I go in life the more grateful I am that you are my mother. You've poured so much of your life into me. Now that I spend my time caring for expectant moms and listening to their fears and helping them with their discomfort, I realize more and more that once you too were occupied with guarding the life growing within you; being careful of what you ate, expressing your concerns to your doctor, and already loving me before you even saw me.

When I was born you named me David; and you made sure I knew my name meant "beloved" and that I was named for a king who was after God's own heart. You gave me a name to live up to.

You encouraged me to develop the musical talents God had given me. You told me about how it thrilled you to feel me stir within you before I was even born whenever music was being played at church. You made our home fill with music. My earliest memories include hearing you sing as you cooked our meals or cleaned our house. You taught me the words to a favorite hymn, "Let Others See Jesus in You," and we sang it together around the house. You were always there to encourage me in my piano lessons and shine with pride at my success. Those seeds grew in me to where today I can't imagine not being part of my church choir or not having music in my home.

You kindled my interest in medicine, and all my life I never wanted to be anything else but a doctor—not because you pushed me in that direction, but because you realized early that I was fascinated by the practice of medicine, and you fed that fascination.

You lifted up our family doctors as role models to me, and I learned that this was an honorable profession. You made it clear to me that sometimes God calls doctors to be missionaries. Though I never got that call, I knew you were preparing me for a life that would be spent in service to others if I followed my dream.

I remember the day you and Dad took me off to college. Your tears reminded me that as your firstborn child left home, life would never again be the same for either of us. While that necessary passage was hard, you never tried to hold me back or cause me to cling to you.

As a grown-up, now I can see you in a different light. I understand some of the sacrifices you made in order to nurture me. I thank you for caring about my self-esteem. I know there were times when I disappointed you and even broke your heart, but you never stopped loving me. As I try to raise my daughter to be a godly woman, I understand exactly why you said and did certain things I swore I would never say and do as a parent. Now I chuckle at myself when I see my daughter roll her eyes at me because I know that someday she too will experience the same revelation that I have . . . and so the cycle goes.

Now we've reached a difficult time in our lives as you lie sick. I consider it a privilege to care for you in my home. I can never repay you for your investment in me, but I'm honored to spend these last days and weeks with you as you teach me that final lesson in life. During those moments when you rest, I can see that you're listening for your heavenly Father to call you home.

I am encouraged once again to know that someday we both will stir together at the sound of God's trumpet and rise to meet each other in the air with Jesus. Together as part of God's family we will make music around His throne for eternity. I will always love you, Mother.

> Your beloved Son,
> David

18

Are You Worthy of Honor?

*A good character is the best tombstone. Those who loved you
and were helped by you will remember you. So carve your
name on hearts and not on marble.*
—C. H. Spurgeon

It was 11 p.m. and I was "history." It had been a particularly stress-filled day, and I could hear the sheets on my bed calling to me. All I wanted to do was to lie down and let them grab me.

The only problem was that our sixteen-year-old son, Benjamin, was sprawled across the foot of our bed. He wanted to talk.

I'm not a perfect father, but I do try to learn from my previous errors. And I have learned when a teenager wants to talk, you'd better seize the moment—even when you're semi-comatose!

I leaned forward on my side of the bed, looked Benjamin in the eye, and said, "What's up, B.J.?" (Only Barbara and I have permission to use this childhood nickname.)

Benjamin proceeded to give me an unbelievable description of a seminar he'd attended on how to counsel his peers about preventing AIDS. He had been selected by his school counselors to be one of six students to represent his high school for the seminar, sponsored by a well-known organization. This conservative organization's official position is that

270

"abstinence" is the best prevention for AIDS. So Barbara and I had signed the parental release form.

At the seminar, five boring minutes were given to abstinence. Then these adult "educators" all but told the kids, "Hey, we know you don't have any character. We know you can't control yourselves. So here's how you can have sex safely and creatively."

They didn't use those exact words—but they might as well have. Benjamin reported that what followed were sixty scintillating, titillating, and descriptive minutes devoted to creative "safe sex." It was the most graphic public description and explanation of heterosexual and homosexual sex that I have ever heard of.

There they sat—shoulder to shoulder—cheerleader and basketball player, Beta Club president and student government vice president, being "sexually abused" by this provocative educational seminar on safe sex.

By the time my son had finished sharing and showing me all the material he had been given, I was fully awake. And angry.

Let me pause and clearly state what I believe about sex education: The best place for it to take place is in the home. It's at home where the values of virginity and moral purity can best be built into a young person's life. And if schools must teach about sex, then parents ought to demand that it be done with clear moral boundaries.

I recognize that some sort of AIDS awareness training is needed—otherwise I wouldn't even have considered letting one of my children attend the seminar. What has happened, however, is that certain groups have taken advantage of the AIDS crisis to push into schools new courses and training that are much too explicit for impressionable teenagers who are curious about sex. These new programs usually ignore that there is no such thing as "safe sex" and ridicule the idea of encouraging abstinence. In effect, teens today are being encouraged to go ahead and have sex.

But Benjamin's revelation was not the end of my surprise. The next day I called the school to object, and in the process I learned that *no other parents had called.* So I called one of the parents from another school and asked if his son had said anything about the seminar. He said they hadn't talked about it at all.

I then proceeded to tell him some of what he had learned. "I can't believe they shared explicit, perverted material like that with our kids," he said. "It really is sick."

When I asked if he was interested in doing anything about it, his response stunned me: "No, I really don't want to talk to him about this. And, no, I don't want to do anything about it in our community."

Since that phone conversation I've done a lot of thinking. And what lingers in my mind is not this father's refusal to take a public stand—that's common today. What disturbed me most was that *he did not even want to talk to his own son* about what he had heard in the seminar.

In other words, he wasn't willing to get involved in one of the most crucial issues of his son's life.

The Flip Side of the Forgotten Commandment

Throughout this book, I have exhorted you as a child to honor your parents. Now, I'd like to challenge you with a question that I once heard Dr. Henry Brandt, psychiatrist from West Palm Beach, Florida, pose to a group of parents. Even though it took place over two decades ago, I have never been able to escape the weight and significance of his question to these parents: "Are *you* worthy of honor?"

The room was strangely quiet. Most had never even considered the question. And many had to answer Brandt with a sheepish, "No . . . I'm not worthy."

For much of this book, you have been challenged to honor your parents for the position they held in your life. You have been encouraged to honor them for what they did right, and not to blame them for what they did wrong. God expects us to honor our parents regardless of their practice.

Now, I'd like for you to consider the flip side of the forgotten commandment: How can you make it as easy as possible for your children to honor you? You may be single or married with no children—it doesn't matter; you can begin the process of becoming a person worthy of honor.

As I wrote this book, it was fascinating to read through the Tributes people sent me. The memories contained in them form a mosaic of what families ought to be. I noticed, too, that over and over, children considered three things important:

1. their parents' involvement.
2. their parents' emotional support.
3. their parents' character.

Let's consider how we can become parents worthy of honor by building these qualities into our lives:

Principle Number One: *Your children will remember your involvement.*

Your children want more than anything else for you to be involved in their lives. They need more than your time—they need your attention. They flourish when you focus on them.

That means more than just showing up at soccer games with a cellular phone in your pocket. Your children need your heart knitted to theirs as they make their choices and hammer out their character. They need you to know what's going on in their lives. They need you to help them think about the clothing they wear, the type of person they date, and the peer pressure they face.

In order to be a parent worthy of honor you can't just "be there." As much as possible, you have to "be *all* there."

That may sound simple, but it's easy for all your hours away from work to be filled with television shows, projects, finances, books, shopping, and housework. If you were able to add up how much time you actually spend focusing on your children each week, you might be shocked to discover your total measured in minutes, not hours. Occasionally I am so exhausted that, when I do arrive home or at one of our children's activities, I am really oblivious to what is going on.

"Being all there" does not mean you have to do it perfectly every time. It does mean that you are keeping the lines of communication firmly open and intact.

A couple of the Tributes I received serve as penetrating reminders:

> Dad, I can still remember afternoons in our backyard pitching the baseball, passing the football, shooting hoops, or doing whatever sport the season called for. . . .

> I thank you for all the wonderful childhood memories: of playing in the sprinkler after a hard day's work in the yard; of going to Playland Amusement Park and riding the roller coaster and shooting darts; of all the wonderful camping trips and water skiing until we dropped; of riding around at Christmas looking at all the pretty lights. Thank you for all the delicious barbecue, and of course the memories would not be complete without remembering how we listened to Kentucky Wildcat basketball games on the radio!

I noticed that these adult children usually did not highlight grand vacations in their lists of favorite memories. Instead they remembered the simpler times—playing games, playing ball, fishing, camping.

Also, I found it interesting that these Tributes rarely mention television, as in, "Thanks for all those times we watched TV together." For many parents today, however, "family time" often means little more than a couple of hours watching a television show or a video rental.

Consider the sad legacy this generation is leaving. In the early eighties, a Michigan State University study reported that one third of four- and five-year-olds would give up their relationship with their dad for television. Too many families allow television to steal both *quantity* and *quality* time.

After one couple returned home from a FamilyLife Marriage Conference, the husband immediately walked into the family room and unplugged the TV. With the cord dangling and wide-eyed kids in tow, he lugged the set to the garage.

In the empty place where the television had once stood, he hung a picture of the family. Their five-year-old son sat down on the floor, staring at the portrait. Then he looked up at his dad and asked, "Does this mean we're going to become a family?"

The Battle for Your Child's Soul

Being involved with your children means more than just doing things with them, however. Involvement means we know what is going on in their souls.

These are days of warfare—a battle is being waged over your child's soul. And if you haven't smelled the smoke of battle recently, you are too far from the front lines.

Sex education is just one battle where the lines are already being drawn. If you and I don't teach our children about sex, the world will.

I believe your children need you to teach them the basics about sex as they enter elementary school. As they prepare for junior high, teach them in advance about the practical boundaries of abstinence, moral purity in dating, and maintaining respect and self-control for the sex drive God has given them. When they are in high school, stay in touch by asking them how they are handling the temptations of immorality. Let them know you want to talk!

One thing Barbara and I particularly want to protect our daughters from is seeking physical intimacy with boys. To accomplish this, we realize it's important for them to develop a close relationship with me, their father. I need to keep giving them plenty of physical and emotional affection.

We also protect them by setting clear expectations for dating—when they can begin, whom they can go out with, how late they can stay out, what types of dates they can have, etc. Many parents let their children begin dating too soon. One recent study found that "the younger a girl begins to date, the more likely she is to have sex before graduating from high school." Ninety-one percent of girls who begin dating at age twelve have sex before graduating from high school, as compared to twenty percent who begin at age sixteen.[1]

Ashley's First Date

Barbara and I allowed our oldest daughter, Ashley, to begin double-dating at age sixteen. And for some time beforehand we made it clear that any boy who wanted to date Ashley needed to come and meet me to have a "little chat" before they went out. We could tell Ashley was rather proud of the idea.

So when the first young man asked her out, Ashley told him he needed to set up an appointment with me. One day after school he rode his motorcycle (?!) to my office. I bought him a soft drink to keep things as informal as possible, and then, after several minutes of small talk, I looked him in the eye. I began to tell him how valuable a woman is, how she is God's finest creation. He nodded dutifully.

Then I said, "You know, Kevin, I was a teenage boy once. And I want you to know that I remember what the sex drive is like for an eighteen-year-old young man." His eyes were getting bigger—he was really listening.

"And I want you to know that I expect you to treat my daughter just like God would have you treat His finest creation —with all respect and dignity. Whether you go out with her one time or one hundred times, I want to be able to look you in the eyes and ask you if you are treating my daughter with respect and dignity—especially in the physical area.

"And you know, Kevin, God may want her to be another man's wife. So you'd better be very careful to keep this relationship pure."

I paused.

"Are we communicating, Kevin?"

His eyes were fully dilated. He nodded. We shook hands

and I commended him on his courage to be willing to meet with me.

Later, as I arrived home, I couldn't help but wonder if I was an "old fuddy-duddy dad." I wondered if I was being too intrusive into the lives of my kids. Then over dinner my doubts evaporated as I shared what had happened with our family.

It wasn't just that Ashley's response was one of appreciation for me. It was that Benjamin, fourteen at the time, put it in context. He said, "Dad, I hope that the father of a girl I ask out wants to meet with me. I'll know I'm at the right house if that happens!"

A Special Challenge to Dads

One more observation stood out to me as I worked on this book. That is, many adults grew up with fathers who were good providers materially but were uninvolved in their kids' lives. Over the past few decades, too many fathers have pulled back from leadership in their families. To a large degree, we who call ourselves "Dads" are responsible for this paralysis of character in our homes.

Too many of us are not leading our families into the battle against evil. Instead, we're passively disengaged—consumed with our careers, preoccupied with our "toys" and hobbies. Too disengaged to get involved with our kids' lives. But real men with real character *act*; they take responsibility head-on. They may not do it perfectly, but they tackle issues and battlefronts courageously. They are men worthy of honor.

Men, we need to hear and heed Paul's words to the church at Corinth: "Be on the alert, stand firm in the faith, act like men, be strong. Let all that you do be done in love" (1 Corinthians 16:13-14).

We've got to encourage one another to be involved and not abandon our kids to the culture. And we've got to do it because God is going to hold us responsible for how we protect our families.

Bill McCartney, head football coach at the University of Colorado, tells of a greeting-card company that gave away free

Mother's Day cards at a penitentiary. All the inmates had to do was to agree to sign and address the card. So great was the response, the company ran out of cards and had to rush in additional boxes.

The leaders of the company then decided to do the same thing for Father's Day. They sent word to the prisoners ahead of time, and this time boxes arrived with an abundance of cards.

But no prisoners showed up. Not one. Not a single person came to send his dad a Father's Day card.

Think about that for a moment. As you probably realize, our prisons are overflowing with men and women who never had a normal, functioning father. Most inmates grew up in homes where the father had abandoned his family responsibilities.

These men did not find their fathers worthy of honor. In fact, I doubt if many could even find their fathers.

If you are a father, your heart needs to be connected to the hearts of your children. That means you may need to cry out in prayer to the Divine Surgeon who specializes in that type of surgery. The last verse of the Old Testament, Malachi 4:6, gives us His promise: "And he will restore the hearts of the fathers to their children, and the hearts of the children to their fathers, lest I come and smite the land with a curse."

God will help you to be worthy of honor and involved in your child's life. Just ask Him to show you ways to reconnect your heart to your children. We need to be men and women of honor by being involved in our children's lives.

Principle Number Two: *Your children will remember your emotional support.*

I will never forget one of my first counseling appointments after we started the FamilyLife ministry. A mom sat in my office and told the story of her eleven-year-old son's relationship with his dad. The father, a hard-driving and successful businessman, constantly criticized the boy:

"You dummy—you left the door open!"

"Look at these grades—that's pitiful!"

"You struck out at the game—I can't believe you did that!"

"Look at your room—it's a mess and *so are you!*"

By my estimate that boy is in his late twenties now. And I'll bet he still hears an inner recording taped repeatedly by the most significant man in his life, a recording that says, "You're a failure! You can't do it! Why try?" Is this father *worthy* of honor?

You may know exactly what I am talking about. Take a moment and reflect back on some of the expectations your parents placed on you. If your parents expected you to be perfect, then you may experience a failure complex—because no one can be!

Do you set unrealistic goals for yourself? Are you driven to perform to gain the approval of others? Do you avoid risky situations because you fear you will fail? Do you hear an inner tape-recording of self-doubt and self-criticism?

You know how painful it feels to hear that inner recording, day after day. But is this the type of recording you are now taping for your children?

Reading through the Tributes, I observed how often adults remembered the positive emotional support they received from their parents:

> I can't remember a time that you didn't accept me. I was always okay. My performance was okay, too, as long as I tried my hardest.

> You encouraged me to develop the musical talents God had given me. You told me about how it thrilled you to feel me stir within you before I was even born whenever music was being played at church. You filled our home with music. My earliest memories include hearing you sing as you cooked our meals or cleaned our house. You taught me the words

to a favorite hymn, "Let Others See Jesus in You," and we sang it together around the house. You were always there to encourage me in my piano lessons and shine with pride at my success. Those seeds grew in me to the point that today I can't imagine not being part of my church choir or not having music in my home.

You were as bound and determined to let me play the drums as I was! You even put up with a decade of having to listen to me practice! Not to mention having to lug those silly drums back and forth all over creation!

The Words They Need to Hear

How often do you tell your children you love them or forgive them? One woman wrote to tell me, "I told [my parents] many times how much I love them, and have only heard my parents tell me those words probably twice—the first when I was forty years old . . . And never the words, 'I forgive.' " Your kids should hear these words so often that they have no idea how often you've said them.

Another way to give your children emotional support is by utilizing the power of the printed word. Letters and notes are tangible reminders to your children that you love and care for them. Young children, especially, will treasure your handwritten notes of affection.

Emotional support is also felt when we physically touch our children. Hugs, tight embraces, and kisses are all the steady practice of a parent who wishes to be worthy of honor.

When our kids were little I used to ask them what kind of a bear hug they wanted: A baby-bear hug, a mama-bear hug, or a papa-bear hug. Each hug increased in intensity and a growl. They usually started out with a baby-bear hug and worked their way up to the papa-bear hug when I'd nearly squeeze the breath out of them.

I've found that if dads give physical and emotional affection when their children are young, it won't be nearly as difficult to do when they become teens. It's difficult sometimes to hug a teenager at times because they act like they don't need it. But that's just a facade.

I'll never forget Barbara hugging our son Benjamin after a rough day at his junior high. She let go—he didn't. He was admitting, non-verbally, "I may be nearly as tall as you, and I may look grown up, and I may act like I don't need affection— but I do!"

By filling and refilling our child's emotional gas tank, you and I become worthy of honor.

Principle Number Three: Your children will remember your character.

Someone has said, "Our children are messengers we send to a time we shall not see." As a parent, what kind of *message* are you sending to the next generation? Are your message and your life worthy of being emulated and honored?

As a parent, you have the incredible responsibility of shaping the moral conscience of the next generation. Even though your children will grow up to make their own choices, the character qualities you model and teach will help mold them and give them direction. In fact, I've noticed that many children, after passing through years of rebellion against their parents, settle into adulthood by adopting many of the same character qualities they once railed against.

Once again, I found these character qualities highlighted often in the Tributes I received:

> You taught me through example to honor and
> respect my elders, to establish a strong work ethic
> and to complete a task with excellence. You are a
> man of your word.

> Mom, you are a woman of strength and
> devotion. Your determination is a beautiful gift from

the Lord. Your perseverance, tolerance, patience, honesty, integrity, and ethics are not to be surpassed. Words such as kind, thoughtful, caring, and gentle were created to describe you. You are loving, giving, compassionate, and generous.

———————————

Mom showed me what it was to have faith in God. She taught me how to love God and worship Him and serve Him.

Mom showed me what generosity and sacrificial giving were all about.

Mom taught me what it meant to be appreciative and grateful. She taught me about being honest. She taught me manners.

What character qualities do you want to pass on to your children? What do you believe in? What are your core values?

You may not have taken the time to answer questions like these. When we held our first FamilyLife Parenting Conference (a weekend seminar for couples and single parents) in 1992, we were surprised to learn that the most popular couples project was "Determining Your Core Values." One conferee spoke for many others when he said, "I'd never put these thoughts on paper before."

The Roman philosopher Seneca said, "You must know for which harbor you are headed if you are to catch the right wind to take you there." If you've determined what your core values are, then you can find creative ways to teach and model them to your children.

A Night of Surprises

Satchel Paige, a baseball Hall-of-Famer and occasional philosopher, once said, "What goes around, comes around."

Barbara and I saw how true these words are at the end of the summer of 1992. During a FamilyLife staff banquet, we were brought up front for a question-and-answer session. But, to our surprise, the master of ceremonies announced that the real purpose of the entire evening was to honor us for our upcoming twentieth wedding anniversary.

Several good friends who had been hiding in the back of the room were brought up to say a few words. But the real highlight came when all six of our children showed up. Little Laura, seven at the time, went first, standing on a chair. She had written a Tribute with the help of her older sisters and brothers: "Thank you, Mom, for all the dresses you made me. For hugs and kisses. For being a great Mom. Dad, thanks for being my ice cream buddy, for the stories you tell at bedtime, and for wrestling with me."

One down, five to go. I looked at Barbara—we both were choking back tears.

Deborah, the next to youngest at age nine and our only adopted child, was the next to stand on the chair and speak. In her quiet, soft voice she thanked her mom for helping her with homework and cutting her hair short. She thanked me for taking her on fishing dates and out to eat. Then she turned to both of us, looked us in the eye with a big grin, and said, "And I want to thank both of you for adopting me when I was a baby."

That did it! Barbara and I were basket cases. Tears were streaming down our faces. We boo-hooed through the four other children.

The evening will go down as one of the greatest privileges we've ever experienced. After all those years of showing children how to honor their parents, we had the opportunity to experience what it was like as parents, to *receive* that honor. It felt great. We had experienced the promise of Ephesians 6:3— "that it may go well with you"—in that we had honored our parents and now we were being honored by our children.

There is much about the command and promise of Exodus 20:12 that I still have to apply and understand. It is my prayer for you that you will begin the process of fulfilling your responsibility to your parents and experience the privileges of obedience.

I pray that you will do what's right and seek to obey God by honoring your parents, and that you will experience God's abundant blessings and favor as a result of your obedience.

Notes

Chapter Three
1. James P. Johnson, "How Mother Got Her Day," *American Heritage Magazine*, May 1970, 16.
2. Charles Panati, *Extraordinary Origins of Everyday Things* (New York, Singapore, Sydney, Tokyo: Harper & Row Publishers, 1987), 60.
3. Panati, 60–61.
4. Michael S. Horton, *The Law of Perfect Freedom* (Chicago: Moody Press, 1993), 134.
5. John MacArthur, *Ephesians* (Chicago: Moody Press, 1986), 312–315.
6. Alan Loy McGinnis, *The Friendship Factor* (Minneapolis: Augsburg Publishing, 1979), 30.

Chapter Four
1. Martin Lloyd-Jones, *Life in the Spirit in Marriage, Home and Work* (Grand Rapids: Baker Book House, 1975), 246–247.
2. Charles J. Sykes, *A Nation of Victims* (New York: St. Martin's Press, 1992), xiv.

Chapter Five
1. Gilbert V. Beers, "A Theology to Die By," *Christianity Today*, 6 February 1987, 11. Used by permission.
2. Henry Bosch, *Our Daily Bread*, 24 July 1973.
3. "FamilyLife Today" radio broadcast, "My Dad II," Crawford Loritts, Jr. (June 18, 1993).

Chapter Six
1. "Toddler's Reign of Terror," *Arkansas Gazette*, 30 July 1982, 1D.
2. Joan France, "A 'Caretaker' Generation?" *Newsweek*, January 29, 1990, 16.

Chapter Seven
1. James Patterson and Peter Kim, *The Day America Told the Truth* (New York: Prentice Hall Press, 1991), 6.
2. "Now a Few Words from the Wise," *Time*, June 22, 1987, 69.
3. "Bill Cosby Has Message for Grads," *The Los Angeles Times*, 18 May 1986, 2A.
4. Larry Crabb, *Inside Out* (Colorado Springs: NavPress, 1988), 77.
5. Suzy Parker, "USA Snapshots," *USA Today*, 3 August 1987, 1A.
6. Gene Dobbins; Johnny Wilson; Wayne Sharp, "Roses for Mama" © 1977 Chappell & Co. All rights reserved. Used by permission.

Chapter Eight
1. J. Wesley Brown, "Good News for Parents," *Christian Century*, 1 May 1981, 513.

Chapter Nine
1. Ivan Maisel, *Dallas Morning News*, 4 August 1992, 17B.
2. Josh McDowell on "FamilyLife Today" radio, to be aired Spring 1994.
3. Ralph Kinney Bennett, "The Greatest Gift I Ever Received," *Reader's Digest*, July 1990, 9.

Chapter Ten
1. Lewis B. Smedes, "Forgiveness: The Power to Change the Past," *Christianity Today*, 7 January 1983, 22.
2. Smedes, 22.
3. Philip Yancey, "An Unnatural Act," *Christianity Today*, 8 April 1991, 36.

4. Smedes, 22.

5. Elaine L. Schulte, "The Day Before My Father Died," *Decision*, June 1981, 27.

Chapter Eleven

1. Ney Bailey, *Faith Is Not a Feeling* (Nashville: Thomas Nelson Publishers, 1978), 42, 45–46.

Chapter Thirteen

1. Gary Allen Sledge, "The Woman in the Kitchen," *Reader's Digest*, September 1989, 85.

Chapter Fourteen

1. Paul Tsongas, "Happy to Be Here," *People*, 3 May 1993, 179.

Chapter Fifteen

1. Dan Allender, *The Wounded Heart* (Colorado Springs: NavPress, 1990), 179.

2. Allender, 238.

3. Allender, 184.

4. Josh McDowell on "FamilyLife Today" radio, to be aired Spring 1994.

5. Bobbie Gee, "Quality of Life," *Buy-Line*, Winter 1991, 5.

Chapter Eighteen

1. Josh McDowell and Dick Day, *Why Wait?* (San Bernardino: Here's Life Publishers, 1987), 79.

HomeBuilders
COUPLES SERIES

The HomeBuilders Couples Series® are the fastest growing small-group studies in the country. This series is designed to help build your relationship on the solid biblical principles found in God's Word.

Building Teamwork in Your Marriage by Robert Lewis
Understand your differences are gifts from God, and learn how you are the unique person equipped to complete your mate.

Building Your Marriage
by Dennis Rainey
Discover and apply God's basic blueprints for a strong, healthy marriage that will last a lifetime.

Building Your Mate's Self-Esteem by Dennis and Barbara Rainey
Learn how to encourage each other and experience new levels of love and fulfillment.

Expressing Love in Your Marriage by Jerry and Sheryl Wunder and Dennis and Jill Eenigenburg
Express God's love in your marriage—seeking His best for one another.

Growing Together in Christ by David Sunde
Discover all the power and joy you and your mate can find together by developing an exciting daily relationship with Christ.

Life Choices for a Lasting Marriage by David Boehi
Identify the key choices for a lasting marriage and renew your minds with the truth of God's Word.

Managing Pressure in Your Marriage by Dennis Rainey and Robert Lewis
Make better choices, plan for the future, and find new solutions for your life and marriage.

Mastering Money in Your Marriage by Ron Blue
Discover how you can make money matters a tool for growth instead of a bone of contention in your marriage.

Resolving Conflict in Your Marriage by Bob and Jan Horner
Learn to transform conflicts into opportunities to energize your marriage and increase your love for your mate.

For more information on these and other FamilyLife Resources contact your local Christian retailer or call FamilyLife at 1-800-333-1433. A free HomeBuilders Information Pack is also available through the FamilyLife "800" number.

FamilyLife™
Bringing Timeless Principles Home
P.O. Box 23840 • Little Rock, AR • 72221-3840
http://www.familylife—ccc.org

A division of Campus Crusade for Christ

"A Weekend to Remember"

Every couple has a unique set of needs. The FamilyLife Marriage Conference meets couple's needs by equipping them with proven solutions that address practi-

cally every component of how to build a better marriage. The conference gives you the opportunity to slow down and focus on your spouse and your relationship. You will spend an insightful weekend together, doing fun couple's projects, and hearing from dynamic speakers on real-life solutions for building and enhancing oneness in your marriage.

You'll learn:

- *Five secrets of a successful marriage*
- *How to implement oneness in your marriage*
- *How to maintain a vital sexual relationship*
- *How to handle conflict*
- *How to express forgiveness to one another*

Our insightful speaker team also conducts sessions for:

- *Engaged/Pre-marrieds*
- *Men only*
- *Women only*

FAMILYLIFE
MARRIAGE CONFERENCE

To register or receive a free brochure and schedule, call FamilyLife at 1-800-999-8663.

FAMILYLIFE™
Bringing Timeless Principles Home